Teaching the Eighteenth Century Now

TRANSITS

LITERATURE, THOUGHT & CULTURE, 1650–1850

A landmark series in long-eighteenth-century studies, *Transits* publishes monographs and edited volumes that are timely, transformative in their approach, and global in their engagement with arts, literature, culture, and history. Books in the series have engaged with visual arts, environment, politics, material culture, travel, theater and performance, embodiment, connections between the natural sciences and medical humanities, writing and book history, sexuality, gender, disability, race, and colonialism from Britain and Europe to the Americas, the Far East, the Middle/Near East, Africa, and Oceania. Works that make provocative connections across time, space, geography, or intellectual history, or that develop new modes of critical imagining are particularly welcome.

Recent titles in the series:

Teaching the Eighteenth Century Now: Pedagogy as Ethical Engagement
Kate Parker and Miriam L. Wallace, eds.

Women and Music in the Age of Austen
Linda Zionkowski with Miriam F. Hart, eds.

Louis Sébastien Mercier: Revolution and Reform in Eighteenth-Century Paris
Michael J. Mulryan

Alimentary Orientalism: Britain's Literary Imagination and the Edible East
Yin Yuan

Thomas Holcroft's Revolutionary Drama: Reception and Afterlives
Amy Garnai

Families of the Heart: Surrogate Relations in the Eighteenth-Century British Novel
Ann Campbell

Eighteenth-Century Environmental Humanities
Jeremy Chow, ed.

For more information about the series, please visit bucknelluniversitypress.org.

Teaching the Eighteenth Century Now

PEDAGOGY AS ETHICAL ENGAGEMENT

Edited by

KATE PARKER AND
MIRIAM L. WALLACE

BUCKNELL UNIVERSITY PRESS
LEWISBURG, PENNSYLVANIA

Library of Congress Cataloging-in-Publication Data

Names: Parker, Kate, 1980– editor. | Wallace, Miriam L., editor.
Title: Teaching the eighteenth century now : pedagogy as ethical engagement / edited by Kate Parker and Miriam L. Wallace.
Other titles: Pedagogy as ethical engagement
Description: Lewisburg, Pennsylvania : Bucknell University Press, [2023] | Includes bibliographical references and index.
Identifiers: LCCN 2023016183 | ISBN 9781684485048 (hardcover) | ISBN 9781684485031 (paperback) | ISBN 9781684485055 (epub) | ISBN 9781684485062 (pdf)
Subjects: LCSH: Europe—Civilization—18th century—Study and teaching (Higher) | Europe—History—1648–1789—Study and teaching (Higher) | Europe—History—1789–1815—Study and teaching (Higher) | College teaching—Methodology.
Classification: LCC CB411 .T425 2023 | DDC 378.1/25—dc23/eng/20230720
LC record available at https://lccn.loc.gov/2023016183

A British Cataloging-in-Publication record for this book is available from the British Library.

♾ The paper used in this publication meets the requirements of the American National Standard for Information Sciences—Permanence of Paper for Printed Library Materials, ANSI Z39.48–1992.

bucknelluniversitypress.org

Distributed worldwide by Rutgers University Press

For our students first, and for all
of our teachers past and present

CONTENTS

Teaching the Eighteenth Century Now

INTRODUCTION

Situating Teaching in/about/around the Eighteenth Century

Kate Parker and Miriam L. Wallace

This collection features scholars with deep expertise in what's often called "the long eighteenth century," defined, at least in part, by a Eurocentric time frame that typically runs from about 1680 to 1832 or so, variously—and never innocently—tagged as the Eighteenth Century, the Enlightenment, the Age of Discovery, the Colonial Period, or Romanticism, depending on the area of focus. But all the contributors to this collection are also, importantly, teachers. Teaching is, in fact, what we do *most* of the time. Yet academic labor is most often tracked across three seemingly mutually exclusive and delimited categories: "scholarship," "teaching," and "service." Whether tenure-track or contingent, this unassailable trifecta forms the basis of our labor assignments and our annual evaluations. Ongoing developments in the scholarship of teaching and learning through the twentieth and into the twenty-first century have taken seriously the scholarly investments of teaching, highlighting the imbrication of intellectual work that blends textual and cultural materials that fascinate us as scholars with the pedagogical approaches that engage developing scholars and culture workers—our students.

We asked the authors featured here to consider what teaching means in this historical moment: a moment of a global contagion that underscores the intersections of health, wellness, and socioeconomic status, and at the same time—and not unrelated—an increasing demand for restitution to repair the centuries of structural violence and intergenerational trauma forced upon Black, immigrant, and Indigenous populations in the Americas and beyond. In the midst of this social and political upheaval, higher education has been called upon to reconsider relevance and differential outcomes in the face of increasingly diverse student populations, to address disappointing efforts to widen the circle of representation and amplify marginalized voices, and to respond to the ongoing politicization of education, all while simultaneously meeting the enrollment and funding challenges of the coming "demographic cliff"—the drop in traditional-age college-bound students.[1]

The chapters in this collection take up these challenges in fascinating and often disparate ways. Acknowledging the difficulties of unfamiliar texts and a general lack of fluency in the culture and history of the eighteenth century, they blend strategies for engaging twenty-first-century Western-educated students with reflections on what we do when we teach—how our pedagogies can be more meaningful, more impactful, and more relevant in the face of massive social, economic, political, and environmental change.

TEACHING AS ACTION

As far back as 1990 Ernest Boyer argued for the value of the scholarship of teaching and learning, arguing that "knowing and learning are communal acts. . . . [G]reat teachers create a common ground of intellectual commitment. They stimulate active, not passive learning and encourage students to be critical, creative thinkers, with the capacity to go on learning."[2] Thirty years later, in this moment of pandemic pedagogy and cultural reckoning, our methods of delivery, our curriculum, and even the parameters of expertise are all under pressure. In our time, the language of "teaching and learning" has pervaded higher education. Attention to learning environments and the complexities of how students acquire, internalize, and process information is all to the good, but sometimes the focus on students' learning has elided the teacher as an active agent in the classroom. At an extreme, this risks evacuating the labor of teaching along with the embodiment of the person who teaches. Scholarly attention to what we *do* when we teach can also serve to make its practice and labor—both institutional and personal, emotional—more visible. By bringing together contemporary academic scholarship with more radical approaches to integrating eighteenth-century content in classroom communities that are often actively presentist, this collection aims to make visible the challenges we face when we teach the eighteenth century *now*.

Indeed, *now* is a moment of increasing scrutiny. The pedagogical activities of college-level instructors are now endlessly quantified and assessed; legislatures across the United States are passing bills to enhance surveillance, proscribe certain (anti-heterosexist, anti-racist, anti-bias) content, and pit students against faculty through ceaseless evaluations and the ever-present threat of being recorded, or reported, for teaching that does not uphold an institutional *status quo*.[3] Public colleges and universities are particularly vulnerable under performance metrics that prioritize "return on investment" in largely economic terms—redefining tenure, relying upon contingent faculty, and reallocating funding to programs with explicitly professional tracks. Private institutions may seem somewhat insulated, but even in so-called ivory towers, similar shifts toward careerism and standardization are under way. This bimodal message means that instructors must constantly negotiate the competing demands of achieving metrics (rather than modeling expert learning or guiding inquiry) and evading accusations of indoctrination. Present-day faculty, it seems, have both too little, and too much, influence through their teaching.

We ask: What about teaching as the hallmark of "generous thinking"?[4] How, and why, should our institutions—not to mention our field—value the intellectual labor of pedagogy? How does teaching the eighteenth century contribute to fostering habits of mind and ethical thinking for a rising generation—one that will need to address the challenges facing our global community, and one that will have to do so largely *without* meaningful personal experiences with an inclusive range of (non-)Western global histories and literatures? What role might we play, as eighteenth-centuryists teaching *now*, to prepare our students to advocate for the world we hope they will live in?

SITUATED: WHO WE ARE

In recent years, academics—as individuals and, to a lesser extent, as institutions—have articulated positionality as a means of acknowledging the situated knowledge(s) and lived experience(s) that form our particular ways of knowing and seeing the world. From Land Acknowledgment statements that recognize occluded histories of occupation, genocide, and theft of land, water, and other resources, to naming those persons lost to racist violence and police brutality, to articulating personal gender pronouns, to simply noting "where we know from,"[5] we strive to make visible those upon whose invisible labor, suffering, and knowledges we have relied. In a collection such as this—in which particular histories, personal commitments and identities, and a wide range of institutional settings are invoked—the debts are large. In many of the chapters, all of which were conceived and written in the wake of protesting police violence followed by the COVID-19 pandemic, the authors are keenly aware of the ways in which the digital world renders less visible the material world from which it originates.

As editors, we write from public, predominantly white institutions (PWIs): the University of Wisconsin La Crosse, a regional comprehensive university that serves a largely rural and under-resourced population in southwestern Wisconsin; and New College of Florida, a public honors college that until recently offered a high-touch and affordable academic experience for students primarily from Florida, including significant first-generation college students. Additionally, both of us are tenured faculty who have served as administrators at our respective institutions, and thus we speak from positions of relative job security and institutional power. Miriam Wallace writes from the west coast of Florida, where local edifices are built upon the raised land made by shell mounds that make physical the long presence of native peoples along the coast and the appropriation of those spaces first by the Ringling family of circus fame, who built mansions along the coastline, and then by successive housing booms. Downtown Sarasota is gentrifying, but the signs of both a white Main Street and a historic Black commercial district just to the north are immediately visible to even a casual visitor and have shaped ongoing discussions about our role in our community. Kate Parker writes from La Crosse, Wisconsin, a small city of 50,000 along the Mississippi River where her institution sits on the ancestral land of the Ho-Chunk people. The city was recently embroiled in a series of controversies over its white supremacist and racist past, including the removal of a twenty-five-foot-high statue of "Hiawatha" that had been a tourist attraction since the 1960s and the uncovering of historical evidence proving that, as a "sundown town," La Crosse openly discriminated against—and attempted to eliminate—its Black residents at multiple junctures in its history.

Our contributors, likewise, speak from varied and diverse standpoints, and their chapters variously acknowledge instructor positionality alongside institutional history, student demographics, and location. Inspired by Eugenia Zuroski and the Black and Indigenous scholars she draws from in her essay "'Where Do You Know From?' An Exercise in Placing Ourselves Together in the Classroom," we collectively recognize teaching as a situated practice in which geographic, historical, institutional, and economic factors "matter"—that is, have material significance. Despite—or, also, because of—this commitment to specific standpoints and perspectives, we hope that many readers in their respective locations will find inspiration and practical suggestions alike in the chapters collected here.

TEACHING IN THE EIGHTEENTH CENTURY

Attention to teaching is particularly appropriate because the eighteenth century was itself obsessed with instruction, didacticism, scientific discovery and geographic exploration, professionalism, and debating the means and purposes of education. From elite women who became "learned ladies" to self-educated writers of the African diaspora, to later-century Sunday schools that taught both religious piety and functional literacy, significant scholarship explores the focus on education and instruction in the period.[6]

Following the invention of literature for children, partly attributed to John Newbery's 1744 *A Little Pretty Pocket-Book*, the later eighteenth century saw an expansion of literature written specifically for children. This literature conceives of the child as reader and of reading as literacy, both in a simple sense and also as a kind of moral and cultural formation. It is perhaps not accidental that early writers for children include figures we associate with sociopolitical reform: Stéphanie-Félicité de Genlis, Anna Laetitia Barbauld, Mary Wollstonecraft, Eliza Fenwick, Edward Baldwin (aka William Godwin). Not one but two "juvenile libraries" were established in London, catering to child readers.

More vexed questions about *who* should be instructed and in what, which kinds of learning were to be open and to whom, as well as who was to be *doing* the instruction, lingered. In the later 1700s, Hannah More and her sister established Sunday schools that combined prayer and scripture reading with basic instruction in reading, writing, and accounts. These were venues for evangelical promulgation, but they also expanded literacy in ways that were seen as threatening and were attacked as "methodistical."[7] Important work has also traced schools for the poor, but also schools for the deaf and the blind, in Britain and France in particular. John Thelwall established a school for students with "speaking defects"—the first of its kind—in London in 1806.

As is being revealed by ongoing "discoveries" about the abuses of schools directed to children who were indigenous, poor, or what we now conceive of as neurodivergent or differently abled, schooling can (of course) be a form of discipline in the Foucauldian sense. We hope that the teaching this volume recounts and promotes is more Freirean "education for liberation"[8]—teaching that aims to engage students across their differences in discovering themselves as knowers and learners in ways that will carry forward into their post-university lives. One question we grapple with, then, is: How does the act of teaching intersect with the "matter" of teaching—the content but also the material effects and outcomes of what we ask students to attempt?

TEACHING ABOUT THE EIGHTEENTH CENTURY

Teaching *about* the eighteenth century is what most of us trained to do. We chose this field because we were drawn to it—by a favorite author, a favorite teacher, or a class that just surprised us with the richness and sheer oddness of the period. Some of us fell into this period when trying to understand later developments, and stayed because the period includes so many seemingly contradictory impulses and founds so much of our current world. The eighteenth century's long afterlives force us to constantly reframe and revise what we know and what we ought to teach. As Rebekah Mitsein writes, "the discipline [of English literature] is continually haunted by its Eurocentric canon."[9] Working to expand that canon, but also to resituate literature, travelogue, natural philosophy, political philosophy, and visual arts, continues to make studying and teaching about the eighteenth century challenging. Suvir Kaul explains, in the case of eighteenth-century English literature, "What we can do, in our individual and collective capacities as teachers . . . , is to teach in a way that does not allow the fissured complexity of these [traditional] texts to be reduced to a species of unexamined Anglophilia. Celebrate the aesthetic achievements that enliven the age, certainly, but recognize that . . . in this period, all documents of 'Englishness' or 'Britishness' are at the same time documents of empire."[10] Kaul's insight resonates beyond literary studies to the entire field. One reason to teach "the eighteenth century," then, is because it is both distant enough to seem strange and yet still present enough to be impactful.

But few of us have students who arrive *knowing* that they want to study "the eighteenth century"—as a historical period, a collection of works and writers, or a tradition of thought. More and more, our institutions no longer hold a commitment to the period as a requirement or even an expectation for an educated graduate. Retirements in the fields that fall under "eighteenth-century studies" are no longer seen as needing replacements. If we think that it *is* important for our present-minded students and colleagues to understand something about the period's impact and long-term significance, it falls to us to build that bridge and articulate why and how we teach about the eighteenth century.

TEACHING EIGHTEENTH CENTURY WHEN YOU DON'T TEACH THE EIGHTEENTH CENTURY

For many of us now, our teaching assignments are various and less tied to our period expertise. The coverage model has never really worked, of course; departments in the single digits and those nearing triple digits all struggle with "coverage." More and more, coverage arguments don't work to convince deans and provosts of the necessity of continuing faculty lines, nor really do they always convince us ourselves.

But we are also newly in a world where many of us believe in the value and power of an expansive eighteenth century that is conflicted at its heart by knowledge-making based in empire building, settler colonialism, scientific experimentation, and globalization. We are newly excited by evolving ways to understand and teach the legacies and impact of this period, only to find ourselves no longer assigned to teach it. Thus, we import eighteenth-century materials, infiltrating our period into topical or interdisciplinary courses that are attractive to students and likely to draw them from adjacent fields in the natural and social sciences and even professional schools. This is both a strategy and a matter of survival.

WHAT IS "EIGHTEENTH CENTURY" AND WHY NOW?

The affordances of the term "eighteenth century" itself are its capaciousness as a loose period—often beginning in the 1600s and ending variously in the early to mid-1800s. To begin with, this period term evades some of the ideological baggage of terms like "Enlightenment," "Age of Johnson," "Romanticism," "Age of Goethe," "les lumières,"—but it also puts a premium on dates that are Eurocentric, and even presupposes (for anglophone scholars) a British-centric way of organizing thought and culture. This organization not only highlights the projects of empire and colonialism, but is also a truly bad fit with forms of Indigenous knowledge, which often operate along different conceptions of time. "Eighteenth century" is a fundamentally diachronic conception that comes with the potential implicit narrative of decline or, more often, given the optimism of the period, progress.[11] Our students are particularly susceptible to narratives of progress, and oddly enough so are syllabuses as a genre. When we build a course, we often do so chronologically and with an implicit sense of building *toward* something. We do well to keep these ideological implications and implicit narratives in mind.

Why then would we want to teach the eighteenth century *now*, in the first half of the twenty-first century, when the old argument that we must know our history to avoid repeating it rings hollow because which "history" we know is increasingly contested? It is perhaps unsurprising that several authors in this volume cite the V21 Collective's call for something like "strategic presentism"—recognizing first that we always necessarily encounter earlier literatures and peoples through our own present, and secondly that there is an ethical call to make a connection to a present. Their statement focuses on the Victorian era, but the pertinent claims resonate for the "long" eighteenth century as well: "Insofar as the world we inhabit bears the traces of the nineteenth century, these traces are to be found not only in serial multiplot narrative, but in income inequality, global warming, and neoliberalism. Presentism is not a sin, but nor are all forms of presentism equally valuable."[12] Just as "strategic essentialism" was a useful riposte to twentieth-century calls to disallow questions of gender, sexuality, and racial and ethnic identity and significance, the call to consider the value of a particular, guarded, and self-aware presentism is worth considering.[13] Who *are* our students now? Without falling into the "study of sameness" that Lynn Hunt warned against in 2002,[14] how do we undercut their assumptions, on the one hand, of the failure of historical change (historical pessimism) and, on the other, of easy progress narratives (as in, this generation has corrected all the errors of the past and purified their terminology)?

And as Nicole Wright has argued, there is a double danger in marketing courses in eighteenth-century and Romantic studies as "vehicles for social justice," even though that strategy increases enrollments. First, she notes, in doing so we "risk buying into the very same narratives endemic to the traditional pedagogical and research approaches they intend to dismantle: Whiggish narratives of inevitable progress from a benighted past to superior present on one hand, and winners/losers of history dichotomies . . . on the other. Both types of narratives can stoke passivity . . . instead of the intellectual inquiry and political consciousness to which some faculty mean to awaken students." Finally, as Wright notes, courses advertised in this way tend to self-select, "failing to attract the students who are least familiar with this history—or most skeptical of its value—and thus arguably need these courses more than do the students who flock to them."[15]

The chapters in this volume also approach teaching aspects of the long eighteenth century in the time of a double pandemic: a global contagion that led to rapid pivoting to teaching in unfamiliar ways and to balancing content delivery with carework (often overlooked in institutionalized approaches to the labor of teaching), *and* a refocusing on the ongoing epidemic of racial injustice that is understood as a threat to health and well-being of Black and other persons of color worldwide. Apparent progress for LGBTQ+ people feels increasingly endangered. These threats are both pressingly *present* and rooted in the struggles of the period we teach and study. As Saidiya Hartman writes, "The past is neither inert nor given. The stories we tell about *what happened then*, the correspondence we discern between today and times past, and the ethical and political stakes of these stories redound in the present."[16]

What, then? How do we teach something called "the eighteenth century" under these conditions? And how might our teaching combine deep and critical engagement with other times, places, and peoples and also encourage ethical engagement between ourselves and the coming generation? One technique is to make the past "matter"—that is, to make it materially present. As several chapters here demonstrate, we seek to retain some of the rich strangeness of a past that impacts all of us but is often not precisely "ours." In that very strangeness and "defamiliarization," perspectives are birthed that review and recast what seems merely "real" or "the way things are" in our own time.

THE CHAPTERS

Teaching is the central labor of most academics, and our instructional mission establishes the conditions under which and in service to which we do our scholarship. In this collection, contributors turn the lens of critical scholarly thinking back on those conditions. Chapters in this collection balance attention to topical scholarship with awareness of teaching as a form of human engagement and shared meaning making, exploring practical approaches to teaching as an activity with an awareness of the stakes. Kate Parker (chapter 3), Diana Epelbaum (chapter 6), and Matthew Reznicek (chapter 7) draw on new fields, such as health humanities, science studies, or sexuality studies, in order to revivify familiar texts. Tiffany Potter (chapter 1), Ziona Kocher (chapter 2), Teri Doerksen (chapter 4), Christine Myers (chapter 5), and Diana Epelbaum (chapter 6) detail instructional options that draw connections from classroom study to active practice, highlighting assignments that encourage collaborative meaning-making and projects that have an afterlife beyond that term's work; these chapters also focus on the work of teaching, and offer practical and embodied or collaborative projects that help students to interrogate what they think they know and to build deeper understanding together. Travis Lau (chapter 8) and Emily Casey (chapter 9) turn the lens back on the experience of the teacher—the ways in which pain and contingency affect us as practitioners and raise the ethical stakes of our teaching.

The chapters in this collection recognize and represent teaching as a serious scholarly activity—one that bridges the sometimes solitary and reflective work of conventional scholarship with the more communal and communicative work of teaching and learning. The authors of this volume's chapters teach under widely variant conditions, yet we share a concern for teaching that is meaningful and experiential, and that has long consequences for students' and our own ethical engagement with the world. The authors include tenured, tenure-track, and contingent faculty, from public, private, and religious institutions, small liberal arts colleges, and comprehensive state and regional universities—and their chapters offer strategies and concerns that are both situated and adaptable. Moreover, while embedded in a range of departments—from English to History to American Studies—many of the chapters have implications for liberal arts core or general education courses of multiple kinds.

The collection opens with four chapters that touch pointedly on particular pedagogical practices and assignments. In chapter 1, Tiffany Potter opens with the question of how to craft assignments that do more than provide a rationale for assessing individual students (and instructors!). What kinds of work might we invite students to do that has a meaningful afterlife? Potter walks us through the question of what makes a good "teaching" edition of a particular text, particularly the challenges of teaching students who often have less time to devote to their studies than was assumed in the past. Potter asserts the value of collaborative editing with undergraduate students because it avoids the kind of "disposable" assignment that ends up in the end-term dumpster and it invites students to discover the tools of scholarly work and to imagine a future of influence and exchange with an expanded audience. In chapter 2, Ziona Kocher advocates for the power of classroom performance to engage students in grappling with the "intricacies of embodiment" on the Restoration stage and, by extension, in colonial America and our own time. Kocher demonstrates how Aphra Behn's difficult play *The Widdow Ranter* opens space for intersectional explorations of gender, race, class, English and colonized positionalities, as well as problems of history and theatricality that are of significant interest to contemporary undergraduates. In chapter 3, Kate Parker explores the affordances, but also the very particular limitations, of trying to teach sensitive content about sexual practices in an online environment at a regional university. The digital realm presents itself as equalizing, when in fact it is anything but. Online instruction may exacerbate not only issues of access but also vulnerabilities and trauma. Turning back to embodied learning, in chapter 4 Terri Doerksen recounts how she opens her class within a rapidly reconfiguring state system by engaging students with a carefully crafted cup of period chocolate. She walks them from that initial sensory experience into the historical moment, tracking from that cup of chocolate through the semester's readings to map out with students the lines of trade, conflict, and enforced labor that made a simple morning indulgence possible for some. Doerksen's chapter links us back to Potter's point about crafting assignments that will live beyond a short term's demands for evidence of student learning. All four of these chapters put the labor and care of teaching back in our view.

Then we turn to three chapters that explore teaching material that seems initially distant in ways that bridge that historical distance, ones we might consider as engaging in "strategic presentism" to positive ends—in chapter 5 (Christine Myers) through the specificities and ongoing impact of the "Scottish Enlightenment," in chapter 6 (Diana Epelbaum) through natural history and science, and in chapter 7 (Matthew Reznicek) through the intersection of health and wealth. The classes they describe reach beyond the current or likely humanities major to attract students rooted in other fields, modeling the value of humanistic study for *all* students without reverting to vague claims of empathy or critical thinking.

Invited to offer a course centered on Adam Smith with the goal of expanding business and economics majors' knowledge of their disciplines, Myers devised a class that both highlighted students' growing command of the period and modeled intellectual debate. Engaging contemporary concerns, from *Hamilton* to the function of universities then and now, Meyers tracks students' discovery of the specific Scottish contributions to Enlightenment ideals and realization of where we continue to fall short.

Teaching in the context of a Jesuit institution, Matthew Reznicek begins his course on poverty and the novel with the Rev. Pedro Arrupe's call to become agents of change who both resist and reform unjust structures. Reznicek's careful unpacking of how he approaches Jane Austen's *Emma*, highlighting the multiple sites of illness in that novel and how health and illness are implicated in the economics of wealth and charity models an intersectional health humanities approach. Reznicek argues for a kind of "strategic presentism" that recognizes that our students are not sealed off from the past, but live with its ongoing effects in health disparities that map onto economic ones.

Diana Epelbaum's chapter gives concrete details of how students in her course "Race and Place in the Natural Histories of the Americas" encounter natural history as a transatlantic cultural practice, intimately tied to European "curiosity, classification, and cultivation" that subtends early ideas about environment and labor. She focuses in particular on engaging those in her class as "student-scholars" who work alongside herself as "teacher-scholar" to discover and learn together. Drawing on a long history of pedagogies of writing and rhetoric that value this kind of collaboration, Epelbaum demonstrates how writing-intensive and WAC (Writing Across the Curriculum) classes like this one model the processes of exploration, discovery, collaboration, and reflection that exemplify the positive legacy of the eighteenth century.

The final two chapters, "Teaching Hurts" by Travis Chi Wing Lau (chapter 8) and "Anticolonial Approaches to Teaching Colonial American Art" by Emily Casey (chapter 9) point the mirror in both directions—toward students' engagement with the material impacts of histories of racial injustice and erasure from literature and culture in the West, and back toward themselves and the pain and ethics of teaching itself.

Lau's chapter focuses on a Restoration and Eighteenth Century survey that, rather than offering an escape from the pain of pandemic, sat with that pain by focusing closely on the period's obsession with bodies and bodily experiences. Lau ends by gesturing to Ramzi Fawaz's "affective curation,"[17] championing a pedagogy that seeks to elicit uncomfortable affective responses in the classroom in order to move through them: "The goal is not to have a painless class. . . . [R]ather, it is about a pedagogical practice that is accountable to pain and the different ways it is lived out among teachers and students" (Lau). In line with the V21 Collective's call for "strategic presentism," Lau's course, like Casey's, examines earlier materials in order to help us account for and "think critically about the past in the present in order to change the present,"[18] harking back to Reznicek's invocation of Rev. Arrupe.

Emily Casey's chapter returns us to the pain of teaching, ratcheting it up a notch by exploring her own work to make teaching American colonial art history into a practice that not only globalizes, but is explicitly anticolonial, asking: "How can we globalize eighteenth-century studies without attending to the histories of imperial violence, settler-colonization, capitalism, and white supremacy, which not only shaped the period but continue to affect our contemporary world?" This concern has additional power because her own status is contingent; her identification with and commitment to her role as teacher are destabilized when her department is closed. Casey importantly argues that "strategies and materials of art history, particularly the practice of prolonged visual analysis, support anticolonial thinking in the classroom and can be applied in other pedagogical contexts," leaving us with a final reflection on how we might learn to respond to this moment of reckoning while also arguing for the value of teaching as a world-changing practice that is itself under attack.

This collection aims to value *both* the labor and the expertise that excellent teaching requires, to highlight the value for all kinds of students of encountering "the eighteenth century" and asking questions about the foundations of knowledge, to empowering students and teachers together to link our contemporary moment to the past while interrogating in both directions. We take the value of focusing on teaching to be in highlighting, first, that teaching undergraduates is real work that has an impact in the world and on the future, and second, that teaching is a form of "generous thinking" that is sometimes under-recognized by institutional metrics. Rather than thinking of ourselves as "mini startups" who "build [our] brands through publishing articles and accruing accolades," these chapters take teaching as an ethical engagement with and among students, facilitated by an expert learner with content and period expertise, who is open to being surprised by students' contributions.[19] And as the final chapters make clear, we as teachers have something to gain in the exchange: teaching is, after all, a two-way engagement. As Jorge Coronado writes, teaching "is not just another task we perform in universities. It *is* the university."[20] The university we long for is one we make together through that engagement; and, for good or ill, its roots are in the period we bring to the fore.

NOTES

1. On the so-called demographic cliff, see, for example, Eric Hoover, "The Demographic Cliff: 5 Findings from New Projections of High-School Graduates," *Chronicle of Higher Education*, December 15, 2020, https://www.chronicle.com/article/the-demographic-cliff-5-findings-from-new-projections-of-high-school-graduates.
2. Ernest L. Boyer, *Scholarship Reconsidered: Priorities of the Professoriate* (New York: Carnegie Foundation for the Advancement of Teaching, 1990), 23–24.
3. Multiple states (Arkansas, Florida, Iowa, Mississippi, Missouri, and South Dakota) have considered prohibiting, or now prohibit, teaching the New York Times's 1619 Project which recounts the impact of slavery on, and contributions of Black Americans to, the history of the United States. Other states have enacted restrictions on teaching "Critical Race Theory" variously understood, or more generally, "divisive concepts," particularly around race, gender, and sex. See Brooke LePage, "These Are the States That Passed Laws Restricting the Teaching of Racial History," *The 74* (September 3, 2021), https://www.the74million.org/article/these-are-the-states-that-passed-laws-restricting-the-teaching-of-racial-history/; and Sarah Schwartz, "Lawmakers Push to Ban '1619 Project' from Schools," *Education Week*, February 3, 2021, https://www.edweek.org/teaching-learning/lawmakers-push-to-ban-1619-project-from-schools/2021/02. In Florida under the 2021 "Viewpoint Diversity" bill, students are encouraged to record faculty lectures and report content they find objectional (this despite the state's two party consent law): "Authorizes a student to record video or audio of class lectures for personal educational use, in connection with a complaint to the public institution of higher education where the recording was made, or as evidence in, or in preparation for, a criminal or civil proceeding." https://www.flsenate.gov/Committees/billsummaries/2021/html/2566. PEN America tracks what they term "educational gag orders" across K-12 and higher education, including the prohibition of information about gender and sexual identities, divisive concepts particularly including race and histories of enslavement, and even social and emotional learning. https://pen.org/educational-censorship-continues-in-2023.
4. Kathleen Fitzpatrick, *Generous Thinking: A Radical Approach to Saving the University* (Baltimore: Johns Hopkins University Press, 2019).
5. See Eugenia Zuroski, "'Where Do You Know From?': An Exercise in Placing Ourselves Together in the Classroom," *MAI: Feminism & Visual Culture* (January 27, 2020), https://maifeminism.com/where-do-you-know-from-an-exercise-in-placing-ourselves-together-in-the-classroom/.
6. See Robert B. Louden, *The World We Want: How and Why the Ideals of the Enlightenment Still Elude Us* (Oxford: Oxford University Press, 2010), chap. 2, "Education," for a useful

overview of key transnational philosophical debates about "schooling" and "education" in the period, particularly questions about universal education and education for practical use or for transformation and moral development.

7. The term "methodistical" is a reference to Methodist practices (rather than those of the Church of England), including lay preaching and personal reading of scriptures. See Anne Stott, "Hannah More and the Blagdon Controversy, 1799–1802," in *Evangelicalism in the Church of England, c.1790-c.1890*, ed. Mark Smith and Stephen Taylor, Church of England Record Society vol. 12 (Woodbridge, UK: Boydell Press 2004), 1–50.
8. See in particular Paolo Freire, *Pedagogy of the Oppressed* (1968), translation, 1970, by Myra Bergman Ramos (New York: Continuum, 1986).
9. Rebekah Mitsein, "Teaching Eighteenth-Century British Literature beyond the Pale," *Studies in Eighteenth-Century Culture* 49 (2020): 131.
10. Nicole Mansfield Wright and Suvir Kaul, "ASECS at 50: Interview with Suvir Kaul," *Eighteenth-Century Studies* 53, no. 1 (2019): 39–40.
11. Contrast Romanticism. As Manu Chander notes, "Romanticism" is less a period term than "an 'ism,' a set of beliefs about, for example, the relationship between the individual and society, or the privileged role of the poet in shaping the mores of a people. As an ideology, 'Romanticism' is portable: we can track the way people were committed to . . . the specialness of poetry and make unexpected connections between disparate communities." See Katarzyna Bartoszyńska, "Texts in Context: Manu Samriti Chander on *Brown Romantics*," *Asymptote* (December 8, 2022), https://www.asymptotejournal.com/blog/2022/12/08/texts-in-context-manu-samriti-chander-on-brown-romantics/.
12. "Manifesto of the V21 Collective," http://v21collective.org/manifesto-of-the-v21-collective-ten-theses/.
13. See also Adela Pinch on "engaged presentism," in "Recent Studies in the Nineteenth Century," *Studies in English Literature, 1500–1900* 54, no. 4 (Autumn 2014): 943. Thanks to Nicole Mansfield Wright for sharing the reference.
14. Lynn Hunt, "Against Presentism," *Perspectives on History* 40, no. 5 (2002): 7–9.
15. Nicole Mansfield Wright, "Resisting 'Resistance': Presentism and Its Discontents," paper presented at the conference "Resistance in the Spirit of Romanticism," University of Colorado, Boulder, September 6, 2018, and at ASECS, Orlando, Florida, March 23, 2018), 6, 7–8. We thank the author for allowing us to cite her unpublished work.
16. Saidiya Hartman, *Lose Your Mother: A Journey along the Atlantic Slave Route* (New York: Farrar, Straus and Giroux 2008), 133.
17. Ramzi Fawaz, "How to Make a Queer Scene, or Notes toward a Practice of Affective Curation," *Feminist Studies* 42, no. 3 (2016): 760.
18. David Sweeney Coombs and Danielle Coriale, "V21 Forum on Strategic Presentism: Introduction," *Victorian Studies* 59, no. 1 (2016): 88. See also "Manifesto of the V21 Collective."
19. Jorge Coronado, "On Entrenched Inequalities in the Research University: Activism and Teaching for Tenured Faculty Members," *PMLA* 136, no. 3 (May 2021): 444.
20. Coronado, "On Entrenched Inequalities," 444.

1

CREATING TEACHING EDITIONS, TEACHING THROUGH EDITING

TIFFANY POTTER

TEACHING IN EIGHTEENTH-CENTURY literary studies has changed over the decades—notably in *what* we teach. In courses on eighteenth-century British fiction, for example, for a lot of different reasons, undergraduate syllabuses these days rarely include the full text of *Clarissa* or *Tom Jones* or *Evelina*, or the complete texts of major philosophical works. As we have reflected on the limited scope of the traditional English canon, such texts have been replaced on syllabuses in many cases by the work of writers like Aphra Behn, Eliza Haywood, Samson Occom, and Olaudah Equiano. As our institutions have changed, and our student populations have expanded—guided by fiscal and educational circumstances different from those of students of old—some of the very long novels and treatises in our courses have been supplanted by shorter texts more easily incorporated into quarter- or semester-length modules. More importantly, our movements toward diversity of voices in our canons and our course materials allow us to engage more effectively with a student audience that is both more diverse and often more sociopolitically informed.

But there are other reasons we need to be constantly revisiting our course choices and the editions we use to teach them. First is the need to counter what Martha Bowden has called "*Oroonoko* syndrome," whereby a single work comes functionally to represent an author and their voice, regardless of whether that work is particularly typical or particularly excellent compared to the writer's other publications. Creating high-quality, accessible new editions of a range of literary texts gives us the resources we need to push back against the shrinking of complex artists into specific pedagogical cubbyholes. Second, we are teaching in a world where mountains of critical work—good and terrible—are instantly at the hand of every student, and where we have to work hard to push some students beyond the belief that Sparknotes, Wikipedia, and AI tools tell them everything they need to know. Worse still are online essay banks full of old essays awaiting purchase, or unethical souls inviting panicking, anxious students to pay for someone else to write for them. And of course we don't know yet where AI tools will take questions of canon, research methods, and academic integrity in the coming months and years. We all had those moments of blank-page abject terror as students, but most of us did not have someone standing at our electronic elbow telling us that salvation is just an essay site or an AI subscription away.

Of course students should not fall to temptation, and of course they should not commit misconduct, but we as teachers have the capacity (and the responsibility), not least through thinking about editions, to design courses that don't just lessen the likelihood of our students' making bad decisions, but, more importantly, offer a more diverse, contextually illuminated, historically engaged learning experience that encourages students to engage with documents, works, or approaches that are not found in every online essay bank and AI web scraping archive. In this chapter, then, I begin with an evidence-based reflection on what our profession seems to agree makes a good classroom edition (canonical or new). I then turn to explaining how we can create a virtuous circle: including a less-canonical text or two on our syllabuses, teaching students to think critically about text choices and how they are positioned in classroom editions, and perhaps even having students create a publicly available edition of a new work—literary, philosophical, or historical—so that other teachers might assign it and other students might learn from it. This approach reflects the circumstances listed above, but also reflects current pedagogical thinking on the benefit of adding to our courses one or more assignments that are not "disposable" (student writes, professor grades, student throws away)—assignments with some sort of renewability or capacity to reach beyond a four-month course.

WHAT MAKES A GOOD TEACHING EDITION?

When we teach, we choose texts that serve our course design and pedagogy, but we also consider access: Can students get the book or document they need? Nearly any eighteenth-century text is now available free in some unedited form of scan from databases like Gale and Hathi Trust if one's institution has access, but—given eighteenth-century typefaces and page design—undergraduates often find it difficult to work from even the clearest scans. Hard copies of these scans are relatively inexpensive on sources like Amazon, but raise the same issues of student-friendliness. Very inexpensive text-only editions like those from Dover offer modern typesetting but no annotation or context. For most of us, something more extensive, but still inexpensive, is optimal.

For this project, I surveyed reviews of classroom editions in *Eighteenth-Century Fiction*, *Eighteenth-Century Studies*, and *The Scriblerian* from 2012 to 2021, seeking to discern any consensus regarding what makes a student edition "good," as well as to note any points of contention. Several of the reviews assert a list akin to what Benjamin F. Pauley describes as "everything one would want from a text for classroom use . . . a reliable text, annotations that are clear and sufficient without being obtrusive, and an intelligent and thoughtful editor's introduction . . . a rich selection of supplementary materials, including a truly surprising number of illustrations, aimed at provoking classroom discussion or simply thoughtful reflection."[1]

The most broadly useful classroom editions have certain obvious qualities: student-focused annotation, a contextual introduction with critical elements, wrapped into an inexpensive, but well-designed and sturdy form, ideally available in identical print and digital formats. Woe betide the "flimsy and unattractive volume"[2] or "sparsely annotated" edition.[3] Well-reviewed editions typically include either contextualizing documents or select critical history or both.

Nearly all of the reviews note whether the base text is authoritative, exactingly transcribed, and either stylistically modernized or not: explicitly student-oriented texts like the Broadview and Norton Critical Editions typically do modernize; blended-audience Penguin and Oxford editions more typically retain original capitalization and the like. Also frequently noted is a strong preference for concise footnotes "rather than those cumbersome endnotes" or end-text glossaries.[4] Reviewers of student-targeted editions argue comprehension and entry-level context are key, rather than bibliographical, historical, and critical completionism. Variants of the term "unobtrusive" recur in reviews as a favorable footnote quality, and with midlevel undergraduate students in mind, preferred annotations have a more explanatory than critical tenor.[5]

Editing is by its nature a critical process that creates interpretive work in every decision, from modernization and annotation content to choices of appendixes and excerpts. The effects and effectiveness of such critical processes impact teachers' selection of textbooks, but those critical implications are often invisible to students, even understood as neutral and benign (a perception addressed in the course module described below). Melvyn New's overview of the classroom genre summarizes the same trends that appear in the review data, while politely leaving room for dissent: "Most important, however, Norton's annotations are footnotes, always preferred by this reader to back notes. Once more, however, this is a matter of taste, as are also differences in the introductory material: Norton's is minimal, as is Oxford's; Penguin's is the most extensive and the most valuable, but again some instructors prefer not to have students swayed by introductory material (not to mention those who will read *only* the introduction)."[6]

Relative brevity of introductory material is consistently praised by reviewers (and, one expects, by students), but the question of interpretation is less consistent: Should a classroom edition have an introduction that offers a specific critical take on the text (typical of mixed-audience critical/classroom editions of recovered or less-canonical texts), or a general introduction to the author, work, genre, and context that sets the teacher an open field for selecting an approach (typical of some Broadview editions)? While some reviews approve of "a useful interpretive lens to guide both teacher and student reading the novel,"[7] others are pleased when an editor "avoids the editorial pitfall of promoting an interpretation of the novel through such passages, leaving the reader to determine how to connect the two."[8]

Reviews of editions with a more critical/scholarly emphasis often express frustration with the fact that critical introductions may appear to students to be exhaustive, though of course they cannot be, and also with the fact that "there are, inevitably, gaps in terms both of scholarly representation and of critical perspective."[9] Other reviews are more brusque on critical positioning. One review, for example, praises "important gains" in terms of pedagogy and points out that the "edition's usefulness is more limited for the researcher. . . . [The] critical apparatus is uneven, at times arbitrary, and it reproduces some long-standing lacunae in criticism. . . . Ideally, the editors would have acknowledged a range of possibility for interpretation, especially in a volume designed for teaching, rather than replicating well-established, outdated assumptions."[10] Perhaps a useful middle ground is identified in Cassander L. Smith's review of what she notes is one of many relatively recent versions of the same text, the *Narrative of the Life of Olaudah Equiano*: "Unlike other editions that mostly target scholars and advanced students, this edition contains a critical apparatus that contextualizes Equiano's story, covering all the basics, without overwhelming the reader. [Brycchan] Carey's introduction, for example, is a concise seventeen pages. In that space, he provides one access point—through the Atlantic slave trade—to help readers enter the narrative and begin to understand its cultural work. He also addresses the book's more technical features related to genre, style, and language."[11]

There is near-universal praise for editions that use appendixes to place a work in its eighteenth-century context. Reviewers praise different things in the same terms: "information about the Grand Tour, art criticism, and other related topics" is valued in a review of Smollett's *Travels through France and Italy* to "allow students and general readers to gain a broader and deeper understanding of Smollett's achievement than was possible with prior editions,"[12] and similarly a review of Mackenzie's *The Man of Feeling* notes the "utility" of a "rich variety of appendixes that supplement the text and provide valuable insights into eighteenth-century sentimentalism."[13] There is consensus that well-chosen historical resources provide a teacher with material that can be used to illuminate the literary text without *telling* students what to think about it. Such materials support active pedagogical practices for students through comparison and illumination in the classroom. The Broadview and Norton Critical Editions are both favored for this element; Norton's marketing material calls this section a part of its "proven three-part format" of "[1] annotated text, [2] historical and cultural contexts: the story behind the story" (i.e., maps, letters, images, contemporary reviews, and responses) and [3] critical essays, where "modern scholars provide an entry point for students' critical engagement."

Norton's stated overarching goal is to help students "understand, analyze and appreciate classic works" in "one trusted, convenient, affordable book."[14]

This last category of "critical essays" separates the Norton teaching editions from others, and reaction is mixed to the selection and inclusion of critical excerpts. Criticism of what is left out is perhaps unavoidable, as in this review of an edition of *Tristram Shandy*: "An editor must no doubt work within restrictions when reproducing published work, but there are one or two Sterne scholars one might have wished present, given their extensive work in the field; and, more pressingly, some areas of discussion are under-represented."[15] In 2019 Melvyn New went so far as to query the inclusion of bibliographies: "How useful are bibliographies in textbook editions? Perhaps Penguin's highly selective 'Further Reading' makes as much sense as the more thorough bibliography offered by Oxford, but the availability of scholarship online may render irrelevant all such listings. More to the point, Norton's primary claim to distinction among textbook editions is its inclusion of 'recent' scholarly essays (here [on *Humphrey Clinker*], nine published between 1982 and 2012/2013. All these essays—and more recent ones—are now just a click away for students."[16] This is true for students at institutions with well-funded libraries well-subscribed to the databases, but not yet universal, so there is a clear benefit to a selection of critical material if one is selecting a text for students with limited library access. But it is also true that critical excerpts and bibliographies are the part of any edition that dates the most quickly. Other than for very widely taught texts like *Oroonoko* or *Pride and Prejudice* or *Robinson Crusoe*—which are likely to receive a second or third or sixth edition in relatively short time—excluding this element would seem to strengthen the long-term effectiveness of an edition (and thus also its resale value for thrifty students).

And this leads to my last question: Exactly how many editions do we really need of the same twenty canonical works? This question too is asked across the reviews. On the gloriously embellished Harvard editions of Austen's works, "we might wonder—we are forced to consider, really—whether it is necessary to spend thirty-five dollars on the big, heavy, gorgeous, lavishly illustrated coffee-table edition from Harvard University Press rather than spending half that on the Norton critical edition, which includes useful critical and contextual materials, or even less: the Oxford edition, with Margaret Doody's excellent introduction, costs a mere US$7.00. Does purchasing this edition—or requiring students to purchase it—make sense? Is it sensible?"[17] Her answer can be summarized as "yes for us, no for our students," and that is the answer for many of us: canonical eighteenth-century texts are kept alive and accessible by new editions that target new types of readers with new approaches and versions of sometimes hard-to-access historical and contextual resources.

The answer is also yes for the not-yet-canonical, texts that may have much to say to our students, and may illuminate new things even for the most experienced scholar. The next section of this chapter turns to the editing of these texts for (and by) students.

With so many archives now fully accessible through databases, significant numbers of new texts are available to help to combat issues like the essay banks and "*Oroonoko* syndrome" discussed above (though the jury is still out on how AI will play out on the accessibility and impact of new texts). The trick, of course, is that it can be hard to get a press to bite on new editions of unknown works, no matter how brilliantly students have responded to the teaching of blotchy scans of archival finds. In my own experience, students have been very open to less-canonical pieces, and genuinely excited to find something where their every thought did not seem already to have been expressed ("How does anyone ever say anything new about *Hamlet*?"). Adding even one of these texts to a course, using a hard-copy edition or scan, can significantly change student experience.

As you will see below, some of my own courses have integrated editing into their teaching practice, but before I choose something for a project, I have typically taught it from scans at least once. Long before I started working on these texts for a press, my students gave their hearts to Elizabeth Cooper's hilarious and witty emotional gamesmanship of a female libertine and a man of feeling in 1735 ("Lady Bellair is my new feminist hero! Can we make t-shirts?"); they followed Eliza Haywood's 1724 alternatingly glamorous and suffering intriguing masqueraders like a darkly comic Netflix series ("so much in such a short book!"); and they wrestled with the shocking brutality of Robert Rogers's 1766 take on Pontiac ("Ponteach"), staging his rebellion and the colonialism it resisted from Pontiac's own point of view, but through the inevitable lens of Rogers's own place in North American imperialism. Each one of these teaching experiences led to published editions with major presses, and they started with editing-related student assignments designed to create opportunities for students to make acknowledged contributions to published scholarship, work that would be available to future students far beyond our own university.

TEACHING THE EIGHTEENTH CENTURY THROUGH CRITICAL EDITING IN THE CLASSROOM

In *Editing Early Modern Women* Sarah Ross and Paul Salzman ask, "How can textual editing upset conventional hierarchies of literary value, while still finding a readership? And, as the print-based editing of both male- and female-authored texts is increasingly complemented or displaced by the electronic edition, how can digital methods of editing, archiving, and amassing early modern texts facilitate multiple editorial and literary-critical aims?"[18] As their book argues, there are not easy answers for these big questions, but there are small steps we can take.

In the past I have taken advantage of years in which I had an editing contract with a press to invite my students to create annotations and share ideas, with the promise that notes that were better than mine would be included in the published edition, with their names on the acknowledgments page. More than fifteen of my students have proudly seen their names in print in my editions, creating a permanent, publicly visible connection between our course together and the larger academic world. As noted above, contracts for new hard-copy editions of rare books are a bit tougher to come by these days, but the value of such editions is not significantly less in other forms and media.

With its goal of intense, independent engagement with course materials and high-impact active learning for the student, a scholarly research paper is still generally a mainstay of assessment design in my courses. But my students write a lot of essays in that form across their degree programs, and I seek to expand the range of ways in which they can communicate their critical talents and knowledge. One of my goals in recent years has been to include assessments that move away from what have been called "disposable" assignments. Disposable assignments are those where the work is written by the student, marked by the professor, and returned to the student, often without much opportunity for it to go beyond the fulfilling of course requirements (and sometimes understood as a product of dispiritingly limited value in the eyes of the students who create the same general form of work ten or twelve times each semester). David Wiley throws down the gauntlet on disposable assignments in harsh terms: "These are assignments that students complain about doing and faculty complain about grading. They're assignments that add no value to the world—after a student spends hours creating it, a teacher spends 30 minutes grading it, and then the student throws it away."[19] He wonders, "What if we changed these 'disposable assignments' into activities which actually added value to the world? Then students and faculty might feel different about the time and effort they invested in them."[20] Engaging with Wiley, Christina Hendricks appreciates the value of innovative nondisposable approaches in assessment, but makes it clear that recognizing disposability does not mean that disposable assignments lack value: they allow students to hone and demonstrate essential skills and cognitive processes, and exams are designed to confirm a student's mastery of the course material. There is enormous value in these outcomes.[21]

What I propose here is not either/or but yes/and—adding another form of active learning and critical engagement with eighteenth-century texts and the critical processes that bring them to modern students. Adding a nondisposable assignment to a syllabus can alter a student's learning by combining two things: authenticity and renewability. Authentic assessment creates what Ashford-Rowe et al. describe as

> connections between real-world experiences and school-based ideas; which within our context translates into the more academic higher education experience. They also present students with the full array of

> tasks that mirror the priorities and challenges found in the best instructional setting. Degree of challenge is a reflection of the authenticity of real-world situations and tasks. Thus, within an authentic assessment activity, students are required to demonstrate their ability to analyse the task and synthesise, from the range of skills and knowledge that they have acquired, those which will be necessary for the completion of a specific outcome, where the approach to the potentially correct response may not always be clear cut or obvious.[22]

An assignment is "renewable" when a student's work has some impact upon or usefulness for other students or a wider population, "provid[ing] an opportunity for longer-lasting influence" or future students' work.[23] Citing Falconer and Littlejohn, Seraphin et al. note that "student-generated instructional materials represent some of the best examples of culturally rich and effective learning objects."[24]

In eighteenth century studies, we can remedy disposability on a small scale by, for example, assigning critical summaries of "recommended readings" to be posted to a shared class resource; or asking students to create, annotate, and post a PowerPoint slide to explain a concept; or holding a term-end class conference, poster display, or "Three-minute term paper" event modeled on the three-minute thesis competition. More broadly, and among many possibilities, one might invite students to write or edit Wikipedia pages for credit or to use the 18thConnect.org tool TypeWright to correct OCR transcriptions that appear in EEBO or ECCO.

The assignment described here creates what can serve as a permanent, publicly accessible academic resource that credits the academic production of current students and invites future students and teachers outside of my university to access texts that are otherwise less accessible and less academically usable: collaborating to create online editions of texts that otherwise languish unread in archives, or by re-editing out-of-copyright literary texts that once were available but are now out of print and nearly impossible to find online or in hard copy.

The critical, scholarly relationship between editing and teaching is not limited to creating a high-quality consumable academic product for eighteenth-century-studies classrooms (though it is excellent when a formal book contract can be part of the process). Editing can also be highly effective as teaching and learning practice in itself, particularly if we use it to invite students to reflect on the disciplinary and cultural assumptions behind the choices that editors make, which are usually invisible to students. In the course module described here, senior undergraduate students follow a scaffolded process: critical analysis of the editions we are using in the course; finding and printing an archival text or texts to be edited as a class project; reflection on the critical positioning and context they think will be most valuable for other students; and then creation of a creative commons-licensed online edition that will be publicly available long after the course is over, including a critical introduction, undergraduate-appropriate annotations, and a selection of informative appendixes and illustrations. It may be a class project, but it does articulate and strive to embody the scholarly reviewers' criteria for a good teaching edition for future students.

COURSE DESIGN

My own institution, the University of British Columbia, is a highly-ranked, competitive Canadian R1 university with some 58,000 undergraduate and 13,000 graduate students, of whom more than 25 percent are international students, coming from more than 160 countries, with China, India and the US the most common countries of origin. UBC does not publish data on students' ethnicities, with the exception of Indigenous Canadian students, who make up 3–4 percent of our population. In a voluntary UBC survey in 2012, approximately two-thirds of students self-identified as members of racialized groups. Our students come from a wide range of economic and social backgrounds. Life in Vancouver is expensive, but for domestic students, tuition typically is not, running under CA$6,000 per year for a bachelor of arts degree in 2023; international students, however, might pay more than CA$40,000 per year. I am conscious of that range of lived experience and economics, and that my teaching benefits significantly from the excellent library and database holdings of a privileged institution. Included below are tips for using this assignment if students do not have access to ECCO or EEBO; in a class larger than the seminar of eighteen to twenty students I describe here; or for a graduate student audience.

Renewable and authentic assignments are not outcomes in themselves, but valuable tools for courses in our discipline: the course that I describe here is not *on* scholarly editing—it's on eighteenth-century British drama—but in this course, one of what might usually be two research essay assignments is replaced by the edition-creation project. Assessment for my course, for example, combines:

- One 300-word critical summary of a relevant scholarly article in the third week of class: each student selects a different work from a list of recommended readings, and summaries are posted to a shared class reference document on the LMS [ours is Canvas] (5 percent of course grade)
- One 10-minute oral presentation, with slides (20 percent)
- A standard 2,500-word critical research essay related in some way to the topic of the presentation (25 percent);
- A grade for contribution to classroom climate, discussion, and peer learning (10 percent)
- The elements of the editorial project (totaling 40 percent) as follows:
    - 5 percent: edition analysis
    - 5 percent: archive search and text markup
    - 10 percent: text creation component (writing footnotes)

10 percent: framing component (500–800 words, with a partner)
10 percent: appendix selection and researched critical headnote (300 words)

For presentations, students sign up for the week in which they will present, and their associated essays are due seven days later. Combining this self-selected due date with the firm timeline and hard deadlines that are essential to meeting the outcomes of the collaborative project enables me to provide a professionalizing team project with a second, more flexible assignment to give students control over their term workload to some degree.

The version of the assignment described here is arranged for a small class of eighteen to twenty students in an upper-level course. The assignment could be scaled up for a larger class in one of two ways: One might have "teams" of fifteen to twenty students each create a separate edition of the same text, using the guide and prompts provided here, perhaps with a class at the end debating any diverging editorial choices. Alternately, scaling up might involve the instructor selecting a grouping of shorter pieces for an "anthology," with smaller teams completing editions of shorter texts around a specific theme or question (essays, broadsheets and magazines, letters or diary entries might work very well here, for example).

ASSIGNMENT ARC

This term-long project is introduced at the beginning of the course so that students are aware at the start that they should be thinking critically about not just the texts, but the editions in which they are reading them. The opening-week setup includes a short introduction to the qualities of a good classroom edition (discussed earlier in this chapter) to raise students' generic awareness and provide a critical vocabulary. If I have time, I review some examples of some slightly hair-raising footnotes and sometimes disturbing introduction comments from old editions to help them to think critically about ostensibly neutral historical introductions.

1. About one-third of the way through the course, after multiple literary texts have been discussed, each student submits a two-page commentary on a past or present edition of one of our assigned texts (a low-stakes introductory step worth 5 percent of the course grade). We spend the next class hour discussing the fact that no edition of a historical text can be entirely neutral. We discuss our analyses, first in small breakout groups—sorted by the text they assessed—unearthing the cultural work being performed by different editions, and the emphases, frameworks, and assumptions that underlie that work. Breakout groups in my class are literally active, bringing students out of their seats to talk together in front of sections of whiteboard, where they live-document their discussion, then circle their four most significant observations and examples,

before a two-minute verbal overview for the rest of the class. Students are encouraged to photograph everyone's whiteboards at the end of class for reference (or the instructor can photograph them and post photos if there is a course website or LMS like Canvas).

2. The course then returns to literary emphases until halfway through the course, when we do text selection and task division. In an undergraduate seminar, I typically preselect a suitable text (relevant to and informed by course content already read, chronologically and geographically appropriate, not available in an annotated classroom or critical edition). In a graduate course, each student might be assigned to use research databases to search out their own text that meets these criteria, reflecting at a more sophisticated level on the theoretical questions behind canon extension. In another low-stakes step, students are assigned to find, download, and generate a hard copy of the assigned text, from the original publication year, using archival resources like the Gale ECCO, Sabin Americana, or Transnational Slavery and Anti-Slavery databases or similar archives (if available). At institutions that do not subscribe to such private databases, the instructor could provide a digital text or photocopy to create the same starting point. After generating their hard copy, students mark it up to highlight terms/ references/ allusions that their experience as students tells them would need a footnote (assuming a second-year undergraduate readership). They are *not* writing annotations yet, however. If the text chosen for the class project exceeds 50 pages or several hundred lines of poetry, it makes sense to break it by chapter, book, or act/scene so that students are reading the whole text, identifying annotation needs in, say, 50 pages, and later actually writing annotations for a set number of pages (depending on the density of citations needed per page in a selected text). The 5 percent for this establishing stage of the assignment includes the finding of the archival copy, highlighting terms for annotation, and listing three things that their reading leads them to think should probably be discussed in an introductory essay.
3. The editing assignment continues in parallel to literary analysis for the rest of the course, with twenty to thirty minutes per week of class time dedicated to our intellectual collaboration. The assignment then has several components: textual annotation, drafting of introduction elements, selection of informative illustrations, selection of illuminating appendixes, and creation of headnotes and annotation for appendixes and illustrations. It sounds like a lot, but not every student does every task: instead, each element is completed by two or three students (depending on class size, with students selecting tasks that suit their interests and, perhaps, other majors like economics, gender studies, history, or French). Then, after assessment, it is all brought together in a google doc, before being migrated to a university-associated page to generate a free, open-access resource. This assignment would work well in a course with an online or blended delivery.

AN EXAMPLE

The chapters in this volume leave me excited by the possibilities of using this editing assignment around the kind of colonizing and conduct texts that inform Behn's *Widdow Ranter*, or to create a growing archive of easily accessible edited versions of lesser-known transatlantic natural histories for Diana Epelbaum's course, or an online anthology of church, medical, and economic documents and women's letters for Matthew Reznicek's approach to *Emma*. But the example I describe briefly here (without wandering too far into the administrative weeds) is for an undergraduate course on performances of power and gender in plays engaging with the masculinist subcultures of Restoration and eighteenth-century libertinism. The course would frame the intellectual and social practices and implications of libertinism with Pepys and modern critical readings, plus poetry by Rochester, Buckingham, and Behn, and then move through canonical plays by Wycherley, Behn, and Etherege, the lesser-known *The Libertine* by Shadwell, one of Fielding's libertine plays, and the revisionist female libertine and man of feeling in Cooper's *The Rival Widows, or Fair Libertine*.

In such a course I might arrange the edition project around a text like Charles Knipe's 1715 two-act afterpiece, *A City Ramble, or The Humours of the Compter* (a play with no later edition, available on Gale's ECCO). Graduate students might be encouraged to go farther: to generate together from archives a collection of broadsheets, poems, essays, letters, journal entries, and the like that convey a sense of the popular perception of the king's privileged and protected libertine circles.

In an undergraduate class of eighteen to twenty students, the course works like this, with each student completing four assessed elements toward our edition:

1. **Archive and planning:**
   - All students would search the archive to find and generate a hard copy of the full text of the 1715 edition of the play.
   - All students would highlight items across the whole (short) play in need of footnotes.
2. **Text creation**
   - In pairs, students sign up for a 15-page text segment, then research and write annotations (for this short text, each section will be annotated by two groups). One group of two to three students researches and writes annotations for the *dramatis personae* and the actors who played each role in the first staging.
3. **Introduction.** Using current scholarship to create a 500- to 700-word piece on Knipe's play, each pair of students takes on one of the following tasks:
   - Research and write a biography of Charles Knipe
   - Research and write a summary of aristocratic libertinism from the Restoration to the early eighteenth century

- Research and summarize attitudes toward Quakers in the early eighteenth century
- Research and summarize the conventions and trends of late-Restoration and early eighteenth-century comedy
- Research and summarize the genre of the afterpiece
- Research and summarize the broader stage trends and environment of the turn of the century
- Research and summarize conservative responses to Restoration comedy (e.g., Collier, Cibber, Shaftesbury)
- Write a piece arguing for the significance of a particular thread or element of the play
- Write a piece arguing for the significance of a second particular thread or element of the play
- Write a piece arguing for the significance of a third particular thread or element of the play
- Create an annotated bibliography as an additional resources page, and edit the cumulative works-cited list generated by the other projects above

4. **Appendixes and Illustrations.** Each student finds *one* historical or archival text, document, or illustration that they feel illuminates the text; they transcribe and annotate a selection of 400–800 words (or generate a clear, cited version of the image), and write a 200-word headnote.

It is possible that more than one student will select the same passage; in that case the best headnote and annotations will end up in our online edition. In preparation for the combination of explanatory and critical elements of a good headnote (and to push back against the "monumentalizing tendency" of headnotes,[25] students read the reflections on "Editing a *Norton Anthology*" by Vincent Leitch et al. As Barbara Johnson puts it in the same symposium, "a headnote has to explain something difficult in simple terms, but it has to convey the difficulty within the simplicity, not just explain it away."[26]

In total, then, each student locates and marks up the play; researches and co-writes eight to ten footnotes; co-writes a 500- to 800-word introduction section; and finds and writes a headnote for an informative appendix text or illustration. As each of the individual elements is completed, assessed, and revised based on the feedback received from the instructor, pieces are added to the master google doc. Each student's non-footnote contributions are credited by initials (TFP), keyed to a list of editors at the end of the document. At the end of the course, I undertake the relatively easy task of changing the document over to a text-based web document, hosted by my university.

I hope that in the future I will be able to hire a tech-savvy graduate student to increase the attractiveness and flexibility of our editions, but tech is not the focus of the assignment. Instead, our class has interrogated the cultural work performed by the apparatus of modern classroom editions; carried out archival, historical, and critical research at a high level; examined the ways in which these different critical methods serve a scholarly project; created a professional-level critical document; and made the document public as an open-access resource for future students. In my experience this assignment is a genuinely authentic and renewable learning experience for students, with a genuine potential benefit to the classes of students who follow them. We hope that our work together not only is a learning experience for our group, but also contributes to the teaching of eighteenth-century literature far beyond our own classroom and long past our time together.

NOTES

1. Benjamin F. Pauley, "Daniel Defoe, *Robinson Crusoe*. Ed. Evan R. Davis" (review), *Digital Defoe: Studies in Defoe & His Contemporaries* 5, no.1 (2013): 152.
2. M-C. Newbould, "*Tristram Shandy* ed. by Judith Hawley" (review), *Eighteenth-Century Studies* 54, no. 2 (2021): 512.
3. Kathleen Lubey, "*Memoirs of a Woman of Pleasure* by John Cleland" (review), *Eighteenth-Century Fiction* 32, no. 3 (2020): 521.
4. Nabil Matar, "The Turkish Embassy Letters: Lady Mary Wortley Montagu, ed. Teresa Heffernan and Daniel O'Quinn," *The Scriblerian and the Kit-Cats* 47/48, no. 2 (Spring 2015): 100.
5. See Pauley, review of *Robinson Crusoe;* Newbould, review of *Tristram Shandy*; and Heather Keenleyside, "The History of Pompey the Little, by Francis Coventry" (review), *Eighteenth-Century Fiction* 23, no. 3 (2011) n.p.
6. Melvyn New, "Thoughts on Reviewing Textbook Editions and Student Companions," *The Scriblerian and the Kit-Cats* 52, no. 1 (2019): 80.
7. Srividhya Swaminathan, "*Captain Singleton* by Daniel Defoe" (review), *Eighteenth-Century Fiction* 33, no. 2 (2021): 325.
8. Lee Kahan, "*Moll Flanders* by Daniel Defoe" (review), *Eighteenth-Century Fiction* 25, no. 3 (2013): 640.
9. Newbould, review of *Tristram Shandy*, 514.
10. Lubey, review of *Memoirs of a Woman*, 522–523.
11. Cassander L. Smith, "*The Interesting Narrative by Olaudah Equiano*" (review), *Eighteenth-Century Fiction* 31, no. 4 (2019): 767–768.
12. Terence N. Bowers, "*Travels through France and Italy* by Tobias Smollett" (review), *Eighteenth-Century Fiction* 25, no. 4 (2013): 799.
13. John Dwyer, "Henry Mackenzie, *The Man of Feeling*. Edited by Maureen Harkin" (review), *Eighteenth-Century Scotland: Newsletter of the Eighteenth-Century Scottish Studies Society* 20 (2006): 28.
14. Norton Critical Editions, https://wwnorton.com/catalog/college/norton-critical-editions, accessed May 9, 2021.
15. Newbould, review of *Tristram Shandy*, 514.
16. New, "Thoughts on Reviewing," 79.
17. Dana Gliserman Kopans, "*Sense and Sensibility: An Annotated Edition*, by Jane Austen" (review), *Eighteenth-Century Fiction* 28, no. 1 (2015): 207.
18. Sarah E. E. Ross and Paul Salzman, eds., *Editing Early Modern Women* (Cambridge: Cambridge University Press, 2016), 3.

19. David Wiley, "What Is Open Pedagogy? Killing the Disposable Assignment," Improving Learning, October 21, 2013, https://opencontent.org/blog/archives/2975.
20. Wiley, "What Is Open Pedagogy?"
21. Christina Hendricks, "Renewable Assignments: Student Works: Adding Value to the World," Flexible Learning, University of British Columbia, October 29, 2015, https://flexible.learning.ubc.ca/news-events/renewable-assignments-student-work-adding-value-to-the-world/.
22. K. Ashford-Rowe, J. Herrington, and C. Brown, "Establishing the Critical Elements That Determine Authentic Assessment," *Assessment & Evaluation in Higher Education* 39, no. 2 (2013): 207.
23. Sally B. Seraphin et al., "A Conceptual Framework for Non-Disposable Assignments: Inspiring Implementation, Innovation, and Research," *Psychology Learning and Teaching* 18, no. 1 (2019): 89.
24. Seraphin et al., "A Conceptual Framework," 94.
25. Victor B. Leitch et al., "Editing a *Norton Anthology*," *College English* 66, no. 2 (Nov. 2003): 175.
26. Barbara Johnson, "Headnotes," *College English* 66, no. 2 (Nov. 2003): 185.

2

PERFORMING AGAINST HISTORY

Teaching Behn's *The Widdow Ranter*

ZIONA KOCHER

APHRA BEHN'S *THE WIDDOW RANTER or, The History of Bacon in Virginia* is a complicated play. Written by one of the most prominent female writers of the period, it was produced posthumously at Drury Lane and was performed only once, in November 1689.[1] While the plot is inspired by the events of Bacon's Rebellion, Behn is unconcerned with presenting an "accurate" historical account, and the details of her drama are significantly different from what played out in the colony. The play's story line itself is confusing at times, and it is easy to get lost in the sea of characters: the cast list includes thirty named roles, as well as numerous unnamed parts. The tragicomic genre can feel disjointed as it swings between heroic romance and comic jabs at the colonizing Virginians. The play's dedication hedges further: "Had our authour been alive she would have committed it to the flames rather than have suffer'd it to have been acted with such omissions as was made and on which the foundation of the play depended."[2]

Despite all of this, or perhaps *because* of it, *The Widdow Ranter* is a rich text for the classroom. It allows space to discuss a wide range of topics, from the intersections of gender, race, and class and the differences between English and colonized spaces on stage to the problem of historical "accuracy" and questions of theatrical "success." Exploring the play through classroom performance brings Behn's play to life, shedding light on the intricacies of embodiment both on the Restoration stage and within the colonial world of the late seventeenth century, all while resonating with our current moment. A performance-based approach leads students to linger in the discomfort produced by this complex play and encourages them to question how our understanding of history is produced.

The Widdow Ranter is often eclipsed by *The Rover* in both anthologies and scholarship, which makes it difficult to incorporate it into a syllabus using a single anthology. Less frequently assigned than Behn's romp through Naples, *The Widdow Ranter* is notable as one of the earliest English plays set in the colonial Americas. It features significant insights into gendered, classed, and racialized hierarchies as they are conceived of in both England and Virginia during the period. This setting makes the play a productive choice for classes focused on drama from the long eighteenth century, as well as those with a focus on early America or transatlantic literature; it works particularly well within a canonical Restoration drama syllabus. Placed after John Dryden's *All for Love* and William Wycherley's *The Country Wife* in a standard survey, students bring a grounding in both tragedy and comedy from the period, and can use what they have learned from these plays to unpack what is both familiar and unfamiliar about the plots and characters of *The Widdow Ranter*. In the context of a broader class about transatlantic literature, it pairs naturally with Behn's *Oroonoko*, as the play's portrayal of Indigenous culture complements and enriches the portrayals found in her novella and in Southerne's dramatic adaptation. The contexts provided by these other texts help students wade through the messiness of Behn's final play and its tense representation of colonization.

Though performance is crucial to helping students understand the play, questions about the physical, printed text and its relationship to the historical record are essential for that engagement to be productive.[3] In a class on Restoration and eighteenth-century drama offered at a small public college to a group of about twelve students, all with some prior experience with college literature courses, I began as guest instructor for a unit on *Widdow Ranter* by examining the play's original title page to introduce students to its primary conflicts. Looking at how the title is structured, students quickly noticed the juxtaposition of the two parts that appear in the largest font: "Widdow Ranter" and "Bacon in Virginia." While students may assume that the subtitle serves as an explanation of the primary title; in this case, however, the split title sets up distinct characters and story lines. Even when students have already encountered Restoration plays featuring distinct and possibly competing plotlines, the tragicomic genre may initially puzzle them because of the contrasting moods and aims within the various subplots. In *The Widdow Ranter*, there are clear connections between the inhabitants of the comic and tragic plots, even if their priorities are nothing alike. Bacon's actions have a clear impact on everyone in the play, and those actions are widely discussed in both the tragic and the comic plots. However, students must still contend with the troubling contrast and overlap between the racialized violence enacted and the comedy that drives the play forward. Most will find that they are uncertain of how to proceed with a play that brings these seemingly opposing stories together—and that very discomfort is an important source of insight.

Students are of course correct to find themselves uncomfortable with the contradictory tones of the overlapping comic and tragic plots, and these feelings should be acknowledged when discussing the play. In "Teaching Hurts" (chapter 8 in this volume), Travis Lau highlights the pedagogical power of pain and discomfort alongside the use of strategic presentism in helping students connect with the texts we teach from the long eighteenth century. Lau's attention to disability in these works while we navigated the ongoing COVID-19 pandemic challenges assumptions about the past as far away and disconnected from our present. Similarly, working through *The Widdow Ranter* as debates about how we teach about race and the need for Indigenous sovereignty play out on the national stage raises crucial questions about how we ourselves understand and (re)produce history. In "Anticolonial Approaches to Teaching Colonial Art Histories" (chapter 9 in this volume), Emily Casey crucially emphasizes the necessity for instructors and students to interrogate and engage their discomfort with their own positions in settler-colonialism. When students read aloud and put thought into how actors in 1689 represented these characters, they not only engage with the text more carefully but find themselves sitting with the unease that comes with embodying characters whose motivations and ethics are counter to their own. They are eager to share how they *feel* about these characters as well as how the characters operate within the plot. Rather than encouraging a shallow understanding based on personal opinion, the examination of such feelings through focus on Behn's drama leads to closer reading and more careful engagement with the history Behn creates and how it is linked to our present moment. By briefly "becoming" these characters who are producing the colonial world we inherit, students may voice a predictable argument about how much better our society is now. However, with the proper context they can recognize colonization as an ongoing process, linking the actions of the colonial government to our own.

Tackling a tragicomedy like *The Widdow Ranter*, it is necessary to unpack students' complicated reactions to the play in discussions about genre and the purpose of drama as *entertainment* when it claims to present *history*. Many students find enjoyment in the play's comic scenes but struggle to reconcile how they crash against moments of racist exoticism and violence. David McInnis suggests that the use of the tragicomic mode operates as "a bid to convey with greater accuracy and affect the full depth of social reality in English Virginia."[4] Assuming that most students have learned about American history in public school classrooms, they may have received a glossy progress narrative of colonization and independence as a positive movement toward freedom. Bacon's Rebellion, both as historical event and as portrayed in Behn's play, however, is messy and complex. Teaching *The Widdow Ranter* is productive because it encourages students to engage with the history of colonization and also asks them to consider *how history is produced*. Jenny Hale Pulsipher argues that in writing the play, "Behn used an interesting story for her own dramatic purpose and felt no great constraint to stick to the record," noting that "there were many reports of the conflict available in England from 1676 on." Instead of presenting a factual account of the rebellion, Behn's changes to the story were "likely made in response to contemporary political and cultural concerns," partially stemming from the playwright's own experiences of getting into trouble for critiquing those in power.[5] The lack of historical accuracy, however, does not undermine the play's potential power. Instead it forces the question of what is "true" in historical accounts: such records are written by specific groups with specific motives and can never be completely neutral. Behn's play might not present an accurate factual accounting of the events of the rebellion, but it certainly attempts to present specific truths regarding the political climate at the time when she was writing.

As students enter the play, it is thus important to establish both a careful skepticism regarding the events it presents and the historical context they need to understand it. We must emphasize to students that knowing every "factual" detail about Bacon's Rebellion will not unlock the play, as it is not meant to be a faithful recounting of these events. At the same time, they should question the "facts" that are known about the event, as well as how those are represented in the historical record. With this context in mind, students can examine how the play produces tensions surrounding race, class, and gender to present a particular political message and specific biases.

Depending on the edition of the play you are using, a brief discussion of the headnote may provide sufficient information about Bacon's Rebellion and the political climate in which the play premiered. The notes in the Routledge and the Penguin Classics editions, for example, outline the play's brief performance history, the stakes of Bacon's Rebellion, and Behn's political loyalties as they relate to her presentation of the historical events. They emphasize the play's complex representation of the varied intersections of race, class, and gender. Focusing in on the play's title character, these editions also provide important context for the Widow's name, giving details about the Ranters as a dissenting religious sect. If the edition used for the course does not have this contextualizing information, a short lecture or textual note to ground the play in history is essential, given its complex combination of historical and imagined events. It may be fruitful to have a student, or a group of students, research this topic and have them share it with the class: though the play differs greatly from the historical incident (as is often the case in history plays), a short presentation would be sufficient to set up the major stakes and how the historical record is being adjusted to present a certain point of view.

When utilizing performance in the classroom, students need to have a firm grasp on this background information to understand the motivations and actions of the characters they attempt to embody.[6] Nathaniel Bacon started the rebellion because of his discontent with the colonial government's actions regarding the Indigenous groups who had been displaced by the colony of Virginia. He led violent raids on Indigenous settlements he considered a threat to the colony and seized power from the colonial governor, Sir William Berkeley. An important detail of Bacon's rise to power that is largely erased in Behn's version of events is the coalition between poor Anglo-European people (many of them indentured servants) and Africans (some enslaved, some indentured, and some free). The backlash from this alliance led to intensified racialized divisions following the suppression of the rebellion, divisions that were encouraged by the colonial government. These divisive actions are some of the many roots of anti-Black racism in the United States, and continue to thrive, impacting current political movements that surround us. With this context in hand, students can fruitfully consider why this important coalition is neither mentioned nor illustrated in Behn's play, as well as how these historical coalitions might intersect with modern political action. It also allows students to tailor their performances of various characters based on their investments in this conflict.

Behn's version of Bacon's rebellion more directly resonates with English monarchical politics of the period, and it is equally important to provide students with information about Behn's Tory sympathies, the tensions surrounding James II, and the events of the "Glorious Revolution." In *The Widdow Ranter*, Bacon becomes a tragic, heroic figure whose love for Semernia, a fictional "Indian queen," contrasts sharply with his desire to destroy the Indigenous society she rules. Desperate to stop Bacon's violence, Semernia dresses as a man and enters the battle, but he kills her before she can reveal herself. Her death leads him to take his own life with poison, and the battle then ends—a notable departure from the truth, which is that he died of dysentery and the rebellion quickly collapsed. This counterfactual heroic ending introduces numerous questions about Behn's view of the rebellion and what Behn intended Bacon to represent to London's theater-going audience. Presenting students with details about Behn's loyalties gives them the tools to explore political allegory (Bacon as figure of the doomed king), the troubled (and troubling) views about colonialism (as beneficial and empowering), the distinct conception of race during the late seventeenth century (as essential character), and what it means to produce "history" as a narrative with a distinct agenda—conversations that have specific and powerful resonances with the times we are living in.

With this historical context in place, the next problem students are likely to face is the complexity of Behn's plotlines. Though it is important for students to engage with the unique qualities of tragicomedy as a genre, when setting up the play it is easier to have students try to untangle the different plotlines and view them as distinct units. There are three major through-lines that students can easily follow over the course of the play: (1) the comic marriage plot centering on the Widdow Ranter and her friends, (2) the comic actions of the colonial council, and (3) the tragic love triangle between Bacon, Semernia, and Cavarnio, the "Indian King." When they are assigned the first two acts of the play for the first class meeting, students can easily identify these plots even without the opening lecture's context. It is fruitful to have them do preparatory work by taking notes about their first impressions of the characters Behn introduces so that when it comes time for class discussion, they are familiar with its various units. It is likely that they will still find the play confusing and complicated, but once they have identified these different pieces it becomes easier for them to weave them back together and they are more prepared to perform short segments of the play.

Once in the classroom, a careful look at *The Widdow Ranter*'s opening is the best place to start to understand how the play fits together. Following Hazard, Act 1, scene 1 aligns the audience with someone who is new to the colonized space of Virginia. The coincidence of Hazard running into Friendly, his friend from England, allows a significant amount of explication, as Friendly explains the colony's culture to Hazard. Asking students to read short sections of this scene out loud enables them not only to work out the major themes explored by the play—marriage and economics, colonial government, class conflicts, racialization, etc.—but also to begin to recognize how the audience of this play was meant to be aligned.

When they read the opening exchange between Hazard and Friendly, questions are raised about the motivations of young English men relocating to Virginia and how men's relationships work. Friendly tells Hazard, "come to my Arms and Heart," opening up a space to dig into conventions of men's relationships. This is useful as the play turns to military action and a plot where a woman secures her husband while dressed as a man.[7] As the scene unfolds, Friendly's opinions on every aspect of Virginian society are exposed, training both Hazard and the audience to properly interpret the groups they will meet over the course of the play. It is important for students to remember that Hazard, due to his class position and previous life in England, exists as an outside observer, watching the events in Virginia unfold through the lens that is provided by his friend, not unlike those who are experiencing the play for the first time.

Following careful attendance to this first scene, informal performances of excerpts from the first two acts help expand the world that Friendly introduces to Hazard. Breaking students into small groups to prepare brief scenes (20–40 lines, depending on how many characters are speaking) to present to the class allows for points of comparison in how characters speak and present themselves. These informal performances did not require preparation outside of class—a short amount of time to refamiliarize themselves with the characters and refresh the play's historical and political context is sufficient to plan these short readings in a class of fifteen to twenty. Highlighting conversations—between Wellman, Dunce, Whimsy, Whiff, and Downright (Act 1, scene 2), Ranter and the serving boy (Act 1, scene 3), and Cavarnio, Bacon, and Semernia (Act 2, scene 1)—gives students space to think about how a wide range of character types are embodied, based on the information provided in the play's first scene. Reading these sections out loud for their classmates emphasizes the differences between these various characters. While the cast list's brief descriptions of who the characters are is helpful, speaking their words out loud emphasizes Behn's tropes and reveals biases embedded in the text to encourage embodied learning and physical memory.

After these brief performances, students are better prepared to highlight the complexities of characterization found in the play's first two acts. Contrasts are found within and across scenes—Ranter and Semernia speak in very different ways despite their parallels within the plot, as do the various members of the Council, particularly when compared to Hazard and Friendly. The tonal shifts can be difficult for students to parse when first reading the play. Having spoken or heard their peers speak these lines and struggle with their diction brings these points home. Such distinctions make it easier to divide up the sizable cast of characters into their particular plotlines, finding the places where they intersect or overlap. Performance is also a good way to identify any misinterpretation early on and course-correct as needed, though our students were often able to make these corrections on their own. One student wrote in their performance reflection, "Slowing down our pace while we digested the text allowed for better comprehension, increased interest and gave a new kind of 'passion' towards these sometimes outlandish plays. . . . [We] also gained a better sense . . . of the scene that we had missed previously when just reading the play." These short oral readings improve understanding of the text and enable students to teach their classmates something new about a scene rather than simply reading assigned text beforehand. The choices they made in presenting these excerpts illustrated a closer attention to the text and a deeper understanding of its goals.

Once students have had the opportunity to present these selected scenes, certain characters begin to stand out. Students are often surprised by the way Behn presents the various cultures that exist within the play, especially compared to how different groupings are presented in plays they have already read. They can effectively recognize the resonances of Antony and Cleopatra's doomed love from Dryden's *All for Love* in the triangle of Cavarnio, Bacon, and Semernia, and the comic quest for advantageous marriage embodied by Hazard and Friendly is familiar from other Restoration comedies. The titular widow, however, is more difficult to place and serves as an important touchstone for students. Her accented speech and talk of Newgate and Bridewell opens up the opportunity to discuss the tensions between transportation and social climbing that becomes a central concern within the play. While Ranter could easily slot into the trope of the greedy and ambitious widow found in much of Restoration comedy, her starting position as an indentured servant and former criminal complicates that assumption. Here Behn presents a culture that resonates with English hierarchies while simultaneously attempting to construct something new within the genre. Our students were generally delighted by the widow, locating her as a potentially queer figure in a play filled with tensions about what conformity looks like in a newly formed social structure. As they see more of her, students began to categorize the ways she rejects and affirms various aspects of her identity and question whether or not her queer gender—embodied not only in her clothing but in her behavior and relationships with other characters—fits in this colonial space. Her position within the play also raises questions about comic closure: as she moves from indentured servant to wealthy widow to the wife of a high-ranking member of the militia, she rejects the return to social order reproduced by many of the other characters as the play ends. She might become a wife, but Dareing's insistence that he prefers her in breeches to petticoats highlights the ways Ranter continues to dodge normative categorization.

Looking at these early scenes, students became similarly invested in the presentation of Cavarnio and Semernia. Given the historical context about colonial America and the aims of Bacon's Rebellion, they found it surprising that the Indigenous people in Behn's play are presented as fairly complex characters rather than as degrading stereotypes. Compared to the white members of the council in particular, the "Indians" speech is formal and elevated, and they are heavily invested in honor and loyalty, rather than in money and power. These observations provided a space to discuss the development of ideas about racialization and othering, and how Behn produces a version of the "noble savage" trope that exploded in popularity during the period. As students read the play, they began to recognize that class heavily impacts how Indigenous characters are presented, and they were able to unpack how intersectional identities operate within this context. While Behn shies away from fully dehumanizing the racialized Other here, she relies heavily upon exoticized imagery that distances the royal couple from the nobility they otherwise embody. Margo Hendricks explains, "Behn openly draws upon . . . cultural difference to mark racial inferiority."[8] Through their consideration of Behn's exoticizing impulses, students struggled with whether this is a positive representation of Indigenous people, and they became invested in picking apart the complexities of these characters and their relationships with the colonizing forces that are intruding upon their world. Though students are interested in Bacon's fate, and the fate of the colony as a whole, the numerous white men who fill the play often become points of comparison rather than the focus of class conversation: students are far more concerned with and intrigued by the various outsiders the play presents.

This investment extends beyond the text of the play and into questions of performance: when students are asked to perform short selections of the play for their classmates, they become more finely attuned to the stage directions, as well as how these different characters would have embodied their different roles. Insightful conversation grows out of the stage directions that describe "Indians *that dance anticks*" and show Sure-Love entering a scene "*fan'd by two negros*" (Behn, *Widdow*, 246, 248). Despite the fact that the historical events of Bacon's rebellion relied heavily on the involvement of enslaved and indentured Africans, these are rarely mentioned in Behn's play. This brief mention in the stage directions, however, raises questions about how bodies that are never given the opportunity to speak were used on stage. There are no Africans with speaking parts in the play, and only a few highly ranked Indigenous characters have major speaking roles, but the stage directions make their physical presence clear. Similarly, Vincent's mezzotint engraving of Anne Bracegirdle performing as Semernia, with her parasol and dress held up by two Black children, surrounded by various markers of exotic wealth, raises questions about the use of racialized people as props and the performance of racial difference.

Looking beyond what is spoken in the play, students can draw important conclusions about who is given a voice in drama and who is used as little more than a prop. This approach to performance also provides space to discuss the practical aspects of presenting race on the Restoration stage, including how race was signified and how gender played into such embodiments. These details enrich the conversation around the history of the play and its performance, drawing attention to details that might otherwise be lost if students read the play as if it were simply a written text. After all, if we only focus on who is speaking, those who are silent can be easily ignored or erased.

Putting *The Widdow Ranter* in conversation with other texts from the period helps students further unpack the ways in which Behn presents an exoticized version of colonial Virginia for a London audience. If *The Widdow Ranter* is taught in a general context—a survey course of the long eighteenth century or pre-1800 literature, or perhaps a class on postcolonial literature and theory—having students read the play alongside Behn's *Oroonoko*, Southerne's *Oroonoko*, Defoe's *Robinson Crusoe*, and/or Equiano's *Interesting Narrative* invites them to compare the methods of representation Behn uses to those found in these other works.

For instance, the presentation of Indigenous royalty in *The Widdow Ranter* has numerous parallels with that of the royal prince in both versions of *Oroonoko*, allowing students to expand their attention to the trope of the noble savage and question the motivations behind these imaginings of African and Indigenous people. Similar comparisons can be drawn using the descriptions of the Indigenous population in Behn's play with those found in *Robinson Crusoe*. Placing these texts in conversations with Equiano's later work highlights crucial differences in how people of color were presented by white authors versus by an African author and abolitionist, who was enslaved to further the production of colonized space and colonial wealth. Such discussion allows for deeper consideration of the political motivations of all of these texts—some of which were primarily intended as entertainment—encouraging students to dig into the purposes of different forms of literature.

If the course is, as mine was, focused on Restoration and eighteenth-century drama, drawing students back to plays they have already read, such as Wycherley's

The Country Wife, not only grounds the play within the canon but draws out the comparisons that Behn herself is making throughout. For example, setting up a Venn diagram of Virginia/Jamestown and England/London allows students to fill in their contrasting interpretations of the different spaces they have encountered while highlighting the central tensions of the plays. The observations made through this activity opens space to challenge the black-and-white nature of these oppositions. In comparing the world of *The Widdow Ranter* to that of *The Country Wife*, for instance, students find that in Virginia, characters are more politically focused and more concerned with class mobility, and the romance plots are driven by love, whereas in Wycherley's London, characters are more socially focused, class distinctions are more stable, and sex is more important than love. In both Virginia and England, however, students notice that concerns about gender fluidity and performance abound, as well as a tension between public and private spaces. While these different categories might be oversimplified, they nevertheless serve as useful touchstones for continuing conversations identifying where these oppositions are reinforced or disputed.

Having acquired a clear picture of the central plots and players, along with a broader understanding of the play's context, students are well prepared for a discussion of the remaining three acts of the play. Their investments in and familiarity with Ranter, Semernia, and Cavarnio can guide the class's focus. Act 3, with its focus on the various colonizing forces as they prepare for the battle that is to come, further affirms what we already suspected about the council and Bacon. Act 3, scene 1, set in the "Country Court," features the lower-class council arguing in circles and drinking heavily, a clear representation of the failures of the existing governing body of Jamestown. This sharply contrasts with the temple scene found in Act 4, scene 1, which presents a different form of ceremony as Cavarnio and Semernia consult oracles who predict the outcome of the coming conflict. This second scene is heavily exoticized and utilized to show the follies of Indigenous religion and tradition. Together this pair of scenes emphasizes the lack of "proper" government in the colony guided by either of the major groups that are present. A comparison of these two scenes allows students to highlight Behn's critiques and further interrogate her position on Indigenous culture. Their observations about Semernia's position in this scene, wherein she reinterprets the oracle's message only to be ignored by her husband, reveal not only a distrust of native religion, but a critique of the patriarchal hierarchy that Behn has reproduced in her representation of Indigenous people.

As the play reaches its climax in Act 4, questions of performance again come to a forefront, as scenes are introduced by lengthy stage directions that set the scene. Asking students to attend carefully to these stage directions emphasizes the importance of spectacle in *The Widdow Ranter*. Part of the appeal of its exotic setting was the lavish, over-the-top visual stimuli the theater could present. Paired with the mezzotint of Bracegirdle, the stage directions at the start of Act 4, scenes 1 and 2, emphasize the sheer number of *things* physically present on the stage and the fact that what is being said is far from the only focus of any given scene. Audiences were coming not only to see the story of the play, but to see all of the *stuff* that was required to convincingly portray what London theatergoers expected of colonized Virginia. In-depth stage directions, particularly those for Act 4, scene 2, also emphasize the collision of different plotlines in the play:

> *Shows a field of tents, seen at some distance thro' the trees of a wood, drums, trumpets and the noise of battel with hollowing. The Indians are seen with battle-axes to retreat fighting from the English and all go off, when they re-enter immediately beating back the English, the* Indian King *at the head of his men, with bows and arrows;* Dareing *being at the head of the English: they fight off; the noise continues less loud as more at distance. Enter* Bacon *with his sword drawn, meets* Fearless *with his sword drawn.* (261)

Whereas these different groups of characters had previously inhabited very specific and separate spaces, they are all brought together here on the battlefield and in the woods. The remainder of the play takes place in these outdoor spaces, and the question of ownership of space becomes a significant point of contention. This conversation can be linked to larger narratives of American colonization and the modern conversation about Land Back movements to discuss how the performance of colonization on stage in the late seventeenth century still echoes through our current moment.

In the context of this highly contentious space, it is helpful for students to map out how the different plotlines, which had previously been so distinct, begin to intersect and overlap as each group participates in the rebellion. Having students perform short excerpts of these scenes helps them better understand the interpersonal relationships that exist against the backdrop of this historical event. Performing the moment where Bacon kills Cavarnio, followed by Bacon's reaction to his actions in Act 4, scene 2, reveals an echo of the homosociality between Hazard and Friendly that students noted at the beginning of the play, emphasizing the intimacy of their relationship. The stage directions say, "*They fight again, wounds on both sides, the* King *staggers,* Bacon *takes him in his arms, the* King *drops his sword*" (262). Bacon holds the King as he dies, and the physicality of this moment mirrors the moment when Semernia dies later in Act 5, scene 3. Having students embody these death scenes back-to-back emphasizes the importance of the physical embodiment of performance and the use of touch on stage to enrich the plot. Another group of students performing Ranter's cross-dressed conversation with Dareing not only raises questions about how Ranter performs gender but models a different version of the love triangle: just as Bacon threatens the relationship between Cavarnio and Semernia, the cross-dressed Widow threatens the relationship between Dareing and Crisante. These various echoes provide students with a wide range of points of comparison. How do love triangles work in tragedy versus comedy? What does it take to "successfully" cross-dress, and who is allowed to do so safely? How do men's relationships operate, and what does their intimacy look like? What types of queer genders are allowed to exist, and how are they embraced or rejected by normative structures?

In discussing the very end of the play, students found that Bacon's death by poison is, like Antony's in *All for Love*, anticlimactic, and preferred to discuss the play's female characters instead. This opened up a space to discuss how Behn as a woman playwright wrote women, and also to expand upon the role of the actress on the Restoration stage. Though Semernia and Ranter never meet in the play, the pair serve as foils for one another: Semernia's accidental death emphasizes tensions surrounding interracial love, whereas Ranter's whiteness allows her to escape her class station and move up through the ranks to marry Dareing. She is an anomaly in the colony, but her ability to pass as a man strangely enables her to live and thrive—a sharp contrast to Semernia's attempts to pass, which instead doom her. Though both roles are relatively minor compared to their male counterparts, it is no surprise that they appeal to contemporary students.

Though the play met little success on the stage, the actresses who filled these roles, Anne Bracegirdle and Elizabeth Currer, were well known during the period. Using tools like *The London Stage Database* in class can provide useful details about the only known performance of the play during the period, while also allowing students to discover the connections between others plays and performers included on their course syllabus.[9] This database provides students with an easily searchable version of *The London Stage, 1660–1800*, an eleven-volume reference text that compiles historical records of theatrical performance during the long eighteenth century. Utilizing a range of search features, students can easily discover details about plays that enrich their understanding of performance and the world of the theater during the period.

In-class experiments with the database can extend into larger assignments, such as a dramaturg packet, which asked students to research the history of the play, provide a biography of one of the performers, and consider how it might be staged for today's audiences. An assignment similar to one created by Misty G. Anderson to help MFAs in theater deepen their understanding of a play's performance history, and imagine what a modern production might look like, can be used in the undergraduate classroom.[10] This assignment requires students to engage with primary and secondary sources and to consider how a play might be received far beyond its original context. If students are asked to stage a scene for a final project (as we did), this packet becomes an invaluable resource in preparing the scene, as it requires an understanding of the play beyond the written text. While informal in-class performances are obviously useful for unpacking specific excerpts, a final project that requires this research alongside a more practiced performance illustrates students' deeper understanding of the plays they have read and serves as a multimodal writing/research assignment. Completing a dramaturg packet and performing an extended scene from *The Widdow Ranter* at the end of the semester allows students to re-engage with the play in the context of everything they have read and to embody the characters with more nuance based on what they have learned while compiling a portfolio about the play's performance history. A post-performance discussion in which students describe and defend the choices they made in planning their scene provides them with space to illustrate their expertise to their classmates. These conversations allow students to teach each other about the texts they have read and proves what they have learned throughout the course.

Despite its failure following its premiere in 1689, *The Widdow Ranter* is a play that particularly rewards performance within the classroom and demonstrates the pedagogical value of simple scene-readings and more polished performances. While historical context and an understanding of genre is critical for students to be able to follow the play's various plotlines and unpack how history is produced, it is through performance that they are able to gain a fuller understanding of its varied cast of characters and the play's rich tensions. In a reflection about their in-class performances, one student beautifully explained the power and importance of bringing these plays to life within the classroom:

> [Performance] gave me a new appreciation of the work, and a stronger reading of it as well. In having to put thought and energy into embodying a character, it feels like you have to look at the play in new ways that make it fresh again. Thinking about character motivations, or their feelings and physicality, adds texture to a work in ways I wasn't anticipating. While logically there's always an awareness that theatre is meant to be performed, I think I get so comfortable in the reading of it that I don't realize the aspect of it I'm missing. This was beyond just viewing, and allowed me to actually step into the world of a play, and it was incredibly engaging.

By providing students with a space to take the lead through performance, their understanding of the material was enriched in a way that can only be attained by embodying it.

This is not to say that performing Restoration drama is easy, but that these classroom performances don't have to be completely "right" in order to be educational. In fact, misfires and slip-ups are the spaces that allow for rich conversation about why a certain line should be read a particular way and how that changes our interpretation. As we teach Restoration drama, it is crucial that we remember that these plays were, primarily, meant to be embodied on a stage. Even though they were published and circulated and read widely, a play is not a novel, and reading it alone in a dorm room will never provide the full picture. Instead, getting students moving around, speaking the words out loud, and interacting as a group while others look on and observe is the best means of finding our way into the plays of the past.

NOTES

1. "London Stage Event: 20 November 1689 at Drury Lane Theatre," *London Stage Database*, https://londonstagedatabase.uoregon.edu/event.php?id=1732, accessed September 14, 2021.
2. George Jenkins, "Dedication to *The Widdow Ranter*," *The Routledge Anthology of Restoration and Eighteenth-Century Drama*, edited by Kristina Straub, Misty G. Anderson, and Daniel O'Quinn (New York: Routledge, 2017), 234. All citations from the play refer to this edition.
3. There are a few editions that make *The Widdow Ranter* more accessible to students. The recent *Routledge Anthology of Restoration and Eighteenth-Century Drama* (2017), edited by Kristina Straub, Misty G. Anderson, and Daniel O'Quinn, includes a headnote with useful context, the complete text of the play with explanatory endnotes, the prologue and epilogue that were printed with the first edition of the play, as well as the prologue and epilogue that were spoken at its original performance. Alongside the play, the editors present Ebenezer Cook's *The Sotweed Factor*, a self-portrait of Nathaniel Bacon, and W. Vincent's mezzotint engraving of Anne Bracegirdle as "The Indian Queen." These additional materials expand the conversation beyond the play, while linking it back to its historical context and performance history. The Penguin Classics edition of *Oroonoko, The Rover, and Other Works* (2003) edited by Janet Todd can be useful for incorporating more of Behn's work: it presents prose, plays, and poems, with a lengthy introduction and chronology to contextualize Behn's life. Though it lacks a headnote, the endnotes to this edition of the play provide significant context to help introduce students to the world of the play. The digitized edition edited by Paul Royster and hosted at DigitalCommons@University of Nebraska–Lincoln (2008) is another excellent resource and a very accessible text for teaching. Like the Routledge edition, Royster's edition includes both prologues and epilogues, but this digital edition was produced to very closely imitate the formatting of the first edition. It therefore provides the opportunity to discuss how printed texts looked in the late seventeenth century without asking students to read an edition from Early English Books Online (EEBO), which may be difficult to read in its entirety and which is not available at all institutions.
4. David McInnis, "Virginian Culture and Experimental Genre in Aphra Behn's *The Widow Ranter*," in *Early Modern Englishwomen Testing Ideas*, edited by Jo Wallwork and Paul Salzman (Farnham: Ashgate, 2011), 104.
5. Jenny Hale Pulsipher, "*The Widow Ranter* and Royalist Culture in Virginia," *Early American Literature* 39, no. 1 (2004): 43.
6. Numerous sources provide historical context about Bacon's rebellion, and it may also be helpful to assign an article that discusses the relationship between the historical event, Behn's politics, and her representation of the rebellion in *The Widdow Ranter*. Thorough examinations of the historical events, and how Behn's political allegiances impacted her presentation of the events in her play, are provided in Heidi Hutner, "Aphra Behn's *The Widow Ranter*," in Heidi Hutner, *Colonial Women: Race and Culture in Stuart Drama*, 89–106 (Oxford: Oxford University Press, 2001); Jenny Hale Pulsipher, "*The Widow Ranter* and Royalist Culture in Colonial Virginia," *Early American Literature* 39, no. 1 (2004): 41–66; and Melissa Mowry, "'Past Remembrance or History': Aphra Behn's *The Widdow Ranter*, or, How the Collective Lost Its Honor," *ELH* 79, no. 3 (Fall 2012): 597–621.

7. Aphra Behn, *The Widdow Ranter or, The History of Bacon in Virginia*, in *The Routledge Anthology of Restoration and Eighteenth-Century Drama*, edited by Kristina Straub, Misty G. Anderson, and Daniel O'Quinn (New York: Routledge, 2017), 239. All subsequent citations to this edition.
8. Margo Hendricks, "Civility, Barbarism, and Aphra Behn's *The Widow Ranter*," in *Women, "Race," and Writing in the Early Modern Period*, edited by Margo Hendricks and Patricia Parker, 225–239 (London: Routledge, 1994), 233.
9. *London Stage Database*, University of Oregon, https://londonstagedatabase.uoregon.edu/, accessed September 14, 2021.
10. Personal communication with Misty G. Anderson, February 11, 2021.

3

LET'S TALK ABOUT (EARLY MODERN) SEX . . . ONLINE

Kate Parker

THIS CHAPTER CENTERS ON AN upper-level seminar cross-listed in the English Department and the Women's, Gender and Sexuality Studies Department with the title "Literature and Culture: Intersectional Feminism and Sexuality." Because of my training as an eighteenth-centuryist, a good portion of the class focuses on both historical accounts of early modern sexuality (with Thomas Laqueur's *Making Sex* as a general, if admittedly vexed, frame) and representations of sexuality in literary texts (including Rochester and Behn, Haywood, Cleland, and Sade). I was scheduled to teach this class in the classroom in Spring 2021, but after COVID-19 hit in early 2020 I was forced to reconceptualize and adapt the course for an online environment. In this chapter I try to recount some of the questions, considerations, and concerns that surfaced as I tried to imagine teaching sex online.

WHERE I KNOW FROM

I work at the University of Wisconsin La Crosse (UWL)—a regional comprehensive institution in the Midwest with a population of about 10,000 undergraduate students, most of whom come from within 200 miles of the university. It is a predominantly white institution (PWI) that occupies the ancestral land of the Ho-Chunk people. Although the student body is overwhelmingly white, cisgender, and straight, many UWL students also identify as marginalized within the dominant structures of U.S. patriarchal capitalism: they are commonly from rural farming communities, and many are first-generation college students and/or Pell grant recipients.[1]

By situating my students' knowledge within the frame of dominant/marginalized identity groups that populate my region of Wisconsin, and my own privilege as a white, cis woman college professor, I make explicit the dynamics that animate and drive my classroom, whether in person or online, and my own positionality vis-à-vis my students in this setting. Inspired by Eugenia Zuroski and the Black and Indigenous scholars from whom she draws, by calling attention to our collective positionality in this way I aim to "make the university classroom a space that overtly and persistently recognizes multiple ways of knowing and sites of learning if we intend . . . to use it as a site to counter histories of misogyny, heteronormativity, racism, classism and colonialism."[2] Even though my students are not typically as diverse as Zuroski's—and posing the question "Where do you know from?" would almost certainly result in a kind of echo chamber that would only alienate the few BIPOC (Black, Indigenous, and people of color), international, and/or LGBTQIA+ students present in any given class—I believe it's still crucial to call students' attention to the relative homogeneity of any predominantly white institutional space. Only by acknowledging the intersecting systems of privilege and oppression within which we all operate is it possible to have a historical account of sex and sexuality and their intersections with gender, race, class, and so on.

All of my syllabuses include an "Instructor Standpoint" document. This document first clarifies my positionality as a professor who advocates feminism, antiracism, and respect for intersectional identities.[3] I list the specific ways in which I inhabit my authority and strive to maintain a healthy classroom "ecosystem"[4] by speaking respectfully, honoring difference, intervening when student comments may unintentionally (or intentionally) reinforce structural inequalities, and centering historically marginalized voices in my course content. I then connect this standpoint explicitly to UWL's student complaint process in a restorative justice framework meant to empower students who feel challenged, or threatened, by my standpoint to either approach me (my preference) or move through the university's system for informal and formal complaints. It also clarifies how I will repair the harm done if I make a mistake—for example, if I inadvertently call a student by the wrong pronouns or use seemingly "inappropriate" language in the classroom. (This is particularly important in a class about early modern sexuality, when students will regularly encounter words like "cunt" that resonate differently in a twenty-first century U.S. context.) I find this document extremely useful—and students seem to find it both illuminating and comforting—but I must acknowledge that students find my actions praiseworthy in large part because they do not find me particularly threatening; I am a relatively young, white, woman professor, and thus I (at least visibly) uphold their expectations of a compassionate, even maternal, authority figure. The use of this document would undoubtedly be more challenging were I to present as a BIPOC, nonbinary, or even LGBTQIA+ instructor. However, I use it to make explicit the unequal dynamics of the classroom in which—regardless of teaching persona and personal commitment to feminist, antiracist teaching—I unquestionably possess privilege and authority over my students, most clearly in my role as evaluator, assessor, and grader of student work.

TEACHING PHILOSOPHY: DIGITAL (PROTO-)FEMINISM

When considered in its most utopian, positive form—the naive view of the internet as "an open, all-inclusive and participatory space"—virtual learning spaces would seem to align themselves with the often equally utopian goals of feminist pedagogy.[5] Cathryn Bailey asks if online feminist pedagogy may serve as "a new doorway into our brick-and-mortar classrooms," particularly as online teaching reflects many of the general goals of feminist pedagogy: "challenging patriarchal power models" through a "nonhierarchical" approach to teaching; the privileging of lived experiences as powerful sources of personal/political knowledge; activism as a vital form of scholarly work; commitment to accessibility and a resistance to intellectual elitism; and so on.[6] And yet, as Kate Levin notes in her powerful account of teaching Eliza Haywood's *Fantomina* as an early feminist text, such utopian goals, however laudable, are almost impossible to maintain, because feminist pedagogy cannot sidestep the disproportionate balance of power endemic to all college classrooms—and, indeed, all institutional spaces, even, or perhaps especially, virtual ones.[7] Digital feminism, which seeks to mobilize virtual spaces for feminist political ends, must also navigate structural inequities, white supremacist and patriarchal discourses, and even online violence against women.[8] So too must online feminist pedagogy. While "digital media were expected to free the female, the queer, the raced, the disabled, and the aged from the expectations that come with embodiment," as Faiza Hirji writes in her article on Islamophobia and online feminist activism, virtual spaces are hardly safe spaces—especially for marginalized identities.[9] Any vision of online feminist pedagogy as more participatory and democratic must be weighed against the pressing realities of heterosexism, racism, and other forms of bias—which may proliferate in an online environment.

As I began to adapt my Intersectional Feminism & Sexuality course for an online, mid-pandemic environment, it seemed to me that the same utopian ideals of feminist teaching also haunt my teaching of protofeminism, in which I exert a kind of blind faith that students will draw meaningful connections between the historically resistant acts of heroines and ingénues like Fantomina, Cloris, Pamela, Fanny, and Eugénie, and the issues of consent, misogyny, and homophobia that frame twenty-first-century discourses of gender equity and identity. I noted that I am always thrilled by any inkling that students are sifting contemporary (even personal, lived) experiences through eighteenth-century filters—and, as evidenced by the work of my fellow instructors cited throughout this chapter, I am not alone in this. But just as the digital world complicates the hopeful ideals of feminism—with questions, for example, of the limits of accessibility, activism, and privacy—it also complicates the teaching of protofeminism, specifically by flattening what is often a rich sensory engagement in an in-person class (filled with images, audio, even movie scenes) to a screenful of text, or video, that seems at best foreign, at worst uninhabitable to your average undergraduate.[10] Further, the "aspirations of the protofeminist within a presentist and praxis-driven frame of the transnational," as Basuli Deb has argued, "define[s] a historical desire for a cross-racial feminist politics of the 'trans' within the empire."[11] But it is much more difficult to see protofeminism as "the transnational, the transgressive, and the transformative" when it is neatly packaged and delivered through virtual spaces that are simultaneously visibly structured and invisibly seamless. Instructure's Canvas, the learning management system (LMS) deployed by the University of Wisconsin system, of which UWL is a part, boasts an ability to "build . . . a seamless learning ecosystem" in which "teaching and learning [are] easier for everyone."[12] The emphasis an LMS like Canvas places on facility and functionality is designed to reduce the productive tension that precisely comes from the kinds of uncertainty, ambiguity, and even discomfort that are necessary to preserve, as Lynn Hunt writes in her column "Against Presentism," the "fruitful tension between present concerns and respect for the past." Protofeminism is animated by such a "fruitful tension"; indeed, Hunt laments how "presentism, at its worst, encourages a kind of moral complacency and self-congratulation," as "interpreting the past in terms of present concerns usually leads us to find ourselves morally superior."[13] In a classroom we stand a chance of convincing students otherwise. In a virtual space, animated by the paratextual language of neoliberalism—literally, surrounded and structured by the superiority of the contemporary digital world over the historically "real"—the force and value of protofeminism is a much more difficult sell.

These two concerns framed my teaching philosophy as I began to explore online versions of my class; and to think through these issues, I turned to other pedagogical works by eighteenth-centuryists whose work on sex and sexuality I admire.[14] Christopher Nagle's questions and concerns in "Beyond Victims & Villains" on teaching Cleland with Haywood and Behn resonate deeply with my own, and his essay centers on teaching a work of pornography (Cleland's *Memoirs of a Woman of Pleasure*) in an in-person classroom, which was also my intention in the online seminar. At the outset of "Beyond Victims & Villains," Nagle sets out rather precisely the stakes I alluded to above; he writes that "the goal [of bringing 'real' erotic narrative into the classroom] is to challenge the seductively familiar and too comfortable binary logic to which conversations about sexual violence and the politics of consent too often fall prey."[15] In order to do this, Nagle considers how Fantomina's "powerful pursuit of female desire" is juxtaposed, for students, against "the question of her agency in the face of such desires," his pedagogical aim being to "avoid both simple celebration of her sexual freedom as well as any reductive moralism about her exploits."[16] Nagle preserves the kind of tensions between a utopian protofeminist ideal (Fantomina as a full and entirely self-actualized sexual agent freed from the "constraints" of eighteenth-century sexual hierarchies) and the kinds of presentist self-congratulation that students routinely fall into when analyzing the behavior of early modern women. This tension is beautifully reversed, in a way, when Nagle introduces discussion of Fanny's brief interludes of "conventional morality" in volume 2 of the *Memoirs*—most famously, in the moral aspersions she casts on the "sodomites" she observes in the brothel.[17] In short, Nagle's essay echoes many of the concerns I have about the dangers of presentism, the limits of protofeminism, and the reductive, binary logic with which students *typically* approach accounts of historical sexuality—and he has developed thoughtful and effective ways to introduce these concerns into the classroom.

Nagle is, of course, speaking of the in-person classroom in his essay. In his postscript, presumably as a nod to COVID-19, Nagle includes some examples of the *online* writing and discussion prompts that he uses to introduce this discussion in the virtual classroom. I can't help but notice that these prompts are relatively tame in comparison to the rich, provocative, complex discussion he describes in great detail throughout in the article. The contrast is stark, it seems to me, between these generalized online discussion prompts and the wide-ranging, explicit questions that animate his in-person class discussions: how students "wrestle with" the democratization of sexual culture; the exploration of "democratic hedonism"; the resistance to any "knee-jerk, black-and-white response to victims and villains," "veering"—rather wildly, one presumes—"between fixing blame and signaling empathy"; learning how to "do justice to the complexities of lived experience" in the #MeToo era. In contrast, asking students to simply explain Fanny's views regarding monogamy and fidelity, for example, seems comparatively straightforward—and is at risk of falling into the very same binary logic that Nagle explicitly seeks to avoid in his in-person teaching.[18]

Let me be clear: I am in *no way* calling Nagle out, here—I deeply admire his teaching and scholarship, and we've sat on panels together (and were both scheduled to appear on the "Pedagogies of Consent" panel at ASECS 2020, from which his excellent article emerged). Rather, I cite these examples because I believe we are struggling with versions of the same problem: How does one preserve the complexity and nuance required to teach early modern sex in a virtual classroom where students not only expect, but the best practices and course management explicitly *encourage*, "seamless," "accessible," and "easy" teaching?

YIELDING, CHEERFULLY OR NOT: THE POLITICS OF CONSENT AND THE VIOLENCE OF THE VIRTUAL CLASSROOM

In May 2021 I was forwarded an email from our university's provost; it was sent to me in my role as the inclusive teaching specialist in our university's Center for Advancing Teaching and Learning (CATL). The subject line of the email was "Of interest (inclusivity and Zoom presence)" and the attached article, published in the journal *Ecology and Evolution*, was aptly titled: "Why Students Do Not Turn

On Their Video Cameras during Online Classes and an Equitable and Inclusive Plan to Encourage Them to Do So."[19] The debate had been raging in CATL—and in the university, more broadly—about whether students should be *required* to turn on their cameras during synchronous class meetings, and the article only served as proof that we were not alone in our confusion. The benefits of synchronous remote learning for student engagement and success are quite clear, when cameras are on and participants are (visibly) accountable to the class meeting; however, there are as many reasons that *requiring* students to be visible on their webcam can exacerbate existing inequities, with perhaps the most significant (for a class about sexuality) being that it can cause intense discomfort for students suffering from anxiety, depression, trauma, and/or other forms of mental illness. The results of the study are quite interesting, but I won't reproduce them at length here. Rather, this exchange inspires a larger pedagogical question I grappled with throughout the pandemic: How do the *nonconsensual* aspects of the COVID-19 moment—forced isolation, compulsory online education, imposed virtual "rules" (like leaving cameras on)—engage students differently in thinking and talking about the sexual politics of consent in eighteenth-century texts?

Leah Grisham, in her article on consent and gender-based violence in Richardson's *Pamela* (the full title of which inspired this section of my chapter), explores the "many ways in which consent can be coerced" as a means of "deepening students' engagement with and interest in the eighteenth century" in the #MeToo era.[20] For Grisham's students, the reading of *Pamela* coincided with a historic moment in the fight for gender equity and against interpersonal violence: Christine Blasey Ford's testimony describing her having been sexually assaulted by Supreme Court Justice nominee Brett Kavanaugh. Because *Pamela* "is mired in issues of consent, sexual violence, resistance and patriarchal supremacy—the very issues that were on display during the Kavanaugh hearing," the students were able clearly to "see the social apparatuses in place that work to strip women of a right to consent to or reject patriarchal ideologies, resulting in the internalization of oppressive hegemony."[21] Issues of consent are often deeply complex, as both the Kavanaugh hearing and the story of Pamela caution. And the realities of internalized oppression mean that women will often mistake, or mischaracterize, nonconsensual sex as consensual, as scholars such as Lynn Phillips have repeatedly demonstrated.[22]

This mischaracterization stems, at least in part, from the internalized oppression of women. Kate Manne characterizes misogyny as "a property of the social environments girls and women navigate," which means that "women as well as men can engage in misogynistic behavior"—including "himpathy"—where "powerful and privileged boys and men who commit acts of sexual violence or engage in other misogynistic behavior often receive sympathy and concern over their female victims."[23] Straying from the policing expectations of a patriarchal society—which Blasey Ford did, for example, when she testified—results in immediate sanctioning, shaming, and even violence, where "women who directly flout [these] norms and expectations . . . may find themselves reliably subject to misogynistic reprisals."[24] Himpathy is one such form these "reprisals" can take, as internalized misogyny: the "threats and punishment leveled at girls and women who resist and challenge the will of male authority figures" are transformed into "the shame and guilt women often feel for not protecting a man who mistreats us." Manne summarizes flatly: "We do not want to hurt him or let him down; we want to be a good girl."[25]

Given such definitions, we can quite easily see how characters like Pamela and even Fantomina not only reflect eighteenth-century sexual mores but exemplify a specific kind of internalized oppression around consensual sex that continues into the twenty-first century: Pamela returns to care for Mr. B after he assaults her, and eventually marries him; Fantomina not only maintains a romantic relationship with her rapist, but in fact encourages and enables his repeated predation. Both do so out of a fear of reprisal *and* a desire to preserve their perpetrator's hypermasculine sense of self. And yet these are not, quite, straightforward examples of internalized oppression. As a concept, internalized oppression embodies the complexities involved in consenting to sex within established gender dynamics—as Nagle observes, within the "binary logic" of heteronormative sex.[26] Fantomina *both* desires Beauplaisir and fears him; she feels pressure to give in to his advances and equally to resist them, at least initially in defense of her reputation. In the first volume, Pamela struggles to reconcile her seeming sexual power over Mr. B with her internalized sense of her own unworthiness (gender intersecting with class); in the second volume, which Grisham also teaches, she grapples with her "high esteem of him" and the often violent and oppressive means by which he controls, ridicules, and demeans her. "Pamela," Grisham writes, "is effectively coerced into consenting to patriarchal rule."[27] And students, especially women-identified students, may relate to this kind of subtle, insidious feeling that, in effect, creates "the specter of sex that is unwanted, and even coerced, but not *by* any particular person," but instead "from patriarchal social scripts and the prevalent sense of male sexual entitlement that would make [refusal] feel rude, even *wrong*."[28] In short: internalized oppression helps students better understand not just this sort of behavior but also other nuances of the story. For example, Fantomina's (admittedly limited) sexual empowerment and Pamela's desperate attempts at cunning deception press back against a too-easy reading of these characters as pure victims of social circumstance.

My seminar students read Manne, including the chapter "Unwanted—On the Entitlement to Consent," alongside *Fantomina*, and in an online discussion were asked to reflect on how intersectional feminism might respond to the overlapping concepts of misogyny, sexism, and "compulsory heterosexuality" (Adrienne

Rich's term for what is now more commonly known as heteronormativity), using Haywood's story as an example. One particular comment stood out to me because the student aligned what they termed the "fishbowl" scene in *Fantomina*—the opening scene in which she surveys the theater, sizes up her options, and determines that dressing as a prostitute is the only way to attract the attentions of Beauplaisir—and the "fishbowl" experience of being on Zoom. The student described it as being "policed in [their] class space" by being asked to not only ascribe to how students are "supposed to act" in an online classroom, but also to "heterosexual norms . . . enforced on us" by mechanisms of, for example, sexualized hypervisibility. That Fantomina, an eighteenth-century heroine, has more agency and physical freedom to move around and occupy a space than this student, a self-identified "lesbian feminist" in the twenty-first century (under pandemic lockdown, of course), struck them as not only deeply problematic, but as clear evidence of the unbroken, systemic nature of historical sexism and misogyny. In the twenty-first century United States, this is not relegated to purely social spaces but in fact infuses more-progressive and liberal spaces like the university. In a follow-up comment I pointed out that a Zoom window also frames a body in a way that offers a limited agency in self-presentation: we can, for example, set our backgrounds, do our makeup, and light our faces (or the opposite) in order to render ourselves in a way that is visually pleasing (but often reinforces patriarchal norms about "acceptable" forms of beauty, etc.). The student agreed, but then argued that such self-presentation is, by association, nonconsensual in a class space in which students are *required* to be on Zoom. (For the record, my class did *not* require cameras on.) For this student, the complexities of sexual (non-)consent were directly aligned with the complexities of nonconsensual class policies regarding the use of Zoom.

In meditating on this student's thought-provoking series of comments, I was reminded again of Kate Levin's article on the teaching of *Fantomina*, in which she explores the professor-as-seducer model, advanced by Jane Gallop and bell hooks. Pedagogy can be a form of seduction, Levin notes, casting herself in the role of a Beauplaisir figure (endorsing, or even enforcing, a particular reading of the text) while her students act as Fantominas, simultaneously intrigued by and resistant to her authoritative "feminist interpretive and pedagogical desires."[29] In a virtual classroom, if pedagogy acts as a form of seduction, it is also haunted by the specter of digital predation—a form of sexual violence so ubiquitous to our socially networked students that it is almost commonplace (if I go by the kinds of examples students offer up in reflections, discussion posts, and papers). From unsolicited "dick pics" on Tinder to explicitly sexual Instagram comments, our students—especially our women-identified and LGBTQIA+ students—are absolutely inundated with nonconsensual sexual harassment: a fact that makes many of my students instinctively hyperaware of their visibility and their self-presentation in any virtual space. Arguing for a feminist politics of consent when students are subjected to—even coerced into—nonconsensual invasions of privacy, exacerbated by an equally nonconsensual compulsory online education and COVID-19 lockdown during which many students described themselves as "imprisoned" or "trapped" in their homes, required a kind of critical self-awareness of my teaching for which I was frankly unprepared. If I were to teach sex online again—in a future lockdown, for example—this would be an absolutely vital conversation to have upfront with students before engaging in conversations about consent in *Fantomina*.

TOO-DANGEROUS LIAISONS: (NOT) TEACHING PORNOGRAPHY ONLINE

In late March 2020, only two weeks into the pandemic lockdown in Wisconsin, a University of Miami professor resigned after sharing his screen during a virtual Zoom class with a tab open to "Busty College Girl."[30] My first thought? *That could have been me*. Granted: I do not troll the internet looking for busty college women, and I am not a sexual predator, but as a sexuality studies scholar I regularly perform Google searches on my work computer that require detailed justification. I am also irrevocably Zoom-challenged. In the first year of the pandemic, I did the following: accidently shared my screen during a professional meeting with a window that showed a graphic of Vesalius's "vagina as penis" (fans of Laqueur will likely call this immediately to mind); taught an entire class with a tab open to an article that read "What Happened to the Porn in Pornography?"; and virtually guest-lectured in a colleague's class with a PowerPoint presentation that featured a French Revolutionary solider riding a horse-sized dick. (I'm pretty sure that last one got widely screenshotted.) To make things even more awkwardly inappropriate, I did all of this from my bedroom, with my own personal *boudoir* framed in the background—the only predictable space of quiet in a tiny house with two kids and four dogs.

In the best of times, being a feminist scholar who works on historical pornography can bring smugly knowing looks, aggressively personal questions, and condescending demands for explanation. I have taken the advice of more seasoned colleagues in the field to *always* be able to justify my required reading: to students, to colleagues, to administrators, and even to parents. My in-person classes begin with detailed content warnings and lengthy back-and-forth conversations about the material, the kinds of institutional support available to struggling students, and the sound pedagogical and political reasons I teach what I teach. I also regularly point out, normalize, and deescalate the use of an escape hatch (the classroom door) at any time, for any reason, with no questions asked. But as I discovered quickly, in a virtual world all these practices magnify tenfold. I have to imagine that absolutely everything I share with my students will be widely shared (nightmarishly perused by parents and grandparents) and/or be subjected to a public, institutional scrutiny I have never before faced in my professional career (I regularly read, and reread, my university's "Appropriate Use of Technology" policy with chills up my spine). Most essentially for my work as a professor who strives to be trauma-informed: the students encountering such texts in the midst of a pandemic where mental health concerns absolutely *skyrocketed* needed specific kinds of individualized personal support. While "the door" in a virtual world may be only a button away, those who pass through it drop into a literal vacuum, and as many of my colleagues lamented, are at a serious risk of disappearing for good.

The spoiler alert: in my initial preparations for this class I had planned to teach two pornographic works: *Memoirs of a Woman of Pleasure* (more colloquially known as *Fanny Hill*) and excerpts from Sade's *La Philosophie dans le boudoir* . . . but I did not teach them. I also had planned to screen a documentary on the pornographic film *Deep Throat* and juxtapose screenshots from a Hardee's Super Bowl commercial with Playboy pull-outs . . . but I did not share these. My pedagogical justification for working with these sorts of texts remained the same: rape culture is rape culture is rape culture—in the eighteenth-century as well as the twenty-first. I knew that I did not introduce these images lightly—for example, simply to be provocative, or to excite or engage students with the eighteenth century, which they might initially assume to be a boring field of literary and cultural study. I know I am justified in using Haywood, Cleland, and Sade to demonstrate the heterosexist visual-textual language of implicit and explicit sexual violence, a historical phenomenon that persists into the present day. I absolutely consider these texts not only vital to a college humanities curriculum, but in fact part of what I'd argue is my particular vocation as an eighteenth-centuryist and a feminist scholar. And yet, despite my firm convictions in what I choose to teach, *and* despite these texts having initially appeared on the syllabus I posted online in January 2021, I made the decision to pull them—all of them—in late March.

I am still thinking through this decision, which is why this section acts as a kind of extended coda, posing more questions than it can possibly hope to answer. But because I face a future in which virtual teaching seems increasingly likely, if not inevitable, and I am not willing to abandon the teaching of sexuality, I am faced with some considerations, which I'll leave here as a means of concluding:

- There is, at minimum, a vexed relationship between the teaching of pornography (particularly via image-sharing) and the internet medium, which enables digital forms of predation that also take the form of (sometimes nonconsensual) image-sharing. This puts instructors at increased risk for public scrutiny and institutionally sanctioned shaming, but also risks retraumatizing students who have experienced sexual violence in any form. Is there a way to mitigate these risks without compromising the integrity of feminist pedagogies of sex and sexuality?
- Online discussions are notoriously more difficult to manage than in-person interactions, and the ability to immediately address or correct offensive remarks

(whether intentional or unintentional) is heavily compromised in a virtual teaching environment. Given this, synchronous Zoom classes are perhaps a more appropriate venue for difficult conversations—and yet these venues can be equally vexed, not only in how they make students hypervisible to classmates, but also in the difficulties they can present for nontraditional students and/or students who have issues with internet access and bandwidth. Are there effective ways to set compassionate discussion guidelines—and uphold them—without requiring students to police one another or policing the discussions as a top-down authority?

- As we all navigated the teaching of literature in a crisis,[31] it became immediately apparent that student support would look *radically* different in such situations. It's not simply that students disappear; it's that they disappear *and* we are profoundly aware of their complete and total isolation and potential lack of any effective support system. In the early days of the pandemic, friends, family, and mental health professionals were only tenuously connected to our students, who were often forced to fend for themselves, emotionally. Even though circumstances might be better as we enter a "post-pandemic" era, can we work to strengthen the virtual structures of support for students with mental health concerns, students from marginalized backgrounds, and others who have found benefits from pandemic responses?
- Perhaps my most pressing question: How can we properly convey nuance, complexity, and ambiguity in a medium that is explicitly made facile and streamlined? Is it possible to maintain accessibility for all users while preserving the kinds of productive tensions that enable the rich and provocative teaching of historical sex? Can accountability to the subject material exist without reductive quizzing, required video-chatting, or the reappropriation of social media for pedagogical purposes?

I continue to think through these questions—to talk with my colleagues, to read and learn from others in my field who are grappling with the same issues. In the end, what I hope for is to sharpen my own self-awareness as an educator to enter into what bell hooks calls "genuine conversation" with my students and colleagues: conversation that is "always about giving . . . about the sharing of power and knowledge . . . fundamentally a cooperative enterprise."[32]

NOTES

1. University of Wisconsin La Crosse, "UWL Factbook," https://www.uwlax.edu/institutional-research/data-resources/fact-book/, accessed July 7, 2021.
2. Eugenia Zuroski, "Where Do You Know From?: An Exercise in Placing Ourselves Together in the Classroom," MAI: Feminism & Visual Cultures, January 27, 2020, https://maifeminism.com/where-do-you-know-from-an-exercise-in-placing-ourselves-together-in-the-classroom/.

3. The phrasing "I advocate . . ." is borrowed from bell hooks, who writes: "To emphasize that engagement with feminist struggle as political commitment we could avoid using the phrase 'I am a feminist' (a linguistic structure designed to refer to some personal aspect of identity and self-definition) and could state 'I advocate feminism.' Because there has been undue emphasis placed on feminism as an identity or lifestyle, people usually resort to stereotyped perspective on feminism. Deflecting attention away from stereotypes is necessary if we are to revise our strategy and direction. . . . It does not engage us in the either/or dualistic thinking that is the central ideological component of all systems of domination in Western society." bell hooks, "Feminism: A Movement to End Sexist Oppression," in *Feminist Theory Reader: Local and Global Perspectives*, ed. Carole R. McCann and Seung-Kyung Kim (New York: Routledge, 2003), 55.
4. I borrow this language from Matthew Kay, whose excellent book has deeply inspired my thinking on classroom discussion dynamics around social justice issues. Matthew R. Kay, *Not Light, but Fire: How to Lead Meaningful Race Conversations in the Classroom* (Portland, ME: Stenhouse, 2018), 13.
5. Kim Barker and Olga Jurasz, "Online Misogyny: A Challenge for Digital Feminism?," *Journal of International Affairs* 72, no. 2 (Spring/Summer 2019): 99.
6. Cathryn Bailey, "Online Feminist Pedagogy: A New Doorway into Our Brick-and-Mortar Classrooms?," *Feminist Teacher: A Journal of the Practices, Theories, and Scholarship of Feminist Teaching* 27, no. 2–3 (2017): 253–254.
7. Kate Levin, "'The Only Beguiled Person?': Accessing Fantomina in the Feminist Classroom," *ABO: Interactive Journal for Women in the Arts, 1640–1830* 2, no. 1 (2012): 4.
8. Barker and Jurasz, "Online Misogyny," 97.
9. Faiza Hirji, "Claiming Our Space: Muslim Women, Activism, and Social Media," *Islamophobia Studies Journal* 6, no. 1 (Spring 2021): 79.
10. I find this is true for my students at UWL, where our bachelor's degree in literature requires only one class in British/American literature prior to 1800; for many literature majors, this will be the first and only time they encounter seventeenth- and eighteenth-century texts.
11. Basuli Deb, "Transnational Complications: Reimagining *Oroonoko* and Women's Collective Politics in the Empire," *Frontiers: A Journal of Women Studies* 36, no. 1 (2015): 33.
12. Instructure, "Teaching and Learning: To the Power of Canvas LMS," https://instructure.com/canvas, accessed July 7, 2021.
13. Lynn Hunt, "Against Presentism," *Perspectives on History: The Newsmagazine of the American Historical Association*, May 2002, https://www.historians.org/publications-and-directories/perspectives-on history/may-2002/against-presentism.
14. While there are many excellent volumes on teaching eighteenth-century literature, I gravitated to *Aphra Behn Online*'s pedagogy section, as I wholeheartedly wish to support their mission and vision as a "open access journal founded on feminist principles and focusing on women's artistic production." University of South Florida Digital Commons, *Aphra Behn Online (ABO): Interactive Journal for Women in the Arts, 1640–1830*, last modified Winter 2022, https://scholarcommons.usf.edu/abo/.
15. Christopher Nagle, "Beyond Victims & Villains: Teaching Cleland with Haywood & Behn," *ABO: Interactive Journal for Women in the Arts, 1640–1830* 10, no. 2 (2020): 1.
16. Nagle, "Beyond Victims & Villains," 3.
17. Nagle, "Beyond Victims & Villains," 4.
18. Nagle, "Beyond Victims & Villains," 5.
19. Frank R. Castelli and Mark A. Sarvary, "Why Students Do Not Turn On Their Video Cameras during Online Classes and an Equitable and Inclusive Plan to Encourage Them to Do So," *Ecology and Evolution* 11, no. 8 (January 2021): 3565–3576.
20. Leah Grisham, "'Yield It Up Cheerfully': Teaching Consent, Violence, and Coercion in Samuel Richardson's Pamela," *ABO: Interactive Journal for Women in the Arts, 1640–1830* 10, no. 2 (2020), http://doi.org/10.5038/2157-7129.10.2.1237.
21. Grisham, "'Yield It Up Cheerfully,'" 3, 1.

22. See Lynn Phillips, *Flirting with Danger: Young Women's Reflections on Sexuality and Violence* (New York: New York University Press, 2000).
23. Kate Manne, *Entitled: How Male Privilege Hurts Women* (New York: Random House, 2020), 9, 5.
24. Manne, *Entitled*, 53.
25. Manne, *Entitled*, 73.
26. Nagle, "Beyond Victims & Villains," 1.
27. Grisham, "'Yield It Up Cheerfully,'" 3.
28. Manne, *Entitled*, 58.
29. Levin, "'The Only Beguiled Person?,'" 1.
30. Chelsea Ritschel, "University of Miami Professor Resigns after Students See 'Busty College Girl' Bookmark during Zoom Call," *Independent*, Thursday, April 30, 2020, 14, https://www.independent.co.uk/news/world/americas/university-miami-professor-zoom-call-busty-college-girl-resign-john-peng-zhang-a9493381.html.
31. University of Wisconsin La Crosse, CATL Teaching Improvement Guide, "Teaching in a Crisis," last updated December 2022, https://www.uwlax.edu/catl/guides/teaching-improvement-guide/how-can-i-improve/crisis/.
32. bell hooks, *Teaching Critical Thinking* (New York: Routledge, 2007), 45.

4

THE CHOCOLATE PROJECT

Recontextualizing Eighteenth-Century Studies in a Time of Downsizing

Teri Doerksen

How do we keep teaching about the fields of literary study we were originally trained in and in which we do our own research, introducing students to all the valuable insight that our periods offer, if we teach in places where traditional literary fields of study are vanishing from the curriculum? At many colleges and universities, tenure-track positions in literature are evaporating, and as colleagues retire, the remaining faculty are taking on more generalist roles. At the same time, the rising costs of postsecondary education have pushed many English departments away from traditional literary and cultural majors and toward career tracks, like teacher training and professional writing. And, of course, many colleges and universities are engaging in a much-needed reconsideration of the curriculum, often very appropriately moving to decentralize the British-and-American focus that has long been dominant in traditional period literary study.

But while the teaching landscape is changing around us, literature and culture remain valuable, even crucial, areas of study. I am an eighteenth-centuryist in a department that no longer offers courses in my period (or any specific period), and I was a key part of the curriculum development process that completely overhauled the way we imagined and presented literary historical periods to our students. I stand behind those decisions for both pedagogical and pragmatic reasons. None of that is to say that eighteenth-century literary and cultural studies are no longer important—not only are they important in their own right, but I am constantly reminded that our period illuminates many issues that are central to understanding where we stand today: social, political, and intellectual turmoil and discovery; conceptions of race and racial identity; colonialism and empire. Nor has the eighteenth century disappeared from our curriculum—it just appears in different contexts, keeping different intellectual company, and I would argue that this reconceptualization benefits both our students and our discipline.

I have an assignment I have devised for my newly christened, period-nonspecific "British Literature and Culture" class. The course is taught at the

300 level, and it draws about equal numbers from the major and the general education program; it is capped at around thirty to thirty-five students, although it has recently run with closer to twenty. The class is not focused on the eighteenth century per se, but the assignment makes use of eighteenth-century literature and culture to help students understand the longer history of British and global literature. I think it is also useful as a metaphor for the challenges that all of us face as our space in the curriculum is redefined, highlighting the interconnectedness and invisible interdependence of our universities, our departments, and our curriculums—and casting light on our future as a discipline.

THE CHOCOLATE PROJECT

When my department last changed our curriculum for the major, the "British Literature and Culture" course replaced all of our British period courses (Medieval, Renaissance, and eighteenth, nineteenth, twentieth, and twenty-first centuries); it is paralleled by World Literature and Culture and American Literature and Culture, all taught as courses that serve both the major and our general education program at the 3000 level. It is designed as a deep dive into a span of 100 to 250 years, at the instructor's choosing, with emphasis on continuing literary influences and cultural continuity across traditional period borders. My current syllabus opens in the 1680s and closes in the 1890s, but when students walk in on the first day of the course they are met by tastes and smells from the eighteenth century, the cultural and literary space I know best. The aroma of warm, nutty chocolate and spices permeates the hallway.[1] As students venture into the classroom, I hand each of them a cup of hot chocolate, prepared adhering as closely as possible to the recipe from Hannah Glasse's 1752 English cookbook *The Art of Cookery, Made Plain and Easy*. While they sit down and take tentative sips, I hand out an assignment called "Breakfast and Empire," along with a copy of the recipe.

Glasse's brief instructions for "How to make chocolate" (figure 4.1) are an odd combination of simplicity and complexity, one brief paragraph that points to a dozen ingredients and hours of labor. The recipe calls for expected ingredients (such as cacao, sugar, and cinnamon) in unexpected forms, *many of them in astonishing quantities*; along with unexpected additions (to our modern palate), including such spices as aniseed, long pepper, achiote, nutmeg, orange flower water, and rose water; nuts like almonds and pistachios; and the rich aromatic additives musk and ambergris:

> **HOW TO MAKE CHOCOLATE.**
>
> Take six pounds of cocoa-nuts, one pound of aniseed, four ounces of long pepper, one of cinnamon, a quarter of a pound of almonds, one pound of pistachios, as much achiote as will make it the color of a brick; three

How to make chocolate.

TAKE ſix pounds of cocoa-nuts, one pound of aniſeeds, four ounces of long pepper, one of cinnamon, a quarter of a pound of almonds, one pound of piſtachios, as much achiote as will make it the colour of brick; three grains of muſk, and as much ambergreaſe, ſix pounds of loaf ſugar, one ounce of nutmegs, dry and beat them, and ſierce them through a fine ſieve: your almonds muſt be beat to a paſte, and mixed with the other ingredients; then dip your ſugar in orange-flower, or roſe-water, and put it in a ſkillet, on a very gentle charcoal-fire; then put in the ſpice, and ſtrew it well together; then the muſk and ambergreaſe; then put in the cocoa-nuts laſt of all; then achiote, wetting it with the water the ſugar was dipt in; ſtew all theſe very well together over a hotter fire than before; then take it up, and put it into boxes, or what form you like, and ſet it to dry in a warm place. The piſtachios and almonds muſt be a little beat in a mortar, then ground upon a ſtone.

Figure 4.1 Hannah Glasse's "How to Make Chocolate," in *The Art of Cookery Made Plain and Easy, Which Far Exceeds Any Thing of the Kind Yet Published*, London, 1784.

> grains of musk, and as much ambergrease, six pounds of loaf sugar, one ounce of nutmegs, dry and beat them, and force them through a fine sieve: your almonds must be beat to a paste, and mixed with the other ingredients; then dip your sugar in orange-flower, or rose-water, and put it in a skillet, on a very gentle charcoal fire; then put in the spice, and strew it well together; then the musk and ambergrease; then put in the cocoa-nuts last of all; then achiote, wetting it with the water the sugar was dipt in; stew all these very well together over a hotter fire than before; then take it up, and put it into boxes, or what form you like, and set it to be dry in a warm place. The pistachios and almonds must be a little beat in a mortar, then ground upon a stone.

While the students puzzle through the recipe and gingerly taste their drinks, I do everything I can to embed them in the sensory experience that would have met the baronet, or the tradesman's daughter, or the squire's family sitting down to a warm cup of chocolate in 1752.

I bring the ingredients in a basket to class, and let the students look at them, smell them, and taste them. I have ordered all of the ingredients that are currently legal and acquirable at a reasonable price—ambergris (a sperm whale excretion) is off the table, of course, and wild deer musk was a hundred dollars more than I was willing to spend. The rest is still pretty impressive, though. Many of the students have never seen crystalized cane loaf sugar, or tasted the richness and depth of flavor that it carries compared to simple white sugar. Achiote is a new concept for most of my (mostly white, northeastern) students, and a fair number of them have never seen or smelled anise, or rose water, or orange-blossom water, or even (to my surprise) nutmeg. I let them taste almonds and pistachios and note the gradations of flavor and texture between the two. Long pepper is a revelation. I order mine directly from India, and it looks and smells like nothing common to the American spice palate—a blend of cinnamon and black pepper notes with overtones of allspice and mace, in a seed pod that looks like catkins, or dried caterpillars. As the students sniff and sample each spice, I invite them to sip the hot chocolate again, searching for the contribution made by that particular flavor or aroma, and then suggest that they taste again afterward, taking in how all the different elements blend together as a whole.

And once they have tasted what the chocolate is like from the consumer's side of the table, I turn them around and ask them to think about the other side. Eighteenth-century British consumer culture (like ours) was a lot like the old story of the swan gliding along on the surface of the water with the feet paddling madly underneath. The chocolate tastes beautiful—rich, creamy, nutty, with overlapping notes of black pepper and cinnamon and licorice and something deeper and earthier from the achiote (and presumably the ambergris and musk). Thinking about the production, on the other hand, is bitter rather than sweet, though just as complex.

We work backward. In class on that first day, we try to work out how many labor hours would be involved in transforming a kitchen full of raw materials into drinkable chocolate. We estimate, as best we can, how long it would take to dry and beat six pounds of cocoa pods into a paste with hand tools, and just what would be involved in shelling and pulverizing the almonds and pistachios. I have a little mortar and pestle, and I have the students try to grind anise and cinnamon bark and achiote finely enough that they could be incorporated into a beverage. We talk about how long it takes to produce charcoal, starting with chopping down the tree. We don't come up with definitive answers, of course, but the students get a glimpse of how much physical labor must have gone on below stairs and out of doors in order to enable ten minutes of pleasant sipping upstairs. The estimate they come up with is never less than about forty labor hours per cup.

Then we take it another step further. As we leave class, I assign each student one ingredient and ask them to come back the next session with the best answers they can find to five questions:

- Where would your ingredient have been grown/produced in the eighteenth century?
- How it would have been produced and by whom?
- Were the people involved in the production free, indentured, or enslaved?
- How would your product have been transported to England?
- How much would it have cost?

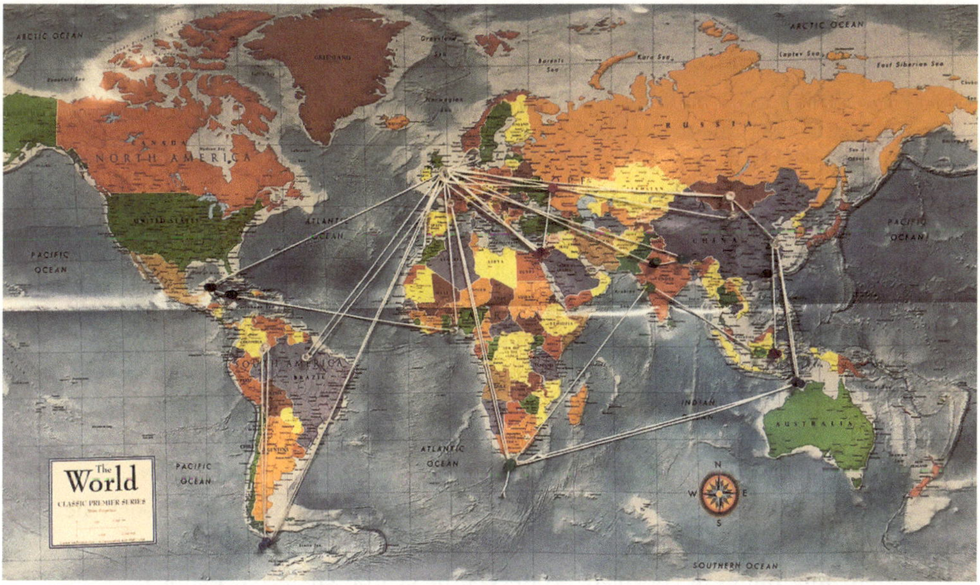

Figure 4.2 Classroom map of production locations and trade routes for chocolate ingredients, ENG 3347 British Literature and Culture, Mansfield University, Fall 2021, courtesy of Teri Doerksen.

When they come back to class the next session, I pin a large world map to the classroom wall and have them place push pins in the geographic areas where their ingredient was produced, and we work together to trace the likeliest trade routes, using pins and string (figure 4.2). There is usually an audible gasp when they connect the loaf sugar and cocoa to the triangle trade, which they know about from their high school history courses, though they often haven't considered the connections between the slave trade and food commerce.

And then we start to count the miles, and the human cost, and the time expended in bringing these things back to London. What have they discovered about the lives of the people harvesting and drying the cinnamon bark? Which native peoples had to be displaced in order to produce nutmeg at scale? What connections did they trace between ambergris and sperm whale hunting? How long would the cinnamon have been in transit from Ceylon? How many enslaved Africans died in the ships en route to harvesting sugar cane in Jamaica? How many lash marks on how many backs to bring cocoa from the Ivory Coast and the West Indies to the breakfast cups in Grosvenor Square? Obviously none of this is easily quantifiable. Nevertheless, we usually end with a map showing tens of thousands of miles traveled; a timeline suggesting years of labor by an overlapping web of many thousands of people in a global network; and a necessarily incomplete accounting of deaths, indentures, enslavements, colonial violence, environmental devastation, backbreaking labor, and grinding poverty.

This assignment sets the tone for the entire semester. We read *Oroonoko* immediately afterward. Aphra Behn's 1688 fictional account of an African prince sold into slavery in Surinam, his love story with the beautiful Imoinda, and both of their tragic deaths leading a slave uprising, has an entirely different valence when the class discourse incorporates a sense of context from the Chocolate Project. One student last year noted that she felt like she was studying the Butterfly Effect in chaos theory—to paraphrase her point, she said that it seemed that, just like a butterfly flapping its wings in Brazil could theoretically cause a tornado in Texas, the trivial desires of unremarkable people for unnecessary delicacies in England were setting in motion a train of events that led inevitably to the utterly avoidable enslavement and death of the main characters.

The connections to the Chocolate Project stay central as we move through the readings in the course. In Alexander Pope's "The Rape of the Lock," the mention of "burning fumes of chocolate" connects the central character, Belinda, to the transatlantic slave trade and the spice fields of India and Indonesia. In Frances Burney's 1778 novel *Evelina*, every time the seventeen-year-old Evelina sits down to breakfast with Maria and Mrs. Mirvan, students are alert to the global implications embedded in trifling acts. The anonymous *Woman of Colour*, an 1808 novel about a biracial heiress who leaves her home in Jamaica to travel to England to marry, takes us back to the West Indies and discussion turns to the multilayered implications of the protagonist's heritage as the daughter of an enslaved worker and the heir to a sugar fortune. Elizabeth Gaskell's *Mary Barton*, with its grim depiction of the life of factory workers in Manchester, spurs comparison to Oroonoko in Surinam and casts into stark relief the luxuriousness of goods like chocolate. As we progress through Wilkie Collins and H. Rider Haggard and Oscar Wilde, the class discourse shows that students see a connectedness between simple actions and global implications that takes on an additional resonance because they can identify the same patterns echoing down the decades.

FACING THE FUTURE: CURRICULAR AND TEACHING CHOICES IN A TIME OF CHANGE

This exercise is useful in the classroom, but I also find it a worthwhile metaphor for the challenges of this historical moment in which we find ourselves—in English in general, and in eighteenth-century studies in particular. The Chocolate Project becomes a centering force for an entire course, and it contributes not only to the knowledge base from which the students operate but also to the modes of inquiry that shape their discourse for the entire semester. In a time of disciplinary and curricular turmoil, I find it useful to think of my knowledge and research as an eighteenth-centuryist centering my teaching in much the same way as the Chocolate Project centers my course, and the kinds of thinking that it encourages are the same ones that can guide all of us as our disciplines and departmental curriculums change.

Different groups of students make meaning in different ways, of course, and develop their own meaningful discourse in response to any class exercise, but at its best the Chocolate Project aims to move students toward a kind of thinking about literature and culture in which they

- Investigate the larger context
- Redefine terms, even the ones they think they know well
- Redefine borders between countries, concepts, and literary periods, and
- Make connections in unexpected places.

My own department's curricular experiences over the last decade or so may serve as a useful touchstone to talk about the kinds of changes that are under way in higher education right now, particularly in the United States. Some of those changes are disorienting and destabilizing, no question, especially as many colleges and universities face declining numbers of English majors and less frequent replacement of retiring faculty. However, I plan to look at the ways that the same guiding questions that emerge from the Chocolate Project can help to make those changes productive and potentially energizing as well.

My department's story is a familiar one, and it represents the kinds of challenges many of us are facing. I was hired twenty-one years ago into a thriving English and Modern Languages department at a small public university in the northeast. Our teaching load is 4/4, with two sections of composition and two of literature every semester. At the time we had twelve tenured and tenure-track English faculty. We grew a bit over the next decade, to thirteen in English.

Then, in rapid succession, we faced the fallout from the 2008 recession, the legislature slashed our system budget, and our geographic area went over a demographic cliff. The English program was repeatedly threatened with "retrenchment," system-speak for firing fully tenured faculty members with years of service to the university. In rapid succession, two English colleagues died in the midst of promising careers, five others retired, and one moved into administration. None of the eight departures were replaced. In only five years (from 2013 to 2018) the department dropped from thirteen faculty in English to five.[2]

We had to reconstruct our curriculum from the ground up. Our approach, in retrospect, mirrored the Chocolate Project: first we looked at the larger context for our situation, then reimagined the way we had defined terms and borders, and finally took on the job of making unexpected connections.

Investigate the Larger Context

Our first impulse as a department was to think of our situation as a unique kind of bad luck. This is an especially distracting kind of magical thinking: bad luck means that you hang on and wait for things to get better instead of making necessary changes. It was important for us to look at the larger picture in order to gain context: the national job market, the national political atmosphere, external funding pressures, regional and accrediting demands.

One glance at the MLA Job Information List over the last decades tells its own story. Between the 2007–2008 academic year and the 2019–2020 hiring year the number of total positions in English has dropped precipitously from 1,826 to 728. Over the same period the percentage of job ads for specialists in British literature have dropped in a similar way, from 27.8 percent in 2007–2008 to 13.4 percent in 2018–2019 (the most recent year available). At the same time, the percentage of advertised jobs requesting more general or approach-based expertise has risen, as is the case with the terms "interdisciplinary" (from 10.9 percent to 11.4 percent) and "cultural studies" (from 11.8 percent to a whopping 17.9 percent). All of this tells us what we already know: our colleagues are retiring, and they are not being replaced at a rate to match the retirements, so departments are looking to cover a lot of terrain with a very few replacement hires.[3]

We also needed to dispel some wishful thinking about our institution in particular. We are located in a part of the northeast where the number of graduating high school seniors eligible to attend college is dropping dramatically, with particularly steep cliffs back in 2012 and coming up in 2026, so there is a smaller pool of potential students to draw upon. At the same time, budgetary support for our state-supported institutions of higher education, as with state institutions in many parts of the United States, has undergone draconian cuts. When I was hired in 2000, my state contributed $6,379 per full-time-equivalent (FTE) student, and we were sixteenth in the nation for student support. By 2008 the state contributed $5,493 per FTE student and we had dropped to thirty-eighth. In 2019 the state had reduced its contribution to $4,302 and we ranked forty-eighth in the nation. Takeaway: the likelihood that new tenure-track lines would be opening up soon was limited.

* * *

All of this is occurring in the context of a national trend of students turning away from the English major in the United States. According to the National Center for Education Statistics, the number of English majors dropped by more than 25 percent from 2008 to 2017,[4] a shift the *Washington Post* referred to as "a great migration."[5]

In other words, the problem is not our department's alone. It is systemic and it will not be solved any time soon.

None of this was reassuring, but it was a critical dose of reality and it inspired us to think productively about what changes to make. Operating with many fewer department members was going to be the new normal, and instead of just aiming to beat back the tide or maintain some kind of stasis, we needed to find productive, innovative ways to locate our strengths and improve our programs with the resources available.

Redefine Terms

Once we faced the reality of the situation, we started back at the very beginning, defining for ourselves what was central to our program and our discipline. We asked fundamental questions: What is an English program? Within that program, what constitutes appropriate "English" study? What content and skills are central to who we are and what we do? How can we make sure our program gives students everything they need, and that we can offer the resulting program in a regular rotation using the assets currently available to us?

Some of the questions had to be answered in the context of external constraints. We had to look at the retirements in our department and assess our expertise with an eye toward the remaining faculty. Some of our "self-definition" had to take into account the requirements of our state department of education for teaching programs in English (e.g., that all prospective English teachers take a certain number of courses in British and American literature). And, of course, we had to take into account growing pressure from students for career preparedness pathways.

We took all of this information and used it to dismantle our existing curriculum in order to rebuild it from the ground up. First we established that instead of a literature major we needed a range of options. We decided to establish two concentration pathways in the major, one in Literary and Cultural Analysis and one in Professional Writing, and to provide all the necessary content area requirements for students pursuing an English education degree. We considered what would be needed to field all of those options, and looked for all the ways we could configure courses to cover learning objectives that would serve more than one concentration.

Redefine Borders

The suddenness and drastic nature of our situation pushed us to redefine both disciplinary and departmental borders.

We first redefined the borders between courses. We restructured courses offerings wherever possible—in my own corner of the curriculum, for example, our two British literature surveys were combined into a single course, and we did away with all of our British period courses to replace them with the British Literature and Culture course I describe above. This gives us flexibility and allows us to offer each course more frequently, while opening up each course to potentially be taught by more than one of us.

We also looked at the borders between our department and general education, and between the major and the other majors on campus. As we rebuilt the courses in the major, we made sure that most of them can also serve as general education offerings so we can offer them in a more robust rotation. At the same time, we talked with other departments on campus that were offering courses that could enrich our major offerings. Our professional writers can now choose from major course options taught by other departments, including marketing, journalism, and professional ethics.

We then necessarily redrew the lines each of us had established around our course responsibilities in the department. Twenty years ago, the expectation was that new hires in our department would represent particular fields and cover a particular subset of our course offerings along with general education courses and composition. I was the eighteenth-century British literature person. I covered (naturally) the eighteenth-century British literature course, along with British surveys and occasional British author and novel courses in addition to Introduction to Literature and a lot of first-year and third-year writing courses. Even then we pushed those boundaries: most of us taught occasional courses outside of our primary field, and all of our faculty were free to propose and teach courses on other topics that might interest students. Generally, though, we were by and large defined by the areas of expertise that had been specified when we were hired.

The sudden loss of so many department members pushed us to redefine all the borders between our areas of study, and to look for all the ways that we could build from our existing expertise and expand the kinds of courses that each person could offer. All of the remaining English faculty members wear a lot of hats, and I would argue that we wear them well. To illustrate, one colleague, whose primary field is civil rights literature, has developed superb courses in drama as a literary genre (to serve our Literature and Culture concentration) and copyediting (to serve our Professional Writing concentration) while still fielding courses in slave narrative and the civil rights novel—she won the Dean's Award for Outstanding Teacher at the university last year. Our world literature specialist is also fully qualified in American literature and professional writing, and he fields a range of courses across all three areas. Our transatlantic twentieth-centuryist covers all the American surveys, most of the upper-division American courses, women's literature, and LGBTQ literature, among other things. All of us have stepped forward to do whatever is needed to provide a thorough and challenging curriculum in all of our concentrations.

Make Connections in Unexpected Places

It turns out that because I know and love eighteenth-century British literature and culture, for me the eighteenth century is everywhere. All of our courses on the literature side of the major are intentionally designed with maximum flexibility in mind. Our British survey now covers all of British literature from Old English to yesterday afternoon, and although I try to bring the same level of expertise to every text we read, the students can tell how excited I am when we get to Alexander Pope and Eliza Haywood and Elizabeth Inchbald. When I teach the Author in Context course, I usually choose Jane Austen, and my students and I immerse ourselves for a semester in Regency England. My next project is to teach the course with Frances Burney as the focal author, and I have a distant dream of trying it with Samuel Richardson. When I teach Genre in Context, I usually teach the history of the novel, and there we are again, revisiting familiar terrain, from Behn to Swift to Richardson to Fielding to Burney.

The fear my colleagues and I shared when we started this process was that the changes we were making would eliminate the disciplines we had studied all our lives. I will admit that I asked to keep the Eighteenth-Century British Literature course on the books for one last extra year, even though I knew it would never be taught again, because I had a hard time letting go (my colleagues humored me, and we left it in the catalogue long enough for me to say a last farewell before consigning it to oblivion). But I needn't have worried. Just as the Chocolate Project touches all parts of my course, the eighteenth century touches all parts of my teaching. Diana Epelbaum argues elsewhere in this volume that "perhaps nothing has the potential to be more relevant for today's college students that the eighteenth century: we just have to help them see it." I would argue that we may need to learn this same lesson ourselves before we can help our students.

SURVIVING AND THRIVING IN A CHANGING LANDSCAPE

Seven years after our department started to face our existential crisis, we are still adjusting to changes as they happen, but we have learned to work together productively and proactively. We are creative, we are nimble, and we are scrappy, and we have well-structured, beautifully integrated, and internally consistent major programs of study that we can field, along with our service courses, with only five faculty members and the equivalent (after administrative course reductions) of four full-time faculty teaching loads (sixteen courses) per semester.

It has been a rough ride. At the same time, though, staying constantly aware of the larger context, being willing to revisit the way we define terms and borders, and making connections across disciplinary and departmental lines has enabled our English program and faculty to be innovative and flexible and resilient. Despite the loss of people power, we have expanded our programmatic offerings to meet the needs of first-generation students who need a clear career trajectory after graduation. We have maintained our Literary and Cultural Analysis major course of study, reinvigorated our grades 7–12 secondary English teaching content pathway, and created a successful and growing Professional Writing concentration. The changes we have made have resulted in a gradual upswing in the number of majors, partly due to successful international recruitment into our program. More transformation is on the horizon: our university has just learned that it will be integrated with two other schools in our system to form a kind of meta-university, with a single English department and a single shared curriculum, but still operating at three different campuses. I am confident that we will meet the challenge.

NOTES

1. Note: Safety is key. My hallway is fairly isolated, so students from other classrooms are unlikely to be within sniffing range, and I contact all my students before the semester starts to check for nut or other food allergies. During COVID times, of course, I changed all of this to meet safety guidelines, and masks and hand sanitizer were the order of the day. I took the students outside to smell and taste, weather permitting.
2. This is a count of the complement of full-time tenured and tenure-track faculty. The adjunct complement dropped during this period as well, from four to five full-time equivalent adjunct positions each year (twelve to sixteen courses per semester) to zero, unless we need to backfill courses for a tenured faculty member on medical leave.
3. "Report on the MLA Job Information List, 2012–13," MLA Office of Research (October 2013); "The MLA Job List, 2018–19," by Natalia Lusin, MLA Office of Programs (November 2020); and "Tables and Figures on the MLA Job List, 2019–20," Reports on the MLA Job List, accessed July 2021.
4. National Center for Education Statistics, "Table 22:10: Bachelor's Degrees Conferred by Postsecondary Institutions, by Field of Study: Selected Years, 1970–71 through 2016–17," Digest of Education Statistics, https://nces.ed.gov/programs/digest/d18/tables/dt18_322.10.asp?current=yes.
5. Heather Long, "The World's Top Economists Just Made the Case for Why We Still Need English Majors: English Majors Are Down 25.5 Percent since the Great Recession, Just as World's Top Economists Say We Need More 'Storytellers,'" *Washington Post*, October 19, 2019. https://www.washingtonpost.com/business/2019/10/19/worlds-top-economists-just-made-case-why-we-still-need-english-majors/.

5
ENLIGHTENED EXCHANGES
An Interdisciplinary Approach to Teaching the Scottish Enlightenment

Christine D. Myers

As an American who studied transnational comparative history in Scotland, I have often been frustrated with the focus in U.S. history textbooks on continental thinkers during the Enlightenment. So, when I was asked by the chair of the Political Economy and Commerce Department at the college where I was teaching to create a course centered on the works of Adam Smith, I jumped at the chance. My colleague's motivation was for business and economics majors to learn more history of their disciplines via a junior-level general education course, but I saw it as a way to feature the many influential Scottish thinkers who are either disregarded by scholars or subsumed under the mantel of Britishness. Because my course was interdisciplinary, my approach invariably included far more than Adam Smith's economic theories. The title I gave it—Enlightened Scots—had a double meaning. Our primary goal was learning about the impact of the Scottish Enlightenment on the world, but I was also trying to enlighten students at a small, private, Midwestern college whose mascot is the Fighting Scots.[1]

Monmouth College's General Education curriculum, as of 2021, included a set of four courses in Integrated Studies, each of which focused on a particular set of learning objectives while fitting overarching criteria.[2] The course taken by students in their junior year was called Reflections, and was intended as a means for them see the value of their liberal arts education in their chosen career path. The first time I taught the course in the spring of 2017 there were twenty-one students, and then in the fall of 2018 there were twenty students, with a relatively even split between men and women each time. They had widely ranging backgrounds and skill sets, plus significant ethnic, racial, and socioeconomic diversity. Though I was a history professor, and this was ostensibly a history course, the first iteration had only one history major and the second had two. The largest contingent in both semesters was business and/or economics majors, owing to the push they received from their home department to select this particular section of Reflections. The rosters also included students majoring in art, chemistry, communications, education, environmental studies, international studies, physical education, political science, public relations, psychology, sociology/anthropology, and theater. Our class met on Tuesdays and Thursdays for 75 minutes, and some students also signed up simply because it fit in their schedules. The graded components of the course included standard items—attendance and participation, two tests and a final exam, a paper near the end of the semester—and a more innovative series of class-wide debates that I called the Enlightened Exchange. The course was segmented into four portions, organized around traditional textbooks and assessments, which I supplemented in various ways.[3]

ESTABLISHING A FOUNDATION OF SHARED KNOWLEDGE

In the first portion of the course, students read *Scottish Enlightenment: The Scots' Invention of the Modern World* by Arthur Herman.[4] The book focuses on ways in which Scottish thinkers led the way in a variety of fields, distinguishing Scots' achievements within the overarching term "British," which also includes England and Wales.[5] Most of the students in the course had little or no previous coursework on any time period of European history, let alone on the Enlightenment; notable exceptions were a student who had taken my course on the French Revolution who happened to be one of two students working on a philosophy minor. As such, during the first three weeks we learned the key figures and advances of the Scottish Enlightenment. To fully understand how the Scottish experience differed from that on the continent, I covered a substantial amount of Scottish history too. Mini-lectures on Scotland as an independent nation before 1707 and after its political union with England and Wales were particularly significant to subjects students would debate later in the semester, with Scotland retaining control over its educational, legal, and religious systems throughout its history. Whether they realized it or not at the time, my critiques of traditional, "Anglocentric" British history worked to pave the way for them to deconstruct what they accept as "fact" based on their schooling thus far.

For students in the United States, Herman's book is engaging because it illustrates the influence of Scottish ideas on America's Founding Fathers.[6] References to American colonial history enable students to attach new content on the Enlightenment to knowledge already in their minds of history they had studied in high school. Inevitably, this introduction reveals gaps in students' past learning, due to oversimplification or an avoidance of contentious material, similar to that noted by Teri Doerksen in chapter 4. Even when Herman does not emphasize such connections, I made them myself to further problematize students' understanding of the past. Shaking the foundations of their worldview gave students the opportunity to repair it with the more nuanced approach we would take during the semester.

For instance, I showed an early performance by Lin-Manuel Miranda of the song "Alexander Hamilton" at the White House during "An Evening of Poetry, Music & the Spoken Word" in 2009.[7] The song opens by describing both Hamilton's half-Scottish parentage and his intellectual accomplishments:

> How does a bastard, orphan, son of a whore
> And a Scotsman, dropped in the middle of a forgotten spot
> In the Caribbean by providence impoverished
> In squalor, grow up to be a hero and a scholar?

By the time I first taught the course in the spring of 2017, *Hamilton* had already taken Broadway by storm and was a cultural phenomenon, even among college students in middle America.[8] Dissecting the lyrics and what they say about obstacles in young Hamilton's life and his tenacity to overcome them makes for a compelling class discussion as students begin to question what character traits and accomplishments society values. That he "started retreatin' and readin' every treatise on the shelf" easily leant itself to specific conversation about the value of education—Enlightened education, specifically—in the development of not only Hamilton as an individual, but the United States as a new country. From there, the students could start to extrapolate on their own about what their goals were and what skills or knowledge they needed to accomplish them.

Students had definite opinions about the racially blind casting of *Hamilton*, raising questions of representation versus historical accuracy. These comments provoked more about intersectionality and gender roles, with me prodding students to ask themselves to react not only to what was presented but also to what (or who) was left out. Hamilton rose up in a way the majority of men and all women were unable to. A natural segue was then possible, to conversations about cultural conflict, discrimination, prostitution, and slavery. While scholars have long argued that "slavery was an inherently 'British' issue, affecting the English, Scots, Welsh, and Irish equally and without regard to regional identity,"[9] the reality was considerably different. One way I teased out this distinction out was by way of Dan Nosowitz's article "How the English Failed to Stamp Out the Scots Language," with its parallels to how the British attempted to eliminate the languages of their Celtic neighbors and countless generations of Indigenous and African peoples.[10] Had I constructed the syllabus in my home department, I would have also assigned readings from Scottish historians who for decades now have been reckoning with the nation's complex role in the slave trade, being both a colonized nation and one of colonizers who perpetuated imperialism.[11] Because I was bound in Enlightened Scots by the strictures of the Integrated Studies curriculum, the need to select texts for a general audience resulted in using popular history and augmenting them with more detailed primary and secondary sources.

If I taught the course now, it would be possible to draw in other examples from popular culture, like the later seasons of *Outlander*, which are set in colonial America and present the Scottish influence on community actions and ethos.[12] The fact that the series consistently pushes back against misogyny, while also highlighting the importance of education for all people regardless of their class, race, or sex, would make its inclusion in the course logical. One reason the Scottish Enlightenment is sometimes overlooked in textbooks is because many academics think it did not amount to tangible changes like those wrought in the French Revolution. The fact that Scotland remains politically tied to England in the twenty-first century, after having failed to break free during the Jacobite Risings in the mid-1700s, leads some to believe it was a failed intellectual movement.[13] What I tried to impress upon my students was the idea that the Enlightenment thinkers in Scotland actually thrived *on account* of the failed rebellions. And the repressive actions of the British government toward the Scots subsequently had a tremendous influence on colonial American leaders. Particularly when teaching in the United States, it's important to bring this intellectual inheritance to the fore.

Another piece introduced early in the semester was the college's Mission Statement, assigned as homework.[14] I've done this at a number of institutions I've worked at, and it always prompts excitable responses from the students, who, more often than not, do not see the education they receive as matching up with the grandiose or idealized language of such documents. In making it a required reading in the formative stage of the students' understanding of the Enlightenment, I could go back to it repeatedly during the remainder of the course. So that students—even those who tend to be quiet during group discussions—would be compelled to engage with the Mission Statement, it was the basis of the take-home portion of their first test of the semester. The question posed was: "To what extent is your education at Monmouth College a product of the Scottish Enlightenment?" We discussed the phrasing of the question collectively, so students knew their answer could embrace the notion that there were undeniable connections between their experiences and the Scottish Enlightenment, they could say such connections were tenuous at best, or anything along the spectrum between those extremes.

What was important in every test question or assignment in the course, unsurprisingly, was that they support their argument with solid examples from the assigned readings or other materials we discussed in class. To push students beyond the obvious examples they might plan to include from our readings alone, on the review sheet for the tests I encouraged the students to look at "the specific learning outcomes of your home department or major/minor or of certain courses you have taken." I hoped this would make the essay as self-reflective as possible, keeping them engaged while writing it. The more they could connect their experience in a business or science course to the philosophies we were discussing, the more likely they would be to integrate the knowledge and not cast it aside as soon as the semester ended. Answers did not need to be long (2–3 pages or 350–650 words); the essay was intended as a starting point from which they could analyze not only the primary and secondary sources we read in class, but also how their own experiences fit within a larger academic and historical context.

Along with having a take-home portion of each test (something that was required by the coordinators of the Integrated Studies structure the course was a part of), students also had an in-class test that was exceptionally open-ended. I used a British format called gobbets, which are essentially chunks of text from assigned readings that students are to engage with in a relatively free-form way.[15] On the review sheet, I gave them the topics of the gobbets. On Test #1 these were: The influence of the Scottish Enlightenment on colonial America; How trade and economics were viewed in the eighteenth century; The movement of people(s)—migration, emigration, and/or immigration; Enlightenment views of religion and the role of religion in society; Perceptions of Scotland/the Scottish people; and Impact of the Act of Union of 1707. They were asked to write about three of the six, and I always encouraged them to study for at least four of them, in case the excerpt I selected caused them to draw a blank for some reason. In covering such a wide array of disciplines, it was possible for students to stick with material they were more comfortable with. My personal teaching philosophy is that examinations should enable students to show you how much they've learned, not seek to reveal gaps in their knowledge. Assessment, in my view, is preferable to traditional testing, particularly in an interdisciplinary course where students' test-taking abilities vary.[16] An emphasis on revealing the students' method of thinking about the material was more important than requiring them to remember a predetermined set of dates or facts.

DEBATING AS A MEANS OF INTEGRATING KNOWLEDGE

During the second portion of the course, we shifted to a new book—Robert Louden's *The World We Want.* The book is organized in two parts—the first five chapters are headed "THEN" and deal with the topics of religion, education, economics, politics, and international relations during the Enlightenment; the second five chapters, headed "NOW," look at the same five topics in current time. The book's subtitle—*How and Why the Ideals of the Enlightenment Still Elude Us*—gives away Louden's conclusion that the hoped-for results of enlightened thinkers in Europe have not come to pass. In his preface Loudon explains: "This in itself may not be news to everyone, but some of the details concerning the extent of the gap did come as a shock to me, and I think that many readers will be surprised to learn that we have often not progressed as much as we think we have—indeed, that in certain central areas of human life things are actually worse now than they were two hundred years ago."[17]

What I chose to do with the book was assign the THEN and NOW chapters on a single topic together. The reading load was anywhere from 23 pages (on religion) to 61 pages (on international relations), with the other three days having 30-some pages of reading. Everyone was expected to do the reading and contribute to the discussion, but specific students would be in front of the room, "fishbowl" style, to propel the conversation.[18] Shifting the responsibility of course prep to them, rather than allowing them to passively absorb information alone, forced the students to engage actively with the material.[19] Even when it was not their day to be in front of the room, knowing they would appreciate constructive comments from their classmates when it *was* their turn was effective motivation all around.[20]

Because the book is *not* focused on Scotland, it provided students with a chance to see how the material they had learned up to that point in the semester about Scottish thought intersected with ideas elsewhere in Europe. Further, it enabled them to see how transnational the intellectual developments were, even during the eighteenth century. Guiding questions for all of the topics were taken from Louden's introduction: "What are the causes of the large gap between Enlightenment ideals and present realities? How can we avoid past mistakes in this area?" and "How and why do the ideals of the Enlightenment still elude us?"[21] The assignment was decidedly *not* a group project, since in my experience many college students are exceedingly resistant to anything that comes with a group grade. I did suggest they confer with the other students who signed up for the same topic, though, in case they wanted to divide their focuses and learn about specific facets of the topic in greater depth. Not surprisingly, the students who collaborated prior to the session were more comfortable when they were in front of the class, if only because they had already verbalized their thoughts to some of their classmates. From my perspective, it was clear that they were benefiting from having an enlightened exchange before the Enlightened Exchange, as I tried to interweave such concepts subtly throughout the semester.

To make sure everyone had accountability for the success of the Exchanges, not just the leaders in the front of the room who were being graded on the day, the assignment sheet included directions for both the presenters and the audience members. Presenters were encouraged to look up additional information on terms and people mentioned in the chapters that we had not learned about in Herman's book. Because Louden's text encompasses the entire Enlightenment, not just Scotland, this simple bit of instruction forced them to delve into a considerable amount of English, French, and Prussian history on their own for the THEN chapter and a great deal of twentieth-century history for the NOW chapter. Audience members had to be prepared to ask questions, a direction that simultaneously warned the students sitting up front to try to anticipate questions they might be asked.

The reflection portion of the assignment came at the end of each Exchange (an example of the low-stakes writing that Diana Epelbaum discusses in greater detail in chapter 6). I handed out a page that included the overarching questions from Louden, followed by a question for the presenters, How do you think you did during the Exchange?, and another for the audience, How would you assess your own contributions to the conversation and attentiveness as an audience member? The final half of the page was blank, as was the reverse side of the page, so students could continue their answer there, my way of indicating they should expand on and contextualize their answers as much as possible. I was pleased that many students had so much to say that they did indeed continue their responses on the back. This thoroughness was driven by the fact that 30 percent of the students' overall course grade was earned through attendance and participation, and the reflections for audience members counted as part of that.[22]

In many cases the audience reflections included justifications of their choice not to speak themselves. Often this was because someone else asked something similar or the presenters dealt with the topic already. Other students admitted that they were not feeling well or were not well prepared, but assured me they "took lots of notes" and "gave eye contact to those speaking if I wasn't writing." Still others admitted to not asking questions because they worried that they would reveal their lack of understanding of a topic and their peers would think they were "ignorant." My feedback on these reflections was gentle and encouraging—asking them questions about how they might prepare for their own day at the front of the room or suggesting they turn their thoughts more inward to question themselves—all in an effort to create a safe environment for students to share, at least with me, what they were struggling with intellectually.

Typically, the students did not take the "easy" way out on their reflections more than once; they were all juniors who knew that they wouldn't get away with that. Some were forthright and insightful each and every time, admitting misunderstandings they had or gaps in their educational background that they now wanted to learn more about. When religion was discussed during the first Exchange, one student remarked that, as a Catholic, her "asking about why there was so much animosity and lack of tolerance [for the Catholic Church] was important for me and my own knowledge." This statement was followed by a parenthetical aside "(They don't really tell you in Catholic school that people really disliked the Catholics for a long time)." Another student noted in his reflection that "religion seemed to be tearing people apart instead of bringing people together" and that he felt the presenters did well to respond to his question with evidence he had overlooked in the text.

I sat in the back of the room each time and said as little as possible. An occasional nudge was needed to get the questioning under way, but they handled it on their own most of the time. The group at the front for the first topic—religion—was the smallest (just three of them), and the first time I taught the course they included the history major and the two philosophy minors I mentioned previously. One was also a student who converted to Catholicism recently, and another was an international student from Kazakhstan, showing the diversity that even a group of three could bring to a discussion of religion. Thankfully, from my viewpoint, they did a fantastic job of preparing and set an extremely high bar for the remaining Exchanges—an observation I made sure to state explicitly to the rest of the class during their semester and to the next contingent of students who took the course the following year.

The subsequent topics gave students from certain disciplines the chance to bring in much of their own knowledge from other courses they'd taken. Education majors had a great deal to say during the second Exchange, as did everyone else based on their own school experiences. Those studying business or economics in our Department of Political Economy and Commerce shone during the third Exchange, on economics. An additional element I didn't anticipate when developing or scheduling the course was that a few of the students were also taking my history course on the European Union. As a result, the days when we discussed economics and international relations included a great number of detailed examples of EU legislation that even the most studious American college student usually knows little about.

The fourth Exchange, on politics, proved to be the most impassioned; it came soon after the contentious 2016 presidential campaign. Several students essentially opted out of that particular conversation because they were uncomfortable talking politics and were worried that it would become *too* heated. In their reflections they commented that they were surprised the group managed to have a calm and civil conversation when all they'd seen portrayed on the news was political differences escalating into shouting matches or even more aggressive actions. As I noted earlier, creating a safe environment for healthy discussion and debate was at the forefront of my mind for this course; it's also an espoused goal at the college and is the first question on every student evaluation.[23] Those students who chose to respond verbally said they felt the environment was positive and welcoming of both comments and questions.

In all the Exchanges, I especially appreciated the students who remarked on the value in studying the assigned topic with the advantage of multiple disciplinary perspectives and having discussions with people of "diverse backgrounds." I hope they will all continue to have respectful, enlightened conversations with people with whom they disagree, and that they will have open minds about the possibility that someone with different training or coming from a different experience might have a solution to a problem they themselves could not solve. As in the Enlightenment itself, no single perspective provides all the answers on a particular topic—this edited collection being a prime example of that point.

CONTEMPLATING THE IMPACT AN INDIVIDUAL CAN MAKE

After the spring or fall break we shifted gears in the course to look at a biography of Adam Smith by Nicholas Phillipson.[24] Along with basic information on Smith's life and works, the biography presents ample discussion of his character and motivations. An added bonus to this particular book selection is that there is an hour-long lecture from the author available on the University of Edinburgh's YouTube channel that we were able to watch, then discuss, during one class period.[25] Interestingly, Phillipson's approach in the lecture is about Edinburgh then and now, so it fit perfectly with the Enlightened Exchanges we had so recently finished. Focusing on Smith's life not only fulfilled the initial request from the Political Economy and Commerce Department but also gave students an individual perspective on the Enlightenment. Herman's book is broad, and Louden's is even more sweeping. A walk through that increasingly familiar territory with a single, remarkably imperfect person, was a shift in scholarship that the students appreciated. Reading excerpts from Smith's works proved revelatory, as what most in the class had learned about his theories had been filtered through centuries of scholarship.[26]

Another beneficial aspect to teaching about Adam Smith is that he was a university lecturer, which opened up the chance for me, as an historian of higher education, to delve into the practicalities of what university study was like in Smith's time. Large topics, like the fact that both secondary and tertiary education were almost exclusively the domain of white men, prompted lengthy debates and much reflection from students (for more on this, see Emily Casey's analysis in chapter 9). My doctoral research had been on the admission of women to universities in the nineteenth century, so I was able to provide numerous counterpoints to this standard narrative and discuss the ways excluded groups tried to access knowledge they were denied. The scientific "justification" for maintaining the hierarchical status quo never ceases to spark productive upset among students. Ultimately, the ways academic knowledge is restricted on account of gender, race, or economic status tells us much about societies regardless of their place in a historical time line.[27]

To make a more practical and less intellectual demonstration of the realities of higher education during the Scottish Enlightenment, on one day during the second iteration of the course I asked for two volunteers. We stepped outside the classroom briefly so I could ask them to try to write down every word I said when I resumed my mini-lecture. I only had them attempt this for a few minutes, then asked that they explain to their classmates what they were doing and how it had gone. As expected, it was a nearly impossible task. We then contemplated the fact that Adam Smith's *Lectures on Justice, Police, Revenue and Arms* were "reported by a student in 1763" and published in 1896.[28] How many times would students need to sit through one of Smith's lectures in order to transcribe them, even if they worked as a team with others? And how thoroughly would they learn the material in the process?

The exercise underscored the difficulties of Enlightenment-era students, who did not have the technology we do today—even items as basic as pencils or spiral notebooks were *not* available, and other items today's college students take for granted, such as electric lighting and laptops, would have been beyond comprehension in the 1700s. Students who tried to preserve Smith's lectures would have marveled at voice-to-text software. It is easy for us to criticize the past for not being more enlightened, yet we often fail to think about the practical difficulties they had in circulating new ideas that would improve society.[29] In the twenty-first century we have the opportunity to truly move to an enlightened, inclusive society, and I hope that this demonstration stays with the students and reminds them make the most of their opportunities and technologies.

As a means of continuing to walk the students themselves through self-reflection on their own educational experiences, the biography led them into their one paper of the semester, which I entitled Enlightened Existence. Just as the Enlightened Exchanges were intended to be equal parts learning about the past and the present while reflecting on both, the Enlightened Existence paper asked them to consider Smith's personality and life choices as the basis for them to reflect upon their own path in life. By this point in the semester they knew that drawing on their experiences was rewarded in the grading process as long as they tied it to materials from class, which encouraged them to continue their introspection. While they were working on the paper, we returned to read the end of Herman's book about the effects the Scottish Enlightenment had on nineteenth- and twentieth-century history. Much of this fourth portion of the course repeated content from Louden's book, thereby functioning as a review for the final exam and way of tying together the threads in the course.

ASSESSING THE PAST AND INFLUENCING THE FUTURE

My students were challenged to learn new content in order to feel prepared to present material to their peers. Because they had to reflect upon the relevance of historic ideas to the present day, they necessarily related it to their own lives, grafting what they learned in the course to what they already knew. The final paper assignment would be easily adapted to other institutions, as would other elements of the course, and readers should feel free to use my materials if they would be helpful. I put all my assignments and syllabuses online because I want them to be part of the public domain. Each course also has a page of "Links Used in Class" that I added to steadily through the semester; all of those links were active at the time the course was taught. The first iteration of the course went extremely well, so I did not find that I needed to tweak it all that much before the second iteration.

To make the most of the course evaluations supplied by the college for all students to complete, I added a question: "What advice would you give to students who take this course in the future?" In this way, students in the second iteration could benefit from their peers' experience and I could get a better idea if what I was attempting in the course was working. Advice included almost entirely recommendations that students do the assigned readings (including specific suggestions to annotate or highlight as they go). One student remarked that the assigned readings were "more engaging than you might think." Another student encouraged those after them to "come prepared for class discussion because it makes the discussion better, which helps the learning process."[30] I pulled these anonymous evaluations up on the screen for all to read, a moment of transparency that is too often lacking with regard to the administrative side of higher education. That the first comment on the list read "Go into it with more of an open mind. Try to connect it to your life and specifically try to connect the philosophers lives to your life" delighted me. Two sentences that succinctly summed up much of the methodology I hoped the course would create.

Rather than rely solely on end-of-semester evaluations, which students often fail to complete, I also incorporated evaluative components in assignments or exam questions.[31] Because this was a course with a primary learning objective of forcing students to reflect on their chosen discipline, giving them the opportunity to argue topics from that disciplinary perspective compelled this analysis. That they were concurrently asked to see the value of their liberal arts education for their chosen career path, as opposed to requirements that were a distraction from attaining their goals, was crucial in their development as students. The Enlightenment, Scottish or other, encompassed all fields of academic study, making it the perfect vehicle for interdisciplinary study. Having students assess the Enlightenment's ongoing relevance in today's world resulted in them pondering where *they* will fit as individuals within that world after graduation.

Ultimately, the question of whether or not students found this Reflections course valuable is best answered by the students' own thoughts in response to a cumulative essay question I put on the final exam: "If a friend or family member asks you what it means to be an Enlightened Scot, what would you say and why?" My favorite answer read as follows:

> To be an Enlightened Scot, you have to be able to ask questions and think critically. It is essential to ask things as simple as why? and how? and what? Every Enlightened thinker we studied from Hume, Smith, Jefferson, Hamilton, Witherspoon and so many more asked these questions. But, that is not enough. You need to go out and look for the answers, engage in conversation, and formulate your own thoughts and opinions. Educating yourself on things you enjoy and things that matter to you all goes into being an Enlightened Scot. . . . I am proud to be an Enlightened Scot

> especially after taking this course . . . it puts a lot more meaning behind my education because it is so much more than a simple #rollscots at a football game but honoring the legacy of what so many brave and Enlightened thinkers left for us to discover and carry on for generations to come.[32]

What made this answer particularly effective was the mixture of examples from various portions of the course, not just required readings but also things like the Lin-Manuel Miranda performance on YouTube. Additionally, the student mixed in some personal experiences, about cheers at football games, to show that they were incorporating the academics into their own lives. There were obviously other thoughtful answers to this question; this one was simply more wide-ranging in the examples they chose to draw upon.

Although this course was taught before the COVID-19 pandemic, it would be adaptable to virtual classroom settings. The discussions of readings, along with the supplemental materials like videos on YouTube, would work well on Zoom or another online platform, though admittedly it might be easier to send students a list of related videos to watch as homework rather than try to cue up the videos during the class period. The Enlightened Exchanges, too, would work well digitally, essentially following the format of an academic conference with panelists who have moderator privileges and audience members participating in Q&A. Reflections on the Exchanges would be best done after the class period, I believe, rather than trying to coordinate collection of them in a compressed time frame. It would still be wise to put a relatively short deadline on the Reflections—having them due by midnight that night, preferably—to get the most impromptu thoughts possible.

A final consideration when teaching about the Scottish Enlightenment is not only the continuing relevance of intellectual theories, but the practical implications of those ideas on the world in the twenty-first century. The Scottish National Party having won yet another majority in the Scottish Parliament in 2021 means that another Scottish Independence Referendum is slated for October 2023.[33] Such a development will make teaching of Scottish elements in traditional courses on the Enlightenment exciting in the years to come, even if an entire course devoted to Scottish thinkers is not feasible at your institution in the way it was at mine (where the "Fighting Scots" are so revered). The COVID-19 pandemic also provided the opportunity for reflection about priorities in life and education, along with reminding us how interconnected the world is. Lessons from the Enlightenment era, including the practicalities of higher education and publication at the time, make for safe places to debate current disparities in the world. Just as innovative ideas circulated from one country to another during the Enlightenment, the same process happens today, albeit with the benefit of faster technologies. Providing students with the means to interrogate sources and thinkers from the past, while teaching them to reassess their own beliefs as they navigate their future, will serve them well.

NOTES

1. A version of this paper was presented at the Canadian Society for Eighteenth-Century Studies and Northeast American Society for Eighteenth-Century Studies Joint Annual Conference in Toronto, Ontario, in 2017.
2. The sophomore- and junior-year courses were eliminated in 2022 in a revamping of the General Education curriculum.
3. The original version of the course can be found at http://cdmyers.info/EnlightenedScots.html, and the second iteration is at http://cdmyers.info/EnlightenedScots2018.html. For obvious reasons, exams are not typically posted online. The additional links I provide to supplemental source materials (images, primary documents, video clips, etc.) may be of use to those looking to add elements to their courses.
4. Arthur Herman, *Scottish Enlightenment: The Scots' Invention of the Modern World* (New York: HarperCollins, 2003).
5. Srividhya Swaminathan, *Debating the Slave Trade: Rhetoric of British National Identity, 1759–1815* (London: Routledge, 2009), 1, 87.
6. Herman, *Scottish Enlightenment*, 77–80, 189–190. Herman devotes much time to Francis Hutcheson, a Scots-Irishman considered to be the "father" of the Scottish Enlightenment. Hutcheson taught Adam Smith at the University of Glasgow and corresponded with David Hume in Edinburgh; all three men are featured in the text and our course.
7. Lori Dorn, "Lin-Manuel Miranda Premiering His Song 'Alexander Hamilton' at a 2009 Poetry Jam at the White House," Laughing Squid, July 8, 2020, https://laughingsquid.com/lin-manuel-miranda-alexander/. Now that *Hamilton* is available on Disney+ it would be possible to expand this section of the course.
8. Melissa Major, "7 Ways 'Hamilton' has Impacted America," PBS/Great Performances, November 16, 2017, https://www.pbs.org/wnet/gperf/hamilton-american-musical-changed-musical-theater/5224/.
9. Swaminathan, *Debating the Slave Trade*, 13.
10. Dan Nosowitz, "How the English Failed to Stamp Out the Scots Language," *Atlas Obscura*, September 28, 2018, https://www.atlasobscura.com/articles/scots-language?utm_source=facebook.com&utm_medium=atlas-page.
11. I suggest starting with T. M. Devine, *Recovering Scotland's Slavery Past: The Caribbean Connection* (Edinburgh: Edinburgh University Press, 2015), and David Alston, *Slaves and Highlanders: Silenced Histories of Scotland and the Caribbean* (Edinburgh: Edinburgh University Press, 2021).
12. A collection of essays that might prove useful is *Outlander's Sassenachs: Essays on Gender, Race, Orientation and the Other in the Novels and Television Series*, edited by Valerie Estelle Frankel (Jefferson, NC: McFarland, 2016).
13. Swaminathan, *Debating the Slave Trade*, 62.
14. Monmouth College, "Our Mission & Values," https://www.monmouthcollege.edu/welcome-home/our-mission-values/, accessed June 22, 2021. Note: The Monmouth College Mission Statement has since been revised.
15. For a basic definition of "gobbet," see Wikipedia, 2022, "gobbet," last modified June 19, 2022, https://en.wikipedia.org/wiki/Gobbet.
16. For more on the pros and cons of testing methods, see Rona F. Flippo, Victoria Appatova, and David M. Wark, "Test Preparation and Test Taking," in *Handbook of College Reading and Study Strategy Research*, ed. Rona F. Flippo and Thomas W. Bean (New York: Taylor and Francis, 2018).
17. Robert Louden, *The World We Want: How and Why the Ideals of the Enlightenment Still Elude Us* (Oxford: Oxford University Press, 2010), vii.
18. "Teaching Strategy: Fishbowl," Facing History & Ourselves, https://www.facinghistory.org/resource-library/teaching-strategies/fishbowl, accessed June 22, 2021.

19. As historian T. Mills Kelly puts it, "Research on student success in college indicates that the more they collaborate with one [an]other (rather than with their professor) in the learning process, the more likely they are to be successful." Kelly, *Teaching History in the Digital Age* (Ann Arbor: University of Michigan Press, 2013), 83.
20. Similarly, once students had taken their turn as discussion leaders, I could see them more willing to comment to keep conversations going for their peers and for me when we returned to a more traditional format.
21. Louden, *The World We Want*, 7.
22. For more on the benefits of reflection and self-reflection in interdisciplinary study, see Joris J. W. Buis, Ger Post, and Vincent R. Visser, *Academic Skills for Interdisciplinary Studies* (Amsterdam: Amsterdam University Press, 2015), 116–123 (chap. 13: "Reflection").
23. Students often answer this question with their thoughts on the climate control in the room. I was pleased that this group understood that a different definition of "environment" was at work in the question.
24. Nicholas Phillipson, *Adam Smith: An Enlightened Life* (New Haven, CT: Yale University Press, 2010).
25. The University of Edinburgh, "Edinburgh Lectures: Nicholas Phillipson," YouTube, March 17, 2011, https://www.youtube.com/watch?v=INiybcmN-YY.
26. Swaminathan, *Debating the Slave Trade*, 22 25.
27. For more on gendered approaches, see my book *University Coeducation in the Victorian Era: Inclusion in the United States and the United Kingdom* (New York: Palgrave Macmillan, 2010).
28. Adam Smith, *Lectures on Justice, Police, Revenue and Arms: Delivered in the University of Glasgow* (Oxford 1763; reprint 1896).
29. Swaminathan, *Debating the Slave Trade*, 5.
30. The course evaluations are anonymous, but my presumption is that this one came from an education major.
31. Knowing which student wrote what was beneficial in understanding what modes of teaching were working for students from various disciplines.
32. Final examination, given on May 7, 2017. The student in question was a cis female majoring in business administration.
33. Lynn Bennie, "New Scottish Government: Key Takeaways from the SNP Deal with the Greens," *The Conversation*, August 31, 2021, https://theconversation.com/new-scottish-government-key-takeaways-from-the-snp-deal-with-the-greens-166841. For more, see Nicola McEwen, "The Union: New (and Old) Challenges for the New Prime Minister," *UK in a Changing Europe*, August 16, 2022, https://ukandeu.ac.uk/challenges-for-the-union/.

6

DESIGN, PEDAGOGY, AND PANDEMIC TEACHING TOOLS IN AN INTERDISCIPLINARY HISTORY OF SCIENCE COURSE

Diana Epelbaum

ON PEDAGOGIES OF ENGAGEMENT

Perhaps nothing has the potential to be more relevant for today's college students than the eighteenth century: we just have to help them see it. In this pedagogy chapter, I detail the design of an undergraduate, interdisciplinary, history of science course entitled "Race and Place in Natural Histories of the Americas."[1] I teach at Marymount Manhattan, a small, creative arts college in New York City, where class sizes are under twenty and space comes at a premium—even as students have access to the unparalleled resources of NYC as "place." The course, part of our upper-level General Education curriculum, takes a cultural-historical approach to tracing the evolution of natural history as practice, science, and genre through the eighteenth century; it frames natural history as a hybrid, transatlantic cultural production embodying European and colonial obsessions with the human–land relation. In the context of global imperialism, and specifically the Atlantic triangle, students from diverse disciplinary backgrounds,[2] some with interest in nature study or history but most fulfilling a requirement, examine circulated discourses about curiosity, classification, and cultivation (among others) alongside early rhetorics of environmentalism and sustainability. The course emphasizes primary sources—some that mediate Indigenous and African knowledges in ways that entangle race and nature, and others on natural history's rooting of science in racial exploitation. Students consider the symbolic resonances of colonized land in the Americas for those who suffered to cultivate it, and for those who resisted bondage through subterfuge, revolt, or marronage.

This chapter outlines course structure, trajectory of readings, learning outcomes, assignment design, assessment instruments, writing-intensive mini-projects, a final multimodal synthesis, and tools of engagement for teaching colonial and early American naturalist texts and art remotely—including social, collective annotation, silent class discussions, facilitated discussion boards, and place-based learning during the COVID-19 pandemic. The chapter reflects on the course's interdisciplinary approach, and considers how, within the undergraduate context, this approach illuminates both the material's cultural-historical exigencies and its contemporary resonances in ways that expose today's injustices—the very framework of "strategic presentism" that Matthew Reznicek spotlights in chapter 7 of this collection.[3] As students time-travel in ways that we as professors are sometimes unable to do, their connections also uncover new directions for research in our field, and in turn, reenter the classroom for further illumination. My students became student-scholars, employed in the active interdisciplinary inquiry that marks eighteenth-century studies. Aligned with tenets of the Scholarship of Teaching and Learning (SOTL),[4] for me this course came to exemplify what it means to work alongside these student-scholars as a teacher-scholar engaged in the "scholarship of teaching."

The students in the course major in a variety of disciplines, and I myself bring interdisciplinary expertise in early American literature, cultures of natural history in the eighteenth century, and rhetoric and writing studies. My own experience as a writing professor and director of an academic writing program—a job that has me steeped in writing, reading, and thinking pedagogies and entails faculty mentorship and training—inspired me to merge the challenging content of this course with best practices in writing instruction. What materialized was a writing-intensive (WI) course in which the principle of "writing to learn," central to Writing Across the Curriculum (WAC) work, facilitated vibrant engagement with the eighteenth century, incredible synthesis projects, and advanced connective work. Eighteenth-century natural history was the very definition of what we might anachronistically now deem "interdisciplinarity," whether embodied in the hybrid genre or in the range of transatlantic practices and peripheral disciplines that informed it. As Teri Doerksen puts it in chapter 4 of this collection, when we teach the eighteenth century through interdisciplinarity, that century "appears in different context, keeping different intellectual company." In Fall 2020, bringing all of our disciplines to bear in the classroom (student and teacher) opened unexpected perspectives on the material, on the eighteenth century, and on cultural and societal resonances today.

COURSE CONSTRUCTION AND UNIVERSAL DESIGN

Following the teaching principle of "universal design," the organization of this course, "Race and Place in Natural Histories of the Americas," is governed by an ethos of flexibility toward inclusivity, accommodation, and student self-direction—all of which are central to the development of the student-scholar. I see careful syllabus construction as a crucial piece of access, for structural design has the power to *include* or *exclude* possibilities for individualized paths of growth. The course's structure, therefore, contains many entry points for exploration and connection

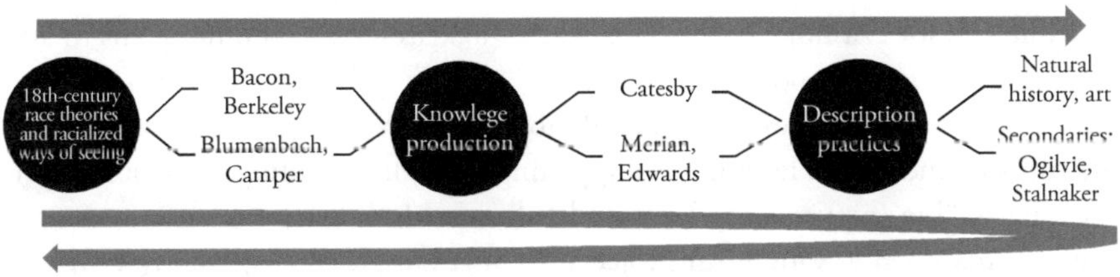

Figure 6.1 Semester iterative progress chart, courtesy of Diana Epelbaum.

that absorb and shape students' interests within flexible assignments, assessments, and low-stakes writing in parallel with course readings. Course readings progress through key lines of inquiry that build upon one another, and that also function iteratively: as understanding of the period's colonialist framework becomes more and more apparent in the primary documents, we return repeatedly to earlier readings and stack them in different ways. Figure 6.1 shows the first three weeks of this progression.

To build expansiveness into a syllabus means giving students a clear, predictable structure for assignments and assessments, thereby deliberately making room for them to play with the material and to work in dialogue with each other, rather than to focus on course requirements and deadlines. This structure includes one part of a place-based, writing mini-project, involving field observation, reflection, or connection to that week's readings due two days before class;[5] a prerecorded "mini-lecture" of ten minutes or less, to be viewed and commented on before engaging with the week's readings; and weekly primary and secondary readings to be annotated in our LMS through Hypothesis, a digital social annotation tool.[6] At the end of each mini-project, students compile two or three parts into a "portfolio" for grading, although they also post each part for class engagement as we go along. The course concludes with a final synthesis, a multimodal project where students are free to synthesize readings and themes of the course in any substantive form.[7] Weeks 11 through 16 on our course schedule are mainly reserved for synthesis project generation, proposals, process oral presentations,[8] peer review, group feedback, drafting, conferencing, and class discussion—time that has proven deeply valuable for revisiting multiple strands of interest from the course.

Just as critical to the equitable classroom as structure is the conceptual shift required for learning access. Central to de-emphasizing grading and redirecting focus on learning, is metacognition, which animated the crafting of this course. Metacognition is reflected in every part of the course design; in the "thinking about thinking" classroom, all processes are transparent, all links are made logical through inquiry, and all tasks are contextualized and given purpose. Assessment instruments, for example, become just that—instruments—and not goals in and of themselves, not "disposable assignments" as Tiffany Potter calls them in chapter 1 of this volume. Assessment does double duty, revealing where students need my support and where learning is happening, as well as leading students to synthesize the "big picture." Students and I discuss these purposes for assessment instruments openly. Our mini-projects, as an example, transparently build on one another from "ways of seeing and describing," to "power imbalances," to "ways of knowing": with each progression, I ask students to stop and reflect together on how this project develops from and connects to the last. Annotation of readings and plentiful low-stakes writing during class time, including freewrites, group work, and class notes, are all fodder for their final synthesis—not distinct, purposeless tasks. Students create their own "thought archives" through writing—what they were thinking, when, in what context, at what point in the term, engaging with which material—and when they return to review these at the end of the term, they find ideas that have been germinating for some time. The synthesis project becomes an opportunity to cultivate these ideas into lush gardens. Principles of recursiveness, building, and "writing to learn" are all bedrocks of writing-intensive pedagogy.

EXPERIENTIAL, PLACE-BASED MINI-PROJECTS

Place-based learning (PBL) inspired mini-project design, as well as a class trip that drew students into the rich archives and exhibits of the American Museum of Natural History, making real the perils of collection and curation and their continued reliance on colonialist taxonomies.[9] Instructors not within reach of the multivalent opportunities of NYC can extrapolate writing-intensive mini-projects that focus on students' own local environments.[10] In particular, Mini-Project 1, "Ways of Seeing and Describing," exemplifies the kind of experiential learning several contributors to this collection find so powerful in the classroom: Teri Doerksen (chapter 4) framed her course through the "Chocolate Project," where students sampled an eighteenth-century chocolate recipe, tracing the transatlantic travel of its ingredients, and Christine Myers (chapter 5) challenged students to faithfully record every word of a course lecture, highlighting the difficulties of knowledge circulation in the period.

Each of three mini-projects follows a similar logic, outlined below, and with experiential learning preceding content engagement. Within the parameters of "no photography" or "no phone use," and alongside primary readings and art from Mark Catesby, Maria Sibylla Merian, George Edwards, and various other images, Part I of Mini-Project 1 asks students to:

- Find a local site in which you can make a "natural" observation.
- Record this observation through textual description (handwriting).

- Illustrate your observation (you may not photograph the organism, ecosystem, or site of observation for reference later; you may not use a photograph instead of an illustration).
- Reflect: What challenges of description did you encounter? What audience context could you rely on when composing your description and illustration, and what context did you have to fill in? How do you think your identity or identities influence your ways of seeing and describing?

Deepening class understanding of these primary readings, Part II of Mini-Project 1 moves from the challenges of description to knowledge production and circulation:

- Create an account on INaturalist.org.
- Post your observation/description in a relevant forum or simply add your observation and ask for feedback.
- For one week, check back in daily, replying to any feedback.
- Reflect: How does communal knowledge collection and production work? How does communal validation and correction change your original observation and/or the description of your observation? What happens if no one reacts to/responds to/takes up the knowledge you produced?
- Revise your description and illustration based on feedback.

Part III of Mini-Project 1 uses secondary readings to frame the experiential immersion and eighteenth-century deep dive of Parts I and II:

- Begin to look at Brian Ogilvie's *The Science of Describing* or Joanna Stalnaker's *The Unfinished Enlightenment: Description in the Age of the Encyclopedia*, if you haven't already.
- Using your experience of observation, description, and collective knowledge production, develop a set of rules for nature description in the twenty-first century (this may now involve photography, of course).
- Reflect: In what ways do your rules include objectivity and subjectivity, and considerations of place-based context and identity-based context?

In Mini-Project 1, students struggled (unexpectedly, they reported) with describing that which their readers could not see. The same questions that eighteenth-century naturalists undoubtedly asked themselves emerged organically: What if your reader is unfamiliar with the scene or specimen you are describing? What shared vocabulary, experiences, or referents can you employ in your description to accurately convey what you see? What role does the visual play? In our era, how do photographs influence the accuracy of description? Are photos always "true to life"?

When students published their sketches, which they typically thought were inadequate, on INaturalist—a platform of photographs, no less—they experienced the joy of a fellow citizen-naturalist taking up their description, or the disappointment of no response. With each identification or comment, the description circulates more broadly. What then happens when no one engages? As a naturalist, what do you do?

EXPANDING THE MEANING OF "TEXT" FOR SYNTHESIS

In their final synthesis projects, Fall 2020 students chose three to five course texts with which to engage, taking up the most potent points of connection they had made throughout the term. They could choose any mode or modes that best spoke to their synthesis, or could choose to write an eight- to ten-page essay. I called the project an "essay" so that students matched, as best as they could, any multimodal project in substance, depth of analysis, and organization to that of an essay; whatever their chosen mode, they had to account for rhetorical situation, audience, and purpose. Much like Christine Myers outlines in chapter 5—where students unpack their college mission statement and home departments' learning outcomes—students in my course had to actively return to syllabus outcomes, our course schedule, and their "thought archives" for a final synthesis essay that was to be:

- inquiry-based (your claim built from texts and questions)
- guided by course outcomes (on our syllabus)
- synthesizing three to five sources we've explored in the class (placing them in conversation)
- closely reading text and at least one work of art
- built from the semester's mini-projects, reading quizzes, class discussions, text annotations, freewrites, class glossary, etc. (anything you've already written may be incorporated)
- demonstrative of deep engagement with course themes and texts

In their proposals and proposal presentations, students were asked to articulate an inquiry and organizational plan, as well as practice a close reading analysis and key syntheses: the proposal served to standardize requirements across projects that differently engaged with the material, and the presentations generated valuable feedback at a critical stage in the inquiry that makes a student-scholar.[11] Many of these passion projects had real-world stakes, were "renewable" and "authentic" (Tiffany Potter, chapter 1 in this volume), as students made TikToks, short films, and fashion portfolios, or wrote papers that they then shared publicly, with family and friends, or within the college community.[12] Short films included "A Game of 2 Truths and a Lie," a narrative musing on the failures of American history education; "If a Gardener is Trans, what does that mean for the Garden?," a film on the gendering of gardening with live, re-created poses of images we examined; "The Lord's Environmental Destruction," a film of striking, repetitive images integrating course themes and texts and audio/visual essay in three parts ("Colonialism," "Indigenous," "African Ways"); and "Black Elk Speaks: A Projection of the Colonial Body," an analysis of white anthropological appropriation of Indigenous voices. Inspired by our field trip to the American Museum of Natural History, and in response to the class's critique of the museum as perpetuating a colonialist worldview, another student created a virtual interactive art exhibit entitled "Race and Science as Tools of Empire: Connecting Climate Perspectives," with course images and short analytic essays for museum captions.[13]

Yet another project, by Julia Squier, "The European Body and Its Separation from Nature," displayed fashion plates of eighteenth-century clothing those in our primary texts would have worn, with half of each figure in the plate silhouetted, half clothed (figure 6.2). The figures with accompanying descriptions constituted a project modeled after Jane Colden's *Botanic Manuscript*, a 1750s flora of upstate New York.

Of her plate based on a French revolutionary image of female collector and cross-dresser Jeanne Baret, Squier writes:

> *Jeanne Baret* holds the uniqueness of attempting to conceal her female body and present it as a male one. Her brown curls are contained by a sailors [*sic*] hat. She wears a white, tie-up undershirt to cover as much of her porcelain skin as possible. On top she wears a matching vest and wide-legged trouser. . . . The stripe pattern is reminiscent of French sailors and allows her to blend in with her crewmates . . . elongating her body. One final layer covers up her small shoulders and curving chest: a navy-blue smock coat that broadens out her shoulders and thickens up her arms to match a more masculine silhouette. [A silhouette is] the outline or general shape of something that tells what it is. When it is manipulated too much, the object in question can become nearly unidentifiable.[14]

A synthesis with authentic stakes included a sharable infographic for Instagram about the sale and seizure of Indigenous land for the creation of Glacier National Park in Montana, an astute critique of the "preservation" movement. A final student used an existing cosplay TikTok account to reach a wider audience, calling his project "The Colonialist Oppression of the 'Other,'" and created short memes and narrative explanation videos incorporating a mix of course themes and texts: TEK (Traditional Ecological Knowledge), Race Theories, Degeneration Theory, Jane Colden, and Contact Zones. As of June 2023 this project had over 5,300 views.[15]

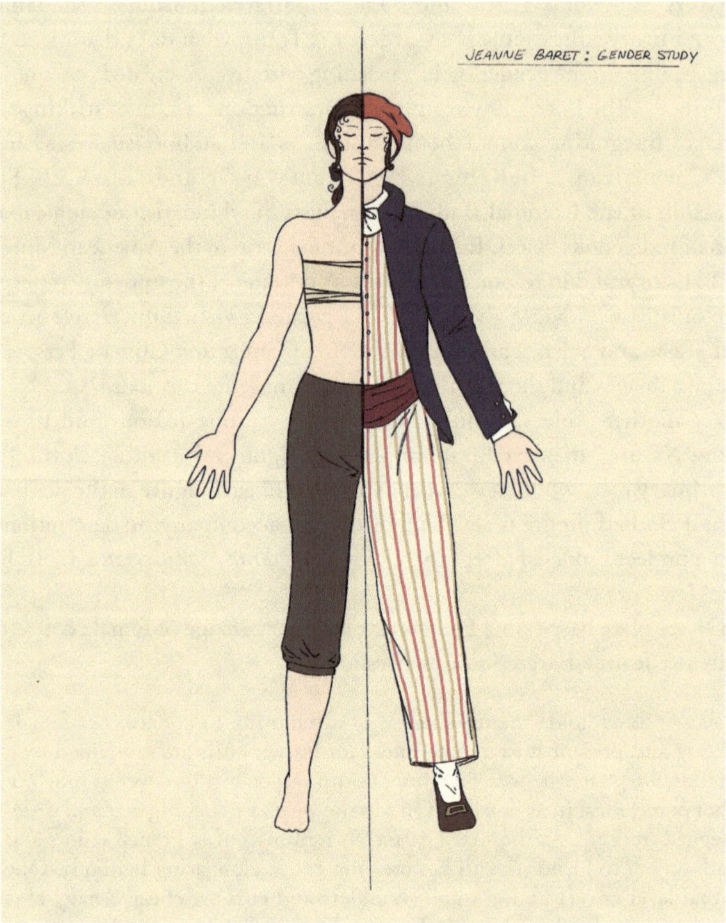

Figure 6.2 "Synthesis Project: Jeanne Baret Gender Study," courtesy of Julia Squier.

How did students come to generate these brilliant projects, to engage deeply with eighteenth-century concepts in exciting, resonant ways? Quite simply, they found, through guided interdisciplinary close reading and analysis of historical records, a methodology with which to approach the period, and with which to read more broadly. Enlarging the meaning and scope of "text"—from natural histories to floras to recipe books (written), from maps to cross-sections to "from-life" plates (visual), from objects to music to place (all "texts" they read at various points in the semester), from gender to race ("texts" of their own in that period, and ours), from that which is present to that which is absent in this small cross-section of eighteenth-century natural history study. In other words, the expansiveness of the material—and hence, the vast network of circulation that constituted natural history practice—was made visible not by comprehensive coverage (an impossibility in our compressed time frame) but through the capacious redefinition of "text."

STUDENTS IN COLLABORATIVE SCHOLARSHIP

Reflected in their final synthesis projects was one of the more astonishing realizations of the Fall 2020 semester: how much both the students' passions and conversations (in class and asynchronous) were shaping the course, and also how much of the course material was organically shaping itself to meet students' passions and conversations—and how vigorously and energetically students created constellations of meaning across time, just as scholars do. For example, in the "anticolonial" frame of the course—aptly distinguished from a "decolonial" frame by Emily Casey in chapter 9 of this volume—most of the primary documents we explored and critiqued routinely dismissed, negated, or erased Indigenous voices. The Fall 2020 group as a whole, however, interrogated this omission at nearly every opportunity, building bridges from week to week, grounding today's anguished identity rhetorics in close readings of eighteenth-century, largely European texts. What began as one or two students' fascination with missing Indigenous voices consumed the class, and guided our approach to reading, thinking, and writing in the material. The intensity of student interest led me to invite two guest speakers—a Western scientist and an Indigenous scientist—to share "Indigenous and Western approaches for understanding shifting seasons." This visit, repeated again in subsequent semesters, delved into how Western science might take responsibility for ethically integrating Indigenous approaches, as well as how *and* whether traditional ecological knowledge (TEK) can be shared with Western scientists and institutions. In Emily Casey's chapter 9 formulation—"decolonial interventions as emphasizing decolonial futurities"—the speaker visit was but one active space of decoloniality within a larger "anticolonial" class. There were, however, many other such spaces, as when our conversation spilled outside of the classroom. One example was when a student emailed to share an Instagram post, writing:

> I came across today from Christie's because I thought it was relevant to our class discourse. . . . I thought it was interesting how Christie's was in a sense celebrating the idea of "cabinets of curiosities" even though the whole concept of the cabinets was to "other" Indigenous cultures and for Imperial colonists to capitalize on conquest and "discovery" in the New World. I was wondering your feelings on this or the rest of the class' feelings. I just think if such a large institution such as Christie's is going to showcase a "Cabinet of Curiosities" it should be contextualizing it too, AT LEAST. I know this "cabinet" includes European "curiosities" but it

> also includes non-European artifacts, and very prominently. Also, the whole concept is just incredibly dated to me and is something I thought our world had evolved past, aka evolved past gawking at "curious" artifacts in a way that holds no contextual meaning or intention of understanding the artifacts other than they inspire awe. I love that your class has made me think critically about these things, even when scrolling down Instagram. I am always looking to rethink my own "colonial gaze."

The post from "christiesinc" with the image of Finch's Cabinet of Curiosities (figure 6.3) boasts, "Discover an eclectic cabinet of curiosities that spans thousands of years of history," and goes on to detail that the cabinet includes "antiqui-

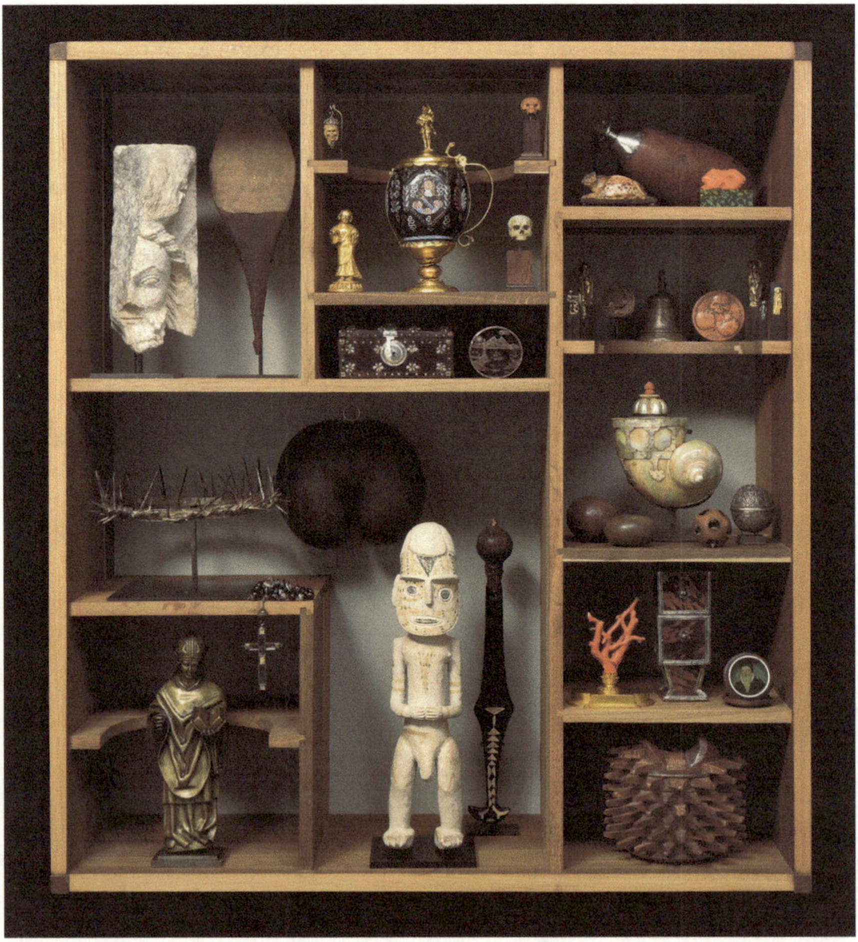

Figure 6.3 "Finch and Co's Cabinet of Curiosities," Instagram post, October 14, 2020. © Christie's Images / Bridgeman Images.

ties, European sculpture and objects, alongside tribal and ethnographic art, natural history, and topographical pictures." With over 2,000 likes, the proffered cabinet "unites historically and geographically important objects and curiosities . . . including a Chinese scholar's wrist rest, an Indian bezoar stone case, a Japanese hand cannon, and Victorian 'Halley's Comet' brooches," noting that "each lot delivers a message and . . . an invitation."[16]

We brought the post to class discussion alongside the same student's critique of the term "New World," an entrée that turned into a spirited and lengthy deconstruction of this term and other terminology students had found problematic in natural history scholarship: "Western" and "Eastern," "virgin wilderness," "Eden." Students debated whether scholars should employ these terms at all, even if doing so critically, and whether even critical employment can cause harm to marginalized cultures. We then turned to discussions of maps, surveys, and the practice of naming as colonialist. At this moment, about halfway through the term, I knew that students had really gotten *close* to the material—that they had gotten so close, that they could simultaneously read in great depth and see the material at a distance, as might a disinterested observer, or an eighteenth-century colonial naturalist, in the field observing and describing a specimen.

Attention to key terms definitions and their evolution throughout the semester is an important facilitator of this immersive, iterative learning, and I challenge students to push against these terms starting on the first day of class, when we begin with the question of vision and description. After introducing the time period, the metacognitive and writing-intensive frames of the course, and after modeling and providing guidelines for annotation, we closely read a range of textual descriptions from published natural histories. As a group, we begin to define "natural history." We then closely read the famous "Battle Lagoon" passage, with an image of an alligator (figure 6.4), from William Bartram's *Travels* (1791) as well as the image of Merian's Surinam Caiman (ca. 1701–1705) (figure 6.5).

Students freewrite their observations, confer in small groups, and begin defining key terms that are framed as fluid. These key terms are words whose definitions students believe they know, but that will become shapeshifters in this class, central to the course content: for instance, "natural history," "place," "race," "science," and "knowledge."

These first definitions launch our posted class glossary, to which we return time and again throughout the term at preplanned critical points and in organic teaching moments to refine our definitions. Other big-concept terms include "the Americas," "cultural history," "transatlanticism," "pseudoscience," "observation," and "description," among others. In a final conversation on day 1, we return to the interdisciplinarity we began with in our introductions by asking how each of the students' disciplines might serve as a lens through which to read that day's texts and images and/or define these key terms. Students come to see that the

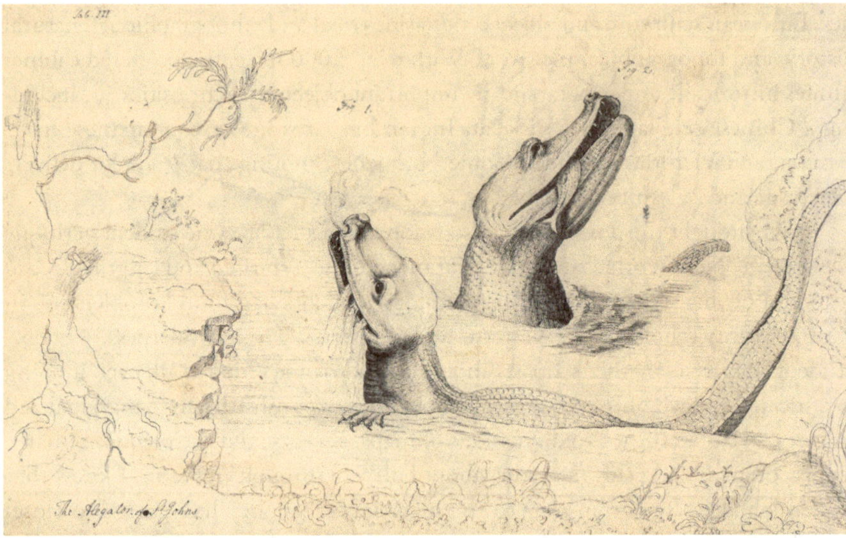

Figure 6.4 William Bartram, "The Alegator of St. Johns," *Botanical and Zoological Drawings of William Bartram, 1756–1788.* © The Trustees of The Natural History Museum, London.

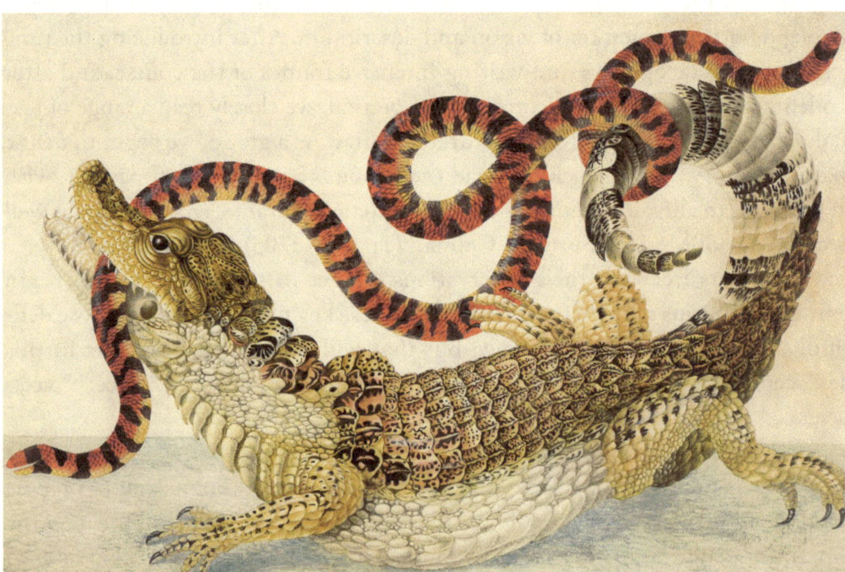

Figure 6.5 Maria Sibylla Merian, "Common or Spectacled Caiman with South American False Coral Snake," ca. 1705–1710. Courtesy of the Royal Collection Trust / © His Majesty King Charles III 2023.

range of disciplines represented constitutes collaborative scholarship, which will exponentially enrich the historiography of natural history that we write together as a class.

Pandemic teaching has in many ways widened the array of written production and participation constituting this historiography. Toward flexibility, accountability, and accommodation, various low-stakes modes of writing energized the classroom: posted freewrites and thought trains, prerecorded mini-lectures with space for reflection,[17] saved chats and posted student class notes, which then became staples of the next two years' courses, online and in-person. I'd like to "zoom" in for a moment on social annotation, which proved a lifeline of participation and a space for truly transformative, asynchronous class discussion. Through Hypothesis, an add-on for your LMS (and also a web-based and private annotation tool), my students participated in vigorous debates and conversations during the week, before we ever came together for each week's class. In response to an excerpt from Brian Ogilvie's *The Science of Describing*[18]—"Fuchs recognized that artistic verisimilitude, and the search for 'glory,' did not always correspond with the naturalist's truth. The perspectival eye of the artist, which rendered an object from a particular viewpoint with 'shadows, and other less necessary things,' was not that of the naturalist, who insisted that the object be represented, as far as possible, in a panoptical fashion" (196)—Student 1 had "two thoughts," namely, "1) what is glory referencing, was this a common goal for naturalists? 2) Interesting how Fuchs noticed that being a naturalist was contradictory because of the inherent bias of the persons [*sic*] life, viewpoints, and just how people see things." Student 2 replied to Student 1, "An artist see's [*sic*] aesthetic, composition, and design qualities. Whereas Fuchs felt these techniques were a distraction and misrepresentation," and Student 3 entered the conversation with, "Yes, he aimed to see the plants in a 'panoptical' fashion which literally translates to 'seeing the whole as one view,' so they were trying to show the totality of the plant in one drawing." In their dialogue, students were *helping each other comprehend* a particularly difficult section of the text in which Ogilvie surveys the debate around the role of illustration in Renaissance natural history. This early reading for the course laid out the parameters for how Enlightenment natural history text and art evolved into a discipline.

In yet another exchange on this same secondary reading, we see students debating the role of artist in the project of natural history, as well as parsing key terms like "naturalist," "scientist," "artist," and "illustrator." In response to Ogilvie's passage "Whereas the artist strove to capture a particular plant at a given moment of its existence, the naturalist wanted to illustrate the plant in general, as it might be observed at different times,"[19] Student 1 distilled to summary: "Differentiation made between science vs. art or naturalists vs. artists." Student 2 replied to Student 1 by narrating an attempt to understand Ogilvie's assertion: "A very interesting take. Personally, I would think the opposite, that the naturalist would want to capture the plant as it is in the moment and the artist would capture the general idea of a plant. Though I see how the two viewpoints can be interchangeable." Student 3 then sought to clarify for fellow classmates, agreeing with part of Student 2's response: "I think at this point in history, artists were more concerned with trying to accurately imitate nature (known in art history as naturalism). The idea of an artist capturing an object in all its phases or all the states it exists in sounds to me like a more recent modernist approach, but I agree, the two viewpoints can be interchangeable." Finally, Student 4 returned to Student 1's equation of "scientist" and "naturalist" and posed an extension question: "I think at this point terms 'naturalist' and 'Scientist' overlap. There isn't much distinction. What exactly is the distinction between artist and naturalist? Artists often study subject matter to understand it, accurately represent it, and of course, add their own stylistic aesthetics." Without my interference, students made meaning together, enlarging their own understanding through their peers' annotations. Before each class session, I read through student annotations, reflections on mini-lectures, and mini-project pieces, highlighting points of confusion, debate, and possibilities for discursive extension in the classroom.[20] Class discussion then unfolded with *all* student voices participating, relying on thoughts they had already spoken on the page.

Social annotation facilitated the archiving of student response in these ways, but also in others. In "silent discussions," we tackled texts together, reading aloud particularly tricky passages one paragraph at a time, and then each of us silently annotating side by side in the social annotation tool (me included). Both during and at the end of this silent discussion, students spent time reading each other's comments, taking notes, and framing thoughts. Sometimes we would then openly discuss, and sometimes we would leave the discussion on the page, in that text's archive. For other texts, especially for art, I frequently began discussion with a basic freewrite that I would post as a "page note" within the Hypothesis page for that text. Students would then reply to me in one thread for reference. Here is a sample directed question I asked when we looked at a series of images across texts, and zeroed in on Bartram's *American Lotus or Water Chinquapin Seed Vessel with Snail and Black Root,* Plate No. 25 (figure 6.6) a complex, busy image that trains the eye to scan multiple coexistent frames.

What's striking you about this image? What are you seeing here? How is transcultural encounter embodied here? Sample replies included profound observations and connections, all fueling fruitful discussion:

Student 1: Over all [*sic*], it feels like a still life. The sense of depth is distorted: the bird sitting on a branch is very small so I want to believe it is further away, however, the shell in the middle ground intersects the base of this plant which makes it appear closer to the viewer.

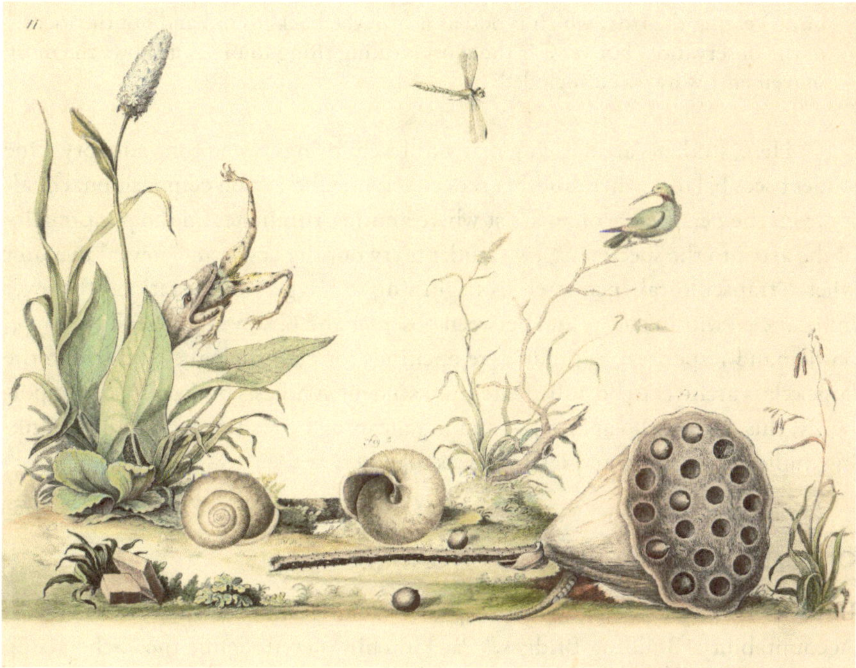

Figure 6.6 William Bartram, *American Lotus or Water Chinquapin Seed Vessel with Snail and Black Root*, © The Trustees of The Natural History Museum, London.

Student 2: There's a lot happening in this image. It doesn't seem, to me, that all of these objects were found in this close proximity to one another naturally. They were either observed individually and then all placed in the image as the artist saw fit, or collected and then purposefully arranged for a drawing later. I think that's a power imbalance there—putting natural objects into an environment they weren't naturally found in?

Student 3: Theres [*sic*] almost a stacked totem-like quality to the composition here that introduces you to each intersecting organism and how they embody the space. In the sky, a flying dragonfly, on a branch a sitting bird, in the grass the eating lizard, on the dirt the snails and roots. Its [*sic*] a meeting of living and dying organisms, of movement and stillness too.

Student 4: The image gives me a sense of balance. Although I think the most striking part of it is the snake eating the frog, it appears to blend with the rest of the drawing. The bird seems to be passively observing the frog being eaten. The snake has the most power here.

Student 5: The most striking thing about this image is how chaotic it is. There is so much movement going on and so many species interacting that it creates a full scene, though I'm not too sure that helps the most in observing the specimens as it makes it very confusing. The part of the image that catches my eye first is the bird(?) eating the frog, which is odd as it is in the background and not the focus of the observation, but yet it is the most striking thing to me as it shows the most movement. Why was it included?

Here, students are noticing many different things, some contradictory. One student sees balance where another sees chaos; one focuses on compositional quality from the perspective of an artist where another ruminates on the positionality of the artist to the specimens; two students try out the key term "power" in a unit where "transcultural encounter" is beginning to trigger consideration of "power imbalances" within nature and between observer and observed. These five-minute, on-demand responses are productive openings for class dialogue, and live in the larger class archive, to be pulled later into student synthesis projects. More importantly, this is how scholars work—making meaning by reading, re-reading, thinking, building, writing, and testing ideas together.[21]

ON THE "SCHOLARSHIP OF ENGAGEMENT"

In their 2013 essay "The Scholarship of Teaching and Learning in an Age of Accountability: Building Bridges," Pat Hutchings et al. define the "Scholarship of Teaching and Learning" (SOTL) as driven by the following values: "internally motivated, voluntary," "faculty-driven," "purpose: inquiry," "focused on knowledge-building," "multiple approaches," "classroom-based outcomes," "linked to practice and improvement," "intellectual and scholarly."[22] The ethos of SOTL was built into the course "Race and Place in Natural Histories of the Americas" before students ever stepped into the classroom, but each of the above values gained its own valence within a space of interplay among them, in their uptake by students. In this space, my students learned and thrived. Ernest Boyer, a lifelong educator who coined the term "scholarship of teaching," outlines "a new paradigm of scholarship" that constitutes, as a whole, this term and the interchangeable "scholarship of engagement," the title of his 1996 speech for the Academy of Arts and Sciences.[23] In the speech Boyer summarizes his proposal that the university professor perform "four essential, interlocking functions," including the "scholarship of discovery," or research pursuits governed by specialization/discipline; the "scholarship of integration," or interdisciplinarity and the pursuit of common inquiries across fields; the "scholarship of sharing knowledge," or the dissemination of knowledge to colleagues in the academy, public audiences, and students; and the "scholarship of application," or the movement from theoretical knowledge to praxis and back again inside and outside of the classroom.[24] Course design and pedagogy are scholarship, both solitary and communal, rooted in intensive research, writing, thinking, and reading. In certain ways, attention to SOTL is more difficult than traditional research because it must respond to the needs of students as they arise, and course material must be shaped by, and speak to, the scholarly interests of a community of a teacher-scholar and student-scholars (you and your students). In this volume, contributors share teaching praxis that is—by virtue of its focus on research, best practices, and on-the-ground experimentation, as well as in its circulation—the definition of "scholarship." By publishing our work, we enter another layer of scholarship, meeting all four of Boyer's pillars of engagement: we are quite literally pursuing the "scholarship of engagement" together. In other words, we train each other to be better *teachers* of the eighteenth century; from our teaching *and* from this mutual training, we grow as *scholars* of the eighteenth century, too—and we learn how to create learning environments in which student-scholars develop alongside us. As Eugenia Zuroski puts it in the Coda to this anthology, we are teaching the eighteenth century now, but our students and fellow scholars are also helping us see "our now as an eighteenth-century phenomenon."

To conclude with the course itself—my student-scholars disentangled, extracted, deconstructed, and analyzed eighteenth-century rhetorics of natural history to reveal present-day echoes I had not always seen. The connections students make to the material we curate for them must become part of the scholarship of our field, for these connections are our ticket to the "scholarship of engagement," to reaching audiences beyond the academy, and to collaboratively building on the interdisciplinarity that so enriches the study of this period. More importantly, we must communally share pedagogies that facilitate engagement and connection for our students, so that our scholarship moves into praxis and back out into the scholarship of our field. And perhaps most important of all, as Boyer says, campuses must be the "staging grounds for action."[25] When participating in courses that center SOTL, students will enter their professional fields and act with their new lenses—as my student said, "I am always looking to rethink my 'colonial gaze'"—to create justice.[26] Indeed, there need not be an intense siloing of professions, or of academic discourses and pursuits from those of the professions, or from public life at all. When our students learn this alongside the content of our courses, we have succeeded.

NOTES

1. Like Emily Casey's art history course on the colonial Americas described in chapter 9, my course covers the period 1492 (Columbus) to 1808 (Behn).
2. In Fall 2020, in an upper-level honors version of the course, students' majors included art history, urban and environmental studies, biology, theater arts, costume design, graphic design, studio art, business, politics and human rights, chemistry, English, and speech therapy. This range of majors enriched the course material immeasurably; accounting for this, I built the course to consider how our own "ways of seeing," positionalities, and disciplinary methodologies impact how we describe, relate, and know, as a microcosm of the intense conflation of fields that characterized natural history study.
3. As Emily Casey writes in chapter 9: "not only does study of the colonial Americas require the context of earlier modern histories, it also reveals that colonial conditions are not only past, but also present."

4. The Center for Engaged Learning at Elon University says of SOTL that it "involves faculty (sometimes in partnership with their students) undertaking systematic inquiry about student learning—informed by prior scholarship on teaching and learning—and going public with the results," Center for Engaged Learning, "What Is SoTL?," October 7, 2021, https://www.centerforengagedlearning.org/studying-engaged-learning/what-is-sotl/. See Alison Cook-Sather, Catherine Bovill, and Peter Felten, *Engaging Students as Partners in Learning and Teaching* (San Francisco: Jossey-Bass, 2014); and Kathleen McKinney, "Searching for Prior Literature for SoTL Projects: Beyond Electronic Data Bases," in *The SOTL Advocate*, April 29, 2015, https://illinoisstateuniversitysotl.wordpress.com/2015/04/29/searching-for-prior-literature-for-sotl-projects-beyond-electronic-data-bases/.
5. Mini-projects included "Ways of Seeing and Describing," "Power Imbalances," and "Ways of Knowing." In the mini-projects, students became observers, naturalists, bodies in "contact zones," and interviewers.
6. This weekly assignment order responded to student feedback from a previous iteration of the course, in which students reported feeling lost in the readings. By first writing in the mini-projects, students engaged the themes of that week's readings ("writing as thinking"), and by viewing the mini-lecture prior to reading, students entered the material with context. These activities were meant as pre-reading strategies, preparing their brains for better comprehension.
7. Student feedback in the first iteration of this course (in Fall 2019) led to the multimodal synthesis project assignment.
8. I have found that process presentations that elicit feedback are enormously more useful for students working through big projects—and for their classmates learning to provide constructive feedback—than are celebratory "final" presentations.
9. In Fall 2019, our class visited the Rare Books Archives of the American Museum of Natural History in New York; in Fall 2020 (and Fall 2021), due to the pandemic, we reserved ticketed entry to the museum and, in pairs, explored individual exhibits, coming together at the end to critique and connect to our course explorations. One of the more poignant moments in this critique was a student's observation that time was represented linearly in the museum, with no conversation across time and no connection to the present; this student observed that we had entered a "time capsule."
10. See Emily Casey, chapter 9, for how local histories, exhibits, and environments can be incorporated into class assignments.
11. In my courses I teach students how to provide and receive constructive feedback through metacognition and feedback workshops, where we dissect and analyze our own feedback practices.
12. One such opportunity at our institution, Marymount Manhattan College, is Honors Day, when students present projects that were competitively selected for presentation; another is the student magazine.
13. See Student 1 (Ashley Pavia). "Race and Science as Tools of Empire: Connecting Climate Perspectives: An Interactive Museum Exhibit," https://www.artsteps.com/embed/5fd9679ad0a711628df1389d/560/315, accessed June 1, 2022. All student projects are shared with permission.
14. Julia Squier, "Jeanne Baret: Gender Study" assignment from "The European Body and Its Separation from Nature."
15. Student 3 (William Bryan). "The Colonialist Oppression of the 'Other': TikTok Cosplay #rpnh," https://www.youtube.com/watch?v=FbygTDd7o0g, accessed June 1, 2022.
16. Christie's (christiesinc). "Finch and Co's Cabinet of Curiosities." *Instagram* (October 14, 2020), https://www.instagram.com/p/CGUng3yHb8F/?utm_source=ig_web_button_share_sheet.
17. I use EdPuzzle, a platform for prerecorded video that enables teachers to build in pauses for student engagement.

18. Brian Ogilvie, *The Science of Describing: Natural History in Renaissance Europe* (Chicago: University of Chicago Press, 2006).
19. Ogilvie, *The Science of Describing*, 196.
20. Sometimes the best place to begin was with students' visceral reactions, here to Lisa Brooks's *The Common Pot: The Recovery of Native Space in the Northeast* (Minneapolis: University of Minnesota Press, 2008), 6: "People had the right and the responsibility to give part of their share to another person." Student 1 commented in response, "again, comparing this to modern Western food waste vs. homelessness and starvation . . . oof," and Student 2 picked up the refrain with, "literally oof."
21. Social annotation has great promise for collaborative class projects like Tiffany Potter's scholarly student editions, explored in chapter 1, this volume.
22. Pat Hutchings et al., "The Scholarship of Teaching and Learning in an Age of Accountability: Building Bridges," *Teaching & Learning Inquiry: The ISSOTL Journal* 1, no. 2 (2013): 38, https://www.jstor.org/stable/10.2979/teachlearninqu.1.2.35.
23. Ernest Boyer, "The Scholarship of Engagement," *Bulletin of the American Academy of Art and Sciences* 49, no. 7 (1996): 26.
24. Boyer, "The Scholarship of Engagement," 26–28.
25. Boyer, "The Scholarship of Engagement," 32.
26. Again, aligned with V21's "strategic presentism" framework, highlighted by Matthew Reznicek in chapter 7, this volume.

7

IT WAS SICKNESS AND POVERTY TOGETHER

Teaching Inequality and Health Humanities in Austen's *Emma*

MATTHEW L. REZNICEK

IN 1973 THE REV. PEDRO ARRUPE, S.J., the Father General of the Society of Jesus, announced a turn in the conception of Jesuit education. "Education for justice," he declared, had become "a constitutive element of the mission" for Jesuit pedagogues so that "our prime educational objective" must be the formation of men- and women-for-others.[1] Arrupe spends the majority of his now-famous address explaining what the term "education for justice" means, drawing specific attention to three key attitudes: "a firm determination to live much more simply," a "firm determination to draw no profit whatever from clearly unjust sources," and "a firm resolve to be agents of change in society; not merely resisting unjust structures and arrangements, but actively undertaking to reform them."[2]

Resisting and reforming unjust structures remains a tall task in today's classroom, but a task that is no less important than it was in 1973. It remains no less important in a classroom on the campus of a Jesuit university, like mine, or of a nonreligious university. Questions of unjust profits and unjust structures dominate today—whether about reparations for slavery, systemic racism in policing, systemic economic inequality, or systemic health care inequalities. These questions have been central to the way I use eighteenth- and nineteenth-century novels to approach the questions of inequality and health humanities in my first-year research writing course, "Poverty and the Novel." As Thomas Piketty notes, money in eighteenth- and nineteenth-century novels by Jane Austen, Honoré de Balzac, Charles Dickens, and Victor Hugo was "everywhere, not only an abstract force but above all as a palpable, concrete magnitude."[3]

Focusing on the intersecting questions of structural inequality and the health humanities, my course "Poverty and the Novel" uses Jane Austen's *Emma* (1815) to challenge students to recognize the ways in which Austen's representation of economics, health and illness, and charity not only reflect ongoing structural inequities but also speak to the challenge Arrupe laid out in "not merely resisting unjust structures . . . but actively undertaking to reform them."[4] Teaching Austen's *Emma* through this focus on inequality and health humanities enables my students to see the ways in which economic status and the social components of health contribute to the unjust structural forces that shape the world around them.

Before providing key definitions of terms, I want to address the obvious ahistoricism of asking Austen's novel to answer for or speak to the socioeconomic realities of the twenty-first century. Or, rather, I want to reframe what might be characterized as ahistoricism in the framework of "strategic presentism." In their introduction to the "V21 Forum on Strategic Presentism" in *Victorian Studies*, David Sweeney Coombs and Danielle Coriale explain that "presentism" typically signifies a naive or complacent "overlook[ing] the alterity of the past."[5] Instead, Coombs and Coriale offer "strategic presentism," which "requires that we think of the past as something other than an object of knowledge that is sealed off, separated from the present by the onrush of sequential time," in order to "help us better understand and address the ways the past is at work in the exigencies of the present, from the recursive afterlives of British imperialism in our own era of war to the long arc of ongoing processes of dispossession under capitalism."[6] Strategic presentism, as a critical framework, "asks us to think critically about the past in the present *in order to change the present*."[7] If strategic presentism challenges critics to see the past in the present in order to change or reform the present, I believe it can help our classrooms become a space in which students bring their world into the examination of the text but also a space from which they can take their development out into the world "in order to change the present" and its "unjust structures and arrangements." Strategic presentism, then, provides the theoretical, critical, and pedagogical framework for an analysis of eighteenth- and nineteenth-century novels that challenges and frees students to look for the historical and social causes of and the potential solutions to today's injustices.

Because I am arguing that employing strategic presentism in discussions and critical assessments of Austen's *Emma* enables students to see more clearly the abstract unjust structures that shape the inequalities of their own world, I want to make clear what those injustices are; I want to be clear about the socioeconomic and health care inequities that shape this course and the world the students inhabit. According to The Commonwealth Fund's report "U.S. Health Care from a Global Perspective, 2019: Higher Spending, Worse Outcomes?," the United States spends "nearly twice as much as the average OECD country" on health care as a share of the economy and yet still "has the highest chronic disease burden and an obesity rate that is two times higher than the OECD average."[8] The contrast between ever-increasing rates of spending on health care and consistently poor health care outcomes demonstrates that "healthcare is only one contributor to health, and it is a small one."[9] The CDC (Centers for Disease Control and Prevention) notes that "only about 20 percent of the nation's health is the result of medical care, while 5 percent is the result of biology and genetics, 20 percent is the result of individual actions, and over 50 percent is caused by the 'social determinants of health.'"[10] More than 50 percent of the contributing factors to American health are determined by the "*conditions of life* people are exposed to because of the way their society is built—how we live, how we work, how we move from place to place, and what we eat and drink," as well as "the *causes or triggers of those conditions of life*—such as government policies, social structure, and the actions of powerful actors and organizations."[11] The current state of health in the United States is fundamentally tied to social structures and the forces that reinforce them.

One key element in health care inequality is income inequality. Richard (Buz) Cooper has detailed the relationship between poverty and health care usage, noting that "poor health and disability are more prevalent in areas of concentrated poverty, and they lead to a greater demand for health care services."[12] This fact is charted through "a continuous gradient over which declining incomes are associated with increasing hospital admissions, with greatest effects in households with very low incomes."[13] Additionally, data show "a systematic increase in life expectancy" for each income decile over the one immediately below it.[14] Thus, the conversation about health care inequality cannot be separated from the current state of economic injustice. As economists like Thomas Piketty, Emmanuel Saez, and Gabriel Zucman have noted, the income gap between the wealthiest 1 percent and the rest of the U.S. population is stark. Saez and Zucman show that today "the top 1% captures more than 20% of national income and the working class barely 12%. In other words, the 1% earns almost twice as much income as the entire working-class population, a group fifty times larger demographically."[15] There was a period of relative equality between 1950 and 1970; Piketty charts that there then followed "a paid rise in inequality in the 1980s, until by 2000 we have returned to a level on the order of [the top decile earning] 45–50 percent of national income."[16] According to Piketty, this rapid divergence can be traced to "powerful forces pushing toward divergence, or at any rate toward an extremely high level of inequality."[17] These forces, summed up in his equation $r>g$ where r stands for the average annual rate of return on capital and g stands for the rate of growth in the economy, result in the capacity of capital, like inheritances and dividends, to grow at a much faster rate than savings derived from income.[18] The growing income inequality in the United States exacerbates pre-existing health conditions.

This intersection of inequality and health care means that any conversations about resisting and reforming health care must be intersectional and structural; they must take into account the social components of health, but also the social structures that make their effects felt so unevenly across our population. Thinking structurally, however, is more difficult than thinking symptomatically or on a case-by-case basis. Barbara Katz Rothman notes that "Americans are good at seeing the individual. . . . We can see the person; in sophisticated, nuanced ways we can understand individuals, their motives, concerns, actions, behaviors. What we are less good at seeing, as a people, is seeing a people: *seeing the whole, seeing the social, the system within which individuals move*."[19] Eighteenth- and nineteenth-century literature, especially novels in the realist tradition, help us to see the whole, the social, the system within which individuals move. By applying the methods, concepts, and content from traditional humanities disciplines, the health humanities aim to perform a "moral function" in the education of medical students and, in this case pre-health undergraduates; that moral function is "to improve health care (praxis) by influencing its practitioners to refine and complexify their judgments (phronesis) . . . based on a deep and complex understanding (sophia) of illness, suffering, personhood, and related issues."[20] Teaching novels like Austen's *Emma* through this framework of strategic presentism and a health humanities focus on structural inequalities can help our students to see and think structurally; once they do, they help us see the unjust structures that continue beyond the realm of Highbury and Regency England, allowing us to begin thinking about how to reform those unjust structures we encounter today.

HANDSOME, CLEVER, AND RICH: THE SOCIAL DETERMINANTS OF HEALTH IN *EMMA*

All of Austen's novels are hyper-aware of income status. In *Mansfield Park* (1816), for example, Sir Thomas Bertram says that his daughters' impoverished cousin Fanny Price "is not a *Miss Bertram*. I should wish to see them very good friends, and would, on no account, authorize in my girls the smallest degree of arrogance toward their relation; but still they cannot be equals. Their rank, fortune, rights and expectations, will always be different."[21] Just as Austen's novels are aware of income and status, they are also remarkably aware of the threat of sickness; illness or poor health features in almost every one of Austen's novels. In *Sense and Sensibility* (1811), for example, Marianne Dashwood develops a "sleepless pain and delirium," after a "restless and feverish night."[22] In *Emma*, however, health and socioeconomic status not only shape the characters' identities but also drive the plot. The protagonist's socioeconomic status and her health are foregrounded within the first sentence, which famously describes Emma Woodhouse as "handsome, clever, and rich, with a comfortable home and happy disposition . . . with very little to distress or vex her."[23] Indeed, Emma is later described as "being the complete picture of grown-up health."[24] These "best blessings of existence" emphasize her status, identifying her as rich and possessing a comfortable home; the lack of anything to "distress or vex her" signals a healthy existence, free from any of the burdens of illness or pain that, as we will see, characterize the lives of so many of the residents of Highbury.[25]

Now, I want to be careful not to suggest that illness is *entirely* and *solely* associated with poverty in *Emma*; as I will show, the characters of Mr. Woodhouse and

Mrs. Churchill clearly show that illness impacts the lives of Austen's wealthier characters. That said, these figures, with their various real and perceived illnesses, exercise an exceptional force within the plot of the novel, highlighting the disproportionate power of these figures and their illnesses. Mr. Woodhouse, John Wiltshire has noted, "is described as 'a nervous man, easily depressed' and his needs influence and perhaps dictate the life of his daughter."[26] The use of "perhaps" seems too cautious; there is little doubt that Emma must reorder her life in order to accommodate Mr. Woodhouse's health (as must even Mr. Knightley at the novel's close). It is this expectation and ability to order the lives of others around one's health that reveals most clearly the power associated with wealth vis-à-vis illness. Emma explicitly admits that "while her dear father lived, any change of condition must be impossible for her" because "such a transplantation would be a risk to her father's comfort," a term "comfort" standing for his health in the novel.[27] This linguistic association of health and comfort is reinforced in the novel's closing pages when Mr. Woodhouse is described as being "so miserable" on the first allusion to Emma's and Mr. Knightley's wedding, and in "less pain" upon second allusion.[28] Equating comfort with health and discomfort with "pain" and "suffering," Austen's representation of Mr. Woodhouse depicts the expectation of health, comfort, and power associated with upper-class status, a nexus of economics, health care, and power that students can use to interrogate the novel and its connection to their own world.[29]

In a similar vein, Mrs. Churchill's ability to exert control over both her nephew, Frank, as well as the entirety of Highbury, through her various bouts of illness reinforces the capacity of the upper-class to reorder the world around their health and comfort. Mrs. Churchill, perhaps even more perniciously than Mr. Woodhouse, reveals the novel's association of class and illness with power, determining the lives of others, especially the lives of those whose lives who are dependent on them. Mrs. Churchill, as Mrs. Weston explains, "rules at Enscombe, and is a very odd-tempered woman; and [Frank Churchill's] coming now, depends upon her being willing to spare him."[30] The rhetoric of ruling and dependency on her being "willing to spare him" echoes language of governmentality, which Foucault describes "population as its target . . . and apparatuses of security as its essential technical instruction."[31] Foucault's conception of governmentality insists that the individual is "no longer pertinent as the objective, but simply as the instrument, relay, or condition for obtaining something at the level of population."[32] Accordingly, Mrs. Churchill's matrix of wealth, inheritance, legitimacy, and names all point to the control over the population, especially when we note that the Churchills believed Frank's father's marriage to Frank's mother to be "an unsuitable connection" and "threw her off with due decorum," aligning this control over Frank with an exercise of power over the legitimate line of the Churchill name and wealth.[33] This ability to exercise control is most clearly rendered through "the wilful or nervous part of her disorder" and her "weaker state of health."[34]

As with Mr. Woodhouse, it is the intersection of wealth, power, and health that enables Mrs. Churchill to exert such exceptional authority in the novel, ordering events and individuals to conform to her comfort.

This presents a marked contrast with two of the impoverished figures who become ill in the novel: Harriet Smith and Jane Fairfax. On the eve of a Christmas-time dinner, Harriet Smith becomes "so much indisposed with a cold."[35] When Emma calls on her the next morning, Harriet is "very feverish and had a bad sore-throat: Mrs. Goddard was full of care and affection, Mr. Perry was talked of, and Harriet herself was too ill and low to resist the authority which excluded her from this delightful engagement."[36] In contrast to Mrs. Churchill, whose illnesses commanded the obeisance of those near her, Miss Smith, who is "the natural daughter of somebody," is subject to an "authority" that "exclude[s]" her from the planned dinner.[37] The language of "authority" again recalls Foucault's concept of governmentality, emphasizing the degree to which the power structures re-emerge in and around illness in Austen's novel. The wealthy, like Mr. Woodhouse and Mrs. Churchill, are able to use their illnesses to orchestrate events; whereas the disempowered, like Miss Smith, become more subject to authority, losing what little agency they had, during their bouts of illness. Indeed, the novel seems to consider Miss Smith's sore throat more of a problem for others in the narrative than it is for her: not only is she "too low and ill to resist the authority which excluded her" from the dinner at Randall's but she is hardly talked about at the party. Her illness becomes more an issue of concern for others as well as an opportunity for performative concern. Of course, the novel is critical of Mr. Elton's response to Harriet's illness, but his response is instructive none the less.

Despite being couched in a rhetoric of concern, Mr. Elton's initial response reveals the degree to which the illness of the poor becomes a threat to the wealthy citizens of Highbury: "A sore-throat!—I hope not infection. I hope not of a putrid infectious sort. Has Perry seen her? Indeed you should take care of yourself as well as your friend. Let me entreat you to run no risks."[38] Mr. Elton, despite his pernicious role in the novel, voices a well-worn concern that the illnesses that beset the impoverished might be communicated to the wealthy, a concern that certainly resonates in the age of COVID-19. This threat of contagion is fundamental to the sense of belonging in the community; as Priscilla Wald explains, "the interactions that make us sick also constitute us as a community," leading to the development of "regulatory norm[s]" that police the boundaries of who is allowed to retain membership within that community.[39] Imogen Tyler draws these regulatory norms into the sociopolitical process of abjection, the process of marking "objects, practices, or persons" disgusting "through the (actual or symbolic) act of expulsion."[40] Harriet Smith is not expelled from the novel or from Highbury because she is ill, but there are repeated attempts to expel her from the evening, from Emma's rank, from affectionate relations with Frank Churchill and Mr. Knightley.

Her illness, and her passivity during her illness, render visible the workings of this sociopolitical act of expulsion.

In a similar vein, Jane Fairfax, "an orphan [and] the only child of Mrs. Bates's youngest daughter," is known throughout the novel for her weak health.[41] Indeed, recounting their meeting in Weymouth, Frank Churchill notes that he thought she looked "ill, very ill—that is, if a young lady can ever be allowed to look ill," adding that she lacks "the fine glow of health."[42] The direct opposite, then, of Emma's "picture of grown-up health," Jane Fairfax also lacks the economic resources of her counterpart. She depends upon a career as a governess, "the sale—not quite of human flesh—but of human intellect," for her survival.[43] Jane's not-so-oblique reference to the slave trade reinforces the relationship between health care outcomes and poverty, but adds an important component for the discussion of another social component of health—race. Sarah Marsh has recently argued that Lord Mansfield's decision in *Somerset v. Stewart* (1772) regarding the forcible removal of an enslaved person on British soil for sale in Jamaica, "while legally distancing Britain from some elements of racial slavery, ultimately permitted it to flourish overseas."[44] Mansfield's complicated ruling enables what Marsh characterizes as "imperial hypocrisy: namely, Britain's legal disdain for slavery at home where it barely existed and silence about slavery in the colonies where it was profitable."[45] As Helena Kelly argues, not only do Austen's references to slavery in *Emma* depend upon the geopolitics of the slave trade located in Bristol, but it is "only the unlikeable characters . . . who can treat the issue so lightly" as to "fling" around the equation of slavery and work as a governess.[46] Taking seriously this equation requires us to follow Manu Samriti Chander and Patricia A. Matthew when they insist that "it should no longer be possible to read Romanticism without attending to the geopolitics of slavery, especially as it is reflected in diverse literary forms."[47]

Attending to the resonances of slavery in this passage, especially as it is framed in connection to the experiences of Mrs. Elton and Jane Fairfax, allows the classroom to begin to explore the ways in which the legacies of slavery continue to shape the world. By creating this "not quite" equivalence, Mrs. Elton relates Jane's precarity to the experience of an enslaved person. This is, of course, an offensive and ridiculous equation, but it highlights the power inequities that continue to shape anxieties in white America. Moreover, it calls attention once again to the relationship between poverty and disempowerment that continues to have a direct impact on health. In particular, because this passage equates slavery with Jane's need to work in order to be able to achieve and maintain health, it opens space for the discussion of Austen, race, and health care inequities for people of color in America. Of course, this comparison is utterly unfair; it enacts what Marsh has described as "the brilliantly imbalanced autonomies of characters who, like James Somerset, are not fully independent persons."[48] Rooting this category of "not fully independent persons" in the Mansfield decision's treatment of Somerset, this racial history helps explicate and excavate the racial roots of ongoing, presentist inequalities in which the autonomy of certain populations continues to be challenged and denied. As Tressie McMillan Cottom powerfully recounts in her essay "Dying to be Competent," the maternal mortality rate for Black women in the United States is "about the same rate as women in countries such as Mexico and Uzbekistan," meaning that Black women are "243 percent more likely to die from pregnancy- or childbirth-related causes than are white women."[49] Exploring the anxiety around equating a white woman with the position of an enslaved African causes us to ask how inequality driven by race and racial structures continue to shape the experience of health and illness.

There are two key moments of Jane's illness: one takes place during a trip to Mr. Knightley's Donwell Abbey, and another follows the catastrophic outing to Box Hill. In both instances, her illness absents her from the main plot of the novel, but it also functions as a rebuke of powerful figures. At Donwell Abbey, her illness is a rebuke of Frank Churchill; after Box Hill, Jane's illness is a rebuke of Emma's behavior toward her aunt, Miss Bates. It is this second instance that is most useful for teaching the novel through the framework of the social components of health and inequality. Emma overhears Miss Bates saying that she will "*say* you are laid down upon the bed, and I am sure are ill enough."[50] The use of "*say*" demonstrates a performative element to Jane's illness, which is not to suggest that she is not ill; rather, this performative element reveals the power of illness to function as a critique. To return momentarily to Wald's claim that "the interactions that make use sick also constitute us as a community," Emma's interactions with Jane and her aunt are what makes Jane ill.[51] Emma, in this case, is the source of corruption rather than the picture of health.

It is important that Emma herself understands this, knowing that Jane's performative illness and retreat is a rebuke of her own behavior rather than a recognition of Jane being the source of contagion. This reverses the power structure that has dominated the representation of illness for the majority of the novel and, significantly, it is joined with Emma's most profound expression of sympathy for Jane. This "picture of her present sufferings," we are told, "acted as a cure of every former ungenerous suspicion, and left her nothing but pity."[52] Jane's illness and her sufferings *cure* Emma of her previous suspicion. Emma is the one who is healed and is thus made capable of rejoining the community without the blemish of illness. Jane's ability to reverse the framework in which illnesses that belong to the poor constitute a form of erasure, and illness that belongs to the wealthy functions as a form of dominance, provides a key instance in teaching this novel via the framework of health humanities and inequality—precisely because it is a disruption of the pattern. So why is Jane's illness different? The answer lies in its therapeutic effect—it produces a lasting form of sympathy in Emma, inoculating her from her previous suspicion.

THE IMPRESSION WILL NOT SOON BE OVER: READING POVERTY, ILLNESS, AND SYMPATHY

Students initially bristle at the concept of sympathy, wondering why Emma cannot instead respond with more empathy. Not only does integrating eighteenth-century conceptions of sympathy in a close reading of a key scene in *Emma* help historicize the novel within its intellectual landscape. Eighteenth-century definitions of sympathy also provide students with a clearer understanding of the range of responses available to Emma in the face of these structural inequalities. As Miranda Burgess has demonstrated, the term "sympathy" in the eighteenth century "designated more than the pity that it implies etymologically, and that is now conventionally associated with it."[53] Sympathy, Burgess continues, "came to mean something like feeling with, as well as feeling for, another," denoting not only a sense of emotional community but also an ethical obligation, what Burgess terms "social feeling.[54]" Underlying Adam Smith's conception of sympathy in his *Theory of Moral Sentiments* (1759) is a question about the "volitional or convolutional notions of sympathy," which is premised on the "quasi-theatrical division of men that makes emotional spectacles of some and sympathetic spectators of others."[55] Smith's framing raises ethical concerns regarding the "suitableness or unsuitableness, . . . the proportion or disproportion" of the sufferer's display of their own suffering.[56] The questions of performativity, of spectacle, and of volitional sympathy are on clear display in Emma's charitable visit to a cottage in volume 1.

> They were now approaching the cottage, and all idle topics were superseded. Emma was very compassionate; and the distresses of the poor were as sure of relief from her personal attention and kindness, her counsel and her patience, as from her purse. She understood their ways, could allow for their ignorance and their temptations, had no romantic expectations of extraordinary virtue from those, for whom education had done so little; entered into their troubles with ready sympathy, and always gave her assistance with as much intelligence as good-will. In the present instance, it was sickness and poverty together which she came to visit; and after remaining there as long as she could give comfort or advice, she quitted the cottage with such an impression of the scene as made her say to Harriet as they walked away,
>
> "These are the sights, Harriet, to do one good. How trifling they make every thing else appear!—I feel now as if I could think of nothing but these poor creatures all the rest of the day; and yet, who can say how soon it may all vanish from my mind? . . . And really, I do not think the impression will soon be over. . . . Well, (smiling,) I hope it may be allowed that if compassion has produced exertion and relief to the sufferers, it has done all that is truly important. If we feel for the wretched, enough to do all we can for them, the rest is empty sympathy, only distressing to ourselves."[57]

This scene provides a perfect opportunity for a close reading in class to work through the ways in which Emma engages in Smithian sympathy: she "entered into their troubles with ready sympathy"; "compassion has produced exertion and relief to the sufferers"; and so on. Asking students to read this scene first for the plot, then for the language of sympathy and suffering, it is useful to have them discuss whether Emma's response was truly about "these poor creatures" or whether it was "empty sympathy, only distressing to [herself]." Then, integrating excerpts from both the first chapter of Adam Smith's *Theory of Moral Sentiments* (1759) as well as Miranda Burgess's "On Being Moved," I ask my students to re-read the passage thinking about the definitions of sympathy as "fellow feeling" and as "quasi-theatrical" in order to query the efficacy of Emma's charity. Is charity enough? Is it a just action, if it is also intended to make the actor feel better? Is there such a thing as "empty sympathy?" Is charity, we ultimately ask, the same as Smith's "fellow feeling," or does charity depend upon "problematize[d] entrenched class hierarchies, signifying the increasing extent to which the gentry and landed aristocracy could not address individually the effects of a transitional economy."[58] In doing so, we often discuss the proliferation of service trips and mission trips that our Center for Service and Justice offers, drawing our conversation about Austen closer and closer to the world that my students inhabit. If, as Danielle Spratt has argued, Emma's "failed acts of philanthropy" indicate "how both local and institutional elites are incapable of addressing societal inequity," this close-reading exercise leads us to the ultimate question of my classroom: How ought we respond to the inequities the in-class conversation reveals?

If sympathy is key to the understanding of inequality in Austen's novel and, as I would argue, key to a critique of our own social response, one way to build on students' reading of this scene is an in-class exercise called "Embodying Social Structures."[59] In this exercise, students or groups of students list every social structure that shapes the world of the novel—gender, race, class, ability, the military, Empire, education, and so forth. Then students chart each of the characters who interact with each of these social structures. For example, Harriet Smith is shaped by the intersection of her class status as an orphan, her modicum of education, her gender, her geographic location; Mr. Weston, similarly, is shaped by gender and class, but also by the institution of marriage and his involvement in the Army as well as the commercial trade in London. Once students have developed this list, they pick one character—Ms. Smith, for example—and change one element of the intersections that shape their identity and re-map their interactions with social structures. What would happen, for example, if Harriet Smith had not been defined by her position as an orphan? What would happen to Mr. Weston if he were not a member of the military? How does each character's position within the social structures of the novel shape their identity? And, ultimately, how does sympathy respond to that intersectionality? This not only helps students see the impact of intersectionality on individual characters' experiences, but also shows them the degree to which social structures themselves respond to different intersectional identities.

TO DO ALL WE CAN FOR THEM: *EMMA* AND INEQUALITY BEYOND THE CLASSROOM

As Pedro Arrupe, S.J., made clear in his 1973 address, the purpose of "an education for justice" must be not only "personal conversion" but also "structural social reform."[60] The outcome of our discussions of health care and economic inequalities cannot simply be recognition but must be a commitment to action. To help students concretize this question, my final assignment focuses not on the representation of poor or sick people in *Emma*, but instead on the ways in which the causes of these inequalities are either revealed or obscured in the novel. To what extent does Austen demonstrate these economic shifts that contribute to the Bates's downward mobility? To what extent does the novel make it clear that Mr. Perry, Highbury's physician, attends more closely to the health of Mr. Woodhouse? In their "Community/Inequality" paper students are given the choice of analyzing either a marginalized community or a specific form of inequality they saw within the novel and then must answer a series of questions, including: Who does this form of inequality affect? What structures produce this inequality? Are those structures revealed or obscured in the novel? How does this mirror the historical reality? and finally, What would a just response be to that inequality, according to Jesuit thought on inequality? This assignment requires students to build on the close-reading skills we have developed through the analysis of the novel, while also asking them to engage secondary sources to assess the historical reality of poverty and health care during the Regency era. Lastly, and most importantly, it asks them to think about how their analysis of a form of inequality demands a response.

This question regarding response is, I believe, the most important part of the assignment, the conversations about the novel, and indeed my class as a whole. This is, to borrow from Arrupe, the "most difficult" part of his charge to the Jesuit educators, because, as he notes, "if we set out to reduce income in so far as it is derived from participation in unjust structures, we will find out soon enough that we are faced with an impossible task unless those very structures are changed."[61] Being able to employ the language of our Mission, however, benefits these conversations precisely because this marks a shift away from the comfortable position of analyzing a Regency-period novel and toward examining our own position in unjust structures. To quote once more from Arrupe, in closing: "Let there be men and women who will bend their energies not to strengthen positions of privilege, but, to the extent possible, reduce privilege in favour of the underprivileged. Please do not conclude too hastily that this does not pertain to you—that you do not belong to the privileged few in your society. . . . In this matter, our basic point of reference must be the truly poor, the truly marginalized."[62] By shifting the focus of the novel not entirely away from Emma herself but to the structures that underlie Highbury society, the structures that enable its health or illness as well as its poverty or its wealth, the intersection of health care and inequality brings to the fore the questions of privilege, marginalization, and of our own response.

Austen's *Emma*, far from being a novel of "empty sympathy," reveals not only "sickness and poverty together," but also the ways in which power functioned in Regency England.[63] Through the prism of strategic presentism, *Emma* can be used to produce conversations that reflect our own world and the inequities that shape it, not only bringing students into the world of the novel but bringing the novel into the world of the students. What's more, by bringing the novel into their world, it helps students "to think critically about the past in the present in order to change the present," and to imagine alternative futures.[64]

NOTES

1. Pedro Arrupe, SJ, "Men for Others," speech, Valencia, Spain, July 31, 1973, https://onlineministries.creighton.edu/CollaborativeMinistry/men-for-others.html.
2. Arrupe, "Men for Others."
3. Thomas Piketty, *Capital in the Twenty-First Century*, trans. Arthur Goldhammer (Cambridge, MA: Belknap Press of Harvard University Press, 2017), 134.
4. Arrupe, "Men for Others."
5. Coombs and Coriale, "V21 Forum on Strategic Presentism: Introduction," *Victorian Studies* 59, no. 1 (2016): 87.
6. Coombs and Coriale, "V21 Forum," 88.
7. Coombs and Coriale, "V21 Forum," 88, emphasis mine.
8. Roosa Tikkanen and Melinda K. Abrams, "U.S. Health Care from a Global Perspective, 2019: Higher Spending, Worse Outcomes?," last modified January 30, 2020, https://www.commonwealthfund.org/publications/issue-briefs/2020/jan/us-health-care-global-perspective-2019.
9. Kathryn Strother Ratcliff, *The Social Determinants of Health: Looking Upstream* (Medford, MA: Polity Press, 2020), 1.
10. Ratcliff, *Social Determinants of Health*, 2.
11. Ratcliff, *Social Determinants of Health*, 2.
12. Richard (Buz) Cooper, *Poverty and the Myths of Health Care Reform* (Baltimore: Johns Hopkins University Press, 2016), 19.
13. Cooper, *Poverty and the Myths*, 19.
14. Ratcliff, *Social Determinants of Health*, 24.
15. Emmanuel Saez and Gabriel Zucman, *The Triumph of Injustice: How the Rich Dodge Taxes and How to Make Them Pay* (New York: Norton, 2019), 6.
16. Piketty, *Capital*, 32.
17. Piketty, *Capital*, 35.
18. Piketty, *Capital*, 34.
19. Barbara Katz Rothman, *The Book of Life: A Personal and Ethical Guide to Race, Normality, and the Implications of the Human Genome Project* (Boston: Beacon Press, 2001), 162.
20. Johanna Shapiro, Jack Coulehan, Delese Wear, and Martha Montello, "Medical Humanities and Their Discontents: Definitions, Critiques, and Implications," *Academic Medicine* 84, no. 2 (2009): 192–193.

21. Jane Austen, *Mansfield Park*, ed. James Kinsley (New York: Oxford University Press, 2008), 9.
22. Jane Austen, *Sense and Sensibility*, ed. John Mullan (New York: Oxford University Press, 2017), 228, 224.
23. Jane Austen, *Emma*, ed. Fiona Stafford (New York: Penguin, 2015), 7.
24. Austen, *Emma*, 38.
25. Austen, *Emma*, 7.
26. John Wiltshire, *Jane Austen and the Body: The Picture of Health* (New York: Cambridge University Press, 1992), 120.
27. Austen, *Emma*, 419.
28. Austen, *Emma*, 452.
29. Austen, *Emma*, 452.
30. Austen, *Emma*, 115.
31. Michel Foucault, *Security, Territory, Population: Lectures at the Collège de France, 1977–78*, trans. Graham Burchell (Basingstoke: Palgrave, 2007), 108.
32. Foucault, *Security, Territory, Population*, 42.
33. Austen, *Emma*, 16.
34. Austen, *Emma*, 296.
35. Austen, *Emma*, 103.
36. Austen, *Emma*, 104.
37. Austen, *Emma*, 23.
38. Austen, *Emma*, 104.
39. Priscilla Wald, *Contagious: Cultures, Carriers, and the Outbreak Narrative* (Durham, NC: Duke University Press, 2008), 2; Imogen Tyler, *Revolting Subjects: Social Abjection and Resistance in Neoliberal Britain* (New York: Zed Books, 2013), 36.
40. Tyler, *Revolting Subjects*, 23.
41. Austen, *Emma*, 153.
42. Austen, *Emma*, 187.
43. Austen, *Emma*, 279.
44. The decision by Lord Chief Justice Mansfield in June 1772 supported the claim that habeas corpus could be used by persons claimed by others as enslaved property in Britain itself to evade being seized, deported, and sold where slavery was legal practice. It was interpreted by many both in Britain and beyond to mean that there was no slavery in Britain under law. See https://www.english-heritage.org.uk/visit/places/kenwood/history-stories-kenwood/somerset-case/; Sarah Marsh, "Changes of Air: The Somerset Case and *Mansfield Park*'s Imperial Plots," *Eighteenth-Century Studies* 53, no. 2 (2020): 212.
45. Marsh, "Changes of Air," 212.
46. Helena Kelly, *Jane Austen: The Secret Radical* (New York: Knopf, 2017), 179–180.
47. Manu Samriti Chander and Patricia A. Matthew, "Abolitionist Interruptions: Romanticism, Slavery, and Genre," *European Romantic Review* 29, no. 4 (2018): 432.
48. Marsh, "Changes of Air," 215.
49. Tressie McMillan Cottom, "Dying to Be Competent," in *Thick and Other Essays* (New York: New Press, 2019), 87.
50. Austen, *Emma*, 354.
51. Wald, *Contagious*, 2.
52. Austen, *Emma*, 355.
53. Miranda Burgess, "On Being Moved: Sympathy, Mobility, and Narrative Form," *Poetics Today* 32, no. 2 (2011): 297.
54. Burgess, "On Being Moved," 297, 300.
55. Burgess, "On Being Moved," 300, 297.
56. Adam Smith, *The Theory of Moral Sentiments*, ed. Ryan Patrick Hanley (New York: Penguin, 2009), 24.
57. Austen, *Emma*, 84–85.

58. Danielle Spratt, "Denaturalizing Lady Bountiful: Speaking the Silence of Poverty in Mary Brunton's *Discipline* and Jane Austen's *Emma*," *The Eighteenth Century* 56, no. 2 (2015): 194.
59. With thanks to Cormac O'Brien (University of California, Davis) for introducing this exercise to me.
60. Arrupe, "Men for Others."
61. Arrupe, "Men for Others."
62. Arrupe, "Men for Others."
63. Austen, *Emma*, 85, 84.
64. Coombs and Coriale, "V21 Forum," 88.

8
TEACHING HURTS

Travis Chi Wing Lau

"AFTER" PAIN?

I compose these reflections at a moment of "afters" that I am only now beginning to process: after navigating the first year of my tenure-track job when I set foot on campus but four times; after teaching remotely a full academic year having never truly been trained to do so; after relocating with my partner from Austin, Texas, to Columbus, Ohio, in the middle of a pandemic; after being vaccinated multiple times. Yet I refuse to claim one "after" that so many institutions, governments, nations, and even public health officials have prematurely claimed: *after the pandemic*. As hundreds of thousands of cases of COVID-19 continue to be reported globally, it feels particularly unethical, if not perverse, to claim afterness when for so many it is still very much the lethal and painful present without the immunological privilege of hindsight. Because my arrival at Kenyon College, a small liberal arts college, coincided with the pandemic lockdown, such conditions continue to inform how I do the vulnerable work of teaching and mentoring students even as my own campus community has collectively moved on after the pandemic.

As a scholar of the eighteenth and nineteenth centuries, I am temporally always after my objects of study. And for my students, many of whom are encountering these historical periods for the first time in my classroom, this sense of after feels that much more disorienting because of the significant differences in form and language. Yet, this last year of encounters with literature of the long eighteenth century helped both my students and me to better understand how that historical distance can be better bridged by what the V21 Collective has called "strategic presentism," that challenges us to "think critically about the past in the present in order to change the present."[1] I deeply share Matthew Reznicek's view (chapter 7 in this volume) that strategic presentism prepares students to intervene in "today's injustices" by understanding their "historical and social causes," which too often get forgotten or erased. Many of my students came to my class expecting to "escape" the pandemic present based on assumptions about an eighteenth-century past somehow freed from the very political and cultural concerns they are living through now. My approach was to interrogate this hermetically sealed model of the past as somehow having nothing to offer us in this pandemic moment aside from aesthetic suspension or a quaint antiquarianism. Rather than cordoning off the past's own pandemic thinking, I wanted to challenge my students to consider what relevant insights for our current COVID moment we might gain in examining how eighteenth-century writers responded to public health crises like the 1665 Great Plague of London or the variolation of smallpox.

In the process of navigating challenging pandemic conditions, we might for good reason want to be outside of our bodyminds to deliberately avoid uncomfortable confrontations with our own anxieties about health and disease.[2] But to challenge this avoidance and to help develop my and my students' vocabularies for talking about embodiment as historically situated, I deliberately structured my survey courses in Restoration and eighteenth-century literature around the very embodiedness of this period's writing—writing that so often unabashedly voices the body and its limits. From Jonathan Swift's scatological satires like "The Lady's Dressing Room" (1732) to Frances Burney's harrowing letter describing her mastectomy without anesthesia (1812) to John Wilmot, Earl of Rochester's witty meditations on impotence in "The Imperfect Enjoyment" (1680), the course explored the long eighteenth century's fascination with the bodily, specifically the bodily at its most vulnerable, grotesque, or even monstrous. As my students emphasized throughout the semester in discussions and in writing, we remain remarkably indebted to the eighteenth century's grammars of the flesh, which continue to animate how Western culture imagines what constitutes proper bodily form and function.

Rather than attempt to give a comprehensive account of my past year of teaching eighteenth-century literature and culture, I instead follow the lead of my own students in their course evaluations to reflect on what they found most urgent and valuable about this material. I had expected students to focus most on works that directly engaged with epidemic crisis, like Daniel Defoe's *A Journal of the Plague Year* (1721), but instead they identified two thematic clusters that transformed their understanding of historical embodiment and its politics: (1) deformity, disability, and defect; and (2) slavery and colonization. Multiple students remarked upon how these two groups—the disabled and the enslaved—shared experiences of physical, affective, psychic, and spiritual pain that revealed unexpected solidarities between these groups that persist into the present: Colonial subjugation very often took the form of deliberately inflicting painful disability upon the enslaved; and the disabled were and still are frequently subjected to institutionalization and abuse. Tracing the shifting language of bodily difference in this period also helped many students see how contemporary disability rights activism and Black antiracist activism uniquely respond to individual and collective pain, both past and present. Pain, my students noticed, underpinned the strategically presentist narrative of the course by offering points of continuity and divergence that they could track into the pain of our present pandemic moment.

In what follows, I consider the limits and affordances of thinking about the long eighteenth century in terms of pain and those who lived with it most. What does it mean to inhabit historical pain alongside, and sometimes in tension with, our own present pains of learning to live in pandemic conditions? I speculate on what an ethics of painful pedagogy might look like, and how it emerges from the vulnerable, sometimes painful, realization, as Marisela Martinez-Cola describes of her own teaching in the pandemic, "that while I cannot control painful situations, I can work to transform personal pain into meaningful pedagogy."[3] I believe this transformation need not disavow, aestheticize, or fetishize pain but instead can center it as foundational to how we might make sense of our pain now and its precarious relationship to the pain of others.

OUR PAIN, OUR INTERDEPENDENCE

The COVID-19 pandemic unexpectedly made some aspects of education more accessible than ever before: courses could be held virtually in asynchronous and synchronous formats that could accommodate faculty and students with different needs and resources; conferences, lectures, and workshops went digital, enabling the participation of even those who would not have been able to attend in person; institutions finally began granting accommodations that disabled students and faculty have been requesting for decades. Yet the gains in access (many of which are already being rescinded and forgotten in the "return to normal") were accompanied by various barriers related to the digital—Zoom fatigue, unstable internet connections, and uncomfortable work environments.

For me, the work of teaching from my own home was no less painful. I have ongoing scoliosis-related disabilities, including chronic pain, vertigo, and brain fog, and spending upward four to six hours in front of my desktop computer for class meetings, grading, and office hours was quite literally painful. Given that institutions do not need to help make home offices accessible because the Americans with Disabilities Act (ADA)'s purview is restricted to on-campus spaces only, I had to invest in making my workspace accessible even before I could sustainably do my job. I had to learn how to manage the new physical and cognitive demands of teaching in this virtual context, which, as many educators have remarked over the past few years, is often labor done unsupported by institutions and without proper training. To acknowledge these challenges and the labor disproportionately thrust upon adjunct faculty, contingent faculty, and graduate students, I have insisted on calling this abrupt turn to Zoom teaching "emergency remote teaching" because so much of it felt like reactionary triage rather than measured and prepared response.[4] For both teachers and students, the pandemic revealed the ways in which education has long been inaccessible, but "we learn about worlds when they do not accommodate us. Not being accommodated can be pedagogy."[5] Such painful, revelatory pedagogy has as much to teach us as it does our students, who co-constitute these spaces of learning and share our pain.

As I prepared to begin my first semester teaching at Kenyon, it felt only right to start with my own pain, if only to acknowledge the pain in the room—that it exists and that it shapes our conditions of learning. For several years now, I have taken the risk of disclosing my scoliosis-related disabilities on the first day of class. I do this not to enforce disclosure as a requirement but instead to frame our work ahead as always shaped by these material conditions that often exist beyond the frame of our Zoom squares. For me (and, as I came to realize, for my students), sometimes the pains of living would make an appearance on screen despite our attempts to keep them out, and I wanted us to practice an ethos of collective and self-care that made space for us to inhabit our bodyminds in whatever messy ways we might need, even if it meant turning off our cameras, stepping away, or having frank conversations about the challenges of being in virtual classrooms. These were not failures of our classroom but the very things that made our scholarly work meaningful and sustainable.

Disclosure, Alison Kafer reminds us, meets a number of different student and faculty needs beyond accommodation: "They might be exploring the possibility of claiming crip identity, or finding their own experiences reflected in a text, or wrestling with the implications of accepting diagnosis; they might be interpreting past experiences through the lens of ableism and yearning for connection to disability activism and resistance."[6] After I made it clear why I was disclosing, students very openly began to share their own experiences with disability and struggles with access that had been newly created or intensified by the pandemic. In witnessing students feeling seen by one another, I have come to believe that there simply cannot be an accessible classroom without this first acknowledgment of how our bodyminds share space and time. I recognize that this is not always the safest approach for instructors, especially those who are underrepresented or contingent, but I believe this cultivates what Mia Mingus has called "access intimacy" or the "elusive, hard to describe feeling when someone else 'gets' your access needs," because the classroom community has made the well-being of our bodyminds a priority even if it simply means acknowledging we are not okay.[7] For the next fifteen weeks, my students and I built and sustained an interdependent community of inquiry and care that held space for vulnerabilities not as pedagogical disruptions but as essential facets of learning in already challenging conditions. Counter to Elaine Scarry's assumption that pain is fundamentally unsharable, my students were learning how to share their pains and share in each other's pains together.[8]

I also wanted to historicize my pedagogical approach within an eighteenth-century context, which in this case took the form of a unit on William Hay's *Deformity: An Essay* (1754) and a selection of smallpox poems written primarily by women, including Mary Jones, Mary Leapor, and Mary Wortley Montagu. These works not only foreground embodiment that displaced (and sometimes permanently exiled) these writers from social life but puts into stark relief, as Keith Wailoo puts it, how historically "pain and its relief defined a high-stakes challenge—a topic not easily controlled by politicians, physicians, judges or any single group" and "incited a steady struggle over who has the right, jurisdiction, and authority to say who is in pain."[9] Students were astonished at these historical examples of disabled people and women explicitly framing their pain as *social* problems, or more specifically as conditions produced by social and structural circumstances like ableism or sexism that could be confronted and changed. These writers understood their pain both as individual experiences of impairment and suffering and as the consequence of being a part of social life that unevenly values bodies and determines which bodies are allowed to be in pain publicly.

In the case of William Hay, his essay articulates not just the pain of his hunchback and blindness after a nearly lethal bout of smallpox in childhood, but also the emotional and psychological pain of having been the object of shame for his guardians, "'who endeavoured to conceal' his deformity after having 'tried every Art to correct the Errors of Nature.'"[10] Yet what unfolds in Hay's *Essay* is hardly just a catalog of ableism's cruelties but instead what many of my students have described as an unexpected example of disability pride well before the formation of disability identity. Hay acknowledges how deformity enabled him to become a parliamentarian and man of letters because of how it taught him to live a life of the mind that is realized through the very hybrid form of the work as memoir, essay in the Baconian tradition, and manifesto against ableism. Hay's seemingly contradictory claim that "Deformity is a Protection to a Man's Health and Person" cleverly naturalizes deformity against its stereotypes as human lack or natural error and acknowledges how it has holistically bettered his well-being—he became increasingly more attentive to his own bodymind's limits and needs in contrast to some of his able-bodied counterparts, who frequently indulged in alcohol and rich foods.[11] Deformity helped Hay develop a form of crip self-awareness that enabled him to survive the very ableist conditions he was so often forced to endure.

Multiple students remarked that Hay's *Essay* anticipates more recent attempts to challenge the duality of mind and body, especially in terms of pain, and also what the disability community has called the social model of disability, where disability here is not intrinsic to Hay's bodymind but produced by eighteenth-century preoccupations with beauty and health as standards by which people are measured. Even when Hay details the mockery and sometimes physical harm he experienced in daily life, he locates in those experiences the foundations for the moral virtue and self-knowledge that enable him to expose the hypocrisy and vices of British culture. This knowledge, grounded in and inextricable from his deformity, is *cripistemology*, a term from disability theory that insists on ways of knowing that emerge directly out of disabled lived experience. Recovering these painful cripistemologies both helps us think about how disability produces knowledges and also invites students to draw on their embodyminded experiences to "produce painful new knowledge, but also to construct analyses about pain that are less painful, and less dangerous to those of us in pain, and, in doing so, to re-imagine our (shared, pained) futures."[12] Beyond theory, this kind of knowledge-making also involves thinking practically about actual campus spaces and how campus cultures and traditions often come with their own unacknowledged forms of inaccessibility, which were further exacerbated by the pandemic.

Many of my students had arrived in my classroom (both in-person and virtual) deeply invested in, and prepared to talk about, gender and its relationship to illness and disability. Smallpox poems like Mary Wortley Montagu's "Saturday; the Small Pox" or Mary Jones's "After the Smallpox" intimately detail the invisible pain of being a woman surviving smallpox.[13] The figure of the "scarred woman" came to emblematize smallpox as a disfiguring tragedy.[14] As opposed to focusing on the symptoms of smallpox itself, in both Montagu's and Jones's poems the speakers expose the cruelty of gendered expectations that unrealistically demand that women preserve their beauty even in the wake of debilitating illness. Many of my woman-identifying students saw themselves in these poems' expressions of gendered pain repeatedly dismissed by friends, family, and caregivers. They identified in these poems a devastating struggle of being disabled twice: by smallpox and then by misogynistic assumptions that these women's pockmarked faces were "proof of their social death," to quote one of my second-year undergraduates. While Flavia in Montagu's "eclogue" laments the potential futures foreclosed for her in an already competitive marriage market that favors the young and beautiful, the speaker of Jones's "After the Smallpox" recognizes how the objectification of women's bodies links beauty to the developing culture of commodity capitalism. Jones indicts the unjust labor of women who are expected to maintain their beauty through the conspicuous consumption of makeup and finery to sell their faces and bodies as advertisement "Signs" for the "nature of the goods within."[15]

During our discussion, I asked whether it mattered that both Flavia and Jones's speaker had in fact survived smallpox. Students observed that both poems underscore how, for the two speakers, physical recovery from smallpox is irrelevant if they are still socially marked as deformed and damaged—a stigmatized subject position that William Hay explicitly refuses This intersection of ability and gender became the focus of many student exam essays that brilliantly argued how womanhood in the eighteenth century was frequently framed in terms of or as disability. Such conflation was literalized by traumatic bodily events like smallpox that could deprive women entirely of their livelihoods and social identities. Making connections across different forms of painful expression helped my students think more expansively about what constitutes disability and its intersections with other forms of identity.

For some of my disabled students (and for me), these were some of the first, if not the only, instances in which they had encountered disability in history.[16] Like other identities that did not become legible as identities until much later, disability is often presumed not to exist in earlier historical periods. Even within disability studies itself, premodern or early modern disability has only recently begun to receive critical attention and in ways that challenge long-standing narratives in the field like disability's relationship to normality. Because disability scholars and activists have rightly pushed back against the medical model of disability, which reduces disability to a problem of the individual's body to be corrected by medicine, historical accounts of disability continue to emphasize the medicalization of disability that culminated in the forced sterilization and institutionalization of disabled people. I did not want to include works like Hay's *Essay* simply to show students that there are many understudied historical precedents to disability. I also wanted to insist upon disabled life as being more than just pain, more than just case histories. Disabled and trans writer Eli Clare, in his own encounters with disability in the archive, mourns how these records—often the only historical evidence we have of disabled people—"transform people into diagnoses and 'expert opinions' . . . personhood itself receding."[17] To undo this receding has become the work of my eighteenth-century classroom.

REGARDING THE PAIN OF OTHERS

My current apartment overlooks the headquarters of the Columbus Division of Police, which became one of the many centers of Black Lives Matter protests in the summer of 2020. Having moved to the city during these protests, I took part in some of the rallies nearby, and I have a vivid memory of two young Black women holding up a hand-painted sign that read, in red letters against black poster board, "Our pain matters." This scene lingered with me well after the rally—the sign demands recognition of pain that was presumed not to matter (or to matter only to a minority) but also does not want to equate Black life with pain or allow such pain to continue. I had inherited the eighteenth-century and Romantic survey courses from my two retired senior colleagues, and in my attempts to revise the courses to include more noncanonical writers of color and women writers, I grappled with the challenges raised by the protestors' sign: at a predominantly white institution, how do I, a non-Black scholar of color, ethically introduce students to Black writing and history without merely rehearsing trauma or speaking for Black people and their experiences? Or, to invoke Christina Sharpe's guiding question, "What happens when we proceed as if we *know* this, antiblackness, to be the ground on which we stand, the ground from which we attempt to speak, for instance an 'I' or a 'we' who know, an 'I' or a 'we' who care?"[18]

Rather than presume that I had clear answers to these big questions, I joined my students in asking these questions again and again over the course of the semester in conjunction with our readings of Black writers and scholars. I drew upon the energetic investments of my students, many of whom were already steeped in the ongoing debates about U.S. race relations. They wanted to know how we arrived at this moment of belated reckoning, but many of them were new to thinking about racial formation in history and its relationship to the painful enterprises of empire and colonialism. One of our most generative discussions focused on the concluding scene of Aphra Behn's *Oroonoko: or, The Royal Slave* (1688), in which Oroonoko is violently dismembered as punishment for leading a slave rebellion against the colonists in Surinam. Having also recently read excerpts of *The Interesting Narrative of the Life of Olaudah Equiano* (1789), students noted the lurid and visceral nature of many narrative accounts we encountered. This "spectacular suffering," to borrow Ramesh Mallipeddi's words, was characterized by "a violation of bodily integrity" and an "invasion of corporeal autonomy" that underscored the extent to which slave bodies were dehumanized as commodities from which planters and colonists could brutally extract labor.[19] Such a framework enabled us to interrogate Behn's spectacularization of pain from her and her narrator's position as white women within the larger context of the British slave trade.

I assigned Mallipeddi's brilliant chapter on Behn's *Oroonoko* to model for students a way of thinking about the "frightful Spectacles of a mangl'd King" beyond its gruesomeness: my students found themselves wondering about the fraught position of Behn's white narrator as a passive witness to such a violent, public display of colonial power.[20] One student drew attention to Mallipeddi's compelling argument for pain's intercorporeal quality in this scene: "In this encounter between the tortured body and responsive feminine imagination, bodily suffering seems contagious and transitive. Pain here does not belong exclusively to the victim, but to the witness as well. Being in the presence of the sufferer is a damaging or overwhelming experience, insofar as the effects of pain threaten the integrity of the observing self."[21] Uncomfortable with the narrator's centering of her own anguish and disgust at the scene of Oroonoko's disfigurement, my student also smartly compared this moment to more contemporary forms of white women's guilt expressed on social media that purported to amplify the messages of Black activism but actually displaced these Black voices. Many of the young white women in my classroom found themselves confronting the unintended consequences of their white guilt and the ways it can dominate the conversation at the expense of the very people they seek to support. Sympathy, what Adam Smith identified as a moral sentiment, was always already racialized in ways often hostile to Black feeling and experience. Sympathy, in other words, was never innocuous.

This strategically presentist comparison to Black Lives Matter helped the class unpack how Black pain and its representations came to structure a moralized, sympathetic set of discourses about slavery and its later abolition often led by white women. As students talked through in later online discussion posts, sympathy in the case of *Oroonoko* is hardly innocuous; Behn's narrator only understands Oroonoko's abuse as a tragedy because he was African nobility with a proximity to whiteness that allowed him to assimilate more easily.[22] To witness pain itself becomes a moral responsibility that implicates all of us in the room as Behn's novella invites us to occupy her narrator's position as passive spectator. *Does Black pain only matter when it is the pain of an exemplary, privileged individual? Who determines the validity of that pain and shapes the response to it?* These questions implicated all of us in the classroom as we navigated a fragmented archive whose enslaved subjects "have disappeared into merchant ledgers, planter inventories . . . [that] renders the processes that put them there indiscernible."[23] Literature reanimates some of these processes, but the kinds of questions we ask before and after that reanimation matter, especially if such questions fail to interrogate those processes or begin to exclude more than they include.

We would confront these questions again in our reading of *The History of Mary Prince*. Born into slavery in Bermuda, Prince lived through extreme forms of mental and physical abuse by her owners, including debilitating work in saltwater ponds that caused her to suffer acute rheumatism for the rest of her life. Dictating the account to Thomas Pringle, Prince described in graphic detail the abuse done to her as an enslaved woman. Many students bristled at Prince's unflinching accounts, which so resembled Behn's depiction of Oroonoko, and some students of color shared family histories full of painful stories like Prince's. "Is this just becoming trauma porn?" a student asked out of frustration at the end of one of our class sessions. Was I inadvertently producing empathy exhaustion through my selection of texts? While I tried to frame our discussion of Prince with multiple content warnings and prefatory reading that contextualized her account in terms of a broader spectrum of Black lived experience in the period, I ultimately found myself still uneasy with the affective intensity of the material and the potentially triggering ways in which I was misrepresenting a history of Blackness defined exclusively by spectacular violence now blanketing the news cycle.[24]

I wanted to affirm that Black pain mattered by exposing my students to examples where bodies "make visible a history (and a historicity) that was already there."[25] But I was also ethically committed to resisting another racist line of thinking of this period related to slavery's dependency on the discipline and disabling of Black bodies: the enduring myth of "black invulnerability" where "those of African descent *cannot* suffer, or at least cannot feel as much pain as people of other races."[26] My students immediately pointed out just how prevalent this myth still is, particularly in Western health care systems, where Black patients disproportionately experience medical providers and caregivers ignoring or questioning their pain and suffering. I particularly admired this presentist connection because the students did not conflate race and disability but instead worked through the historical co-constitution of anti-Blackness and ableism as two facets of the British colonial project.

In retrospect, I do not feel I successfully addressed the "trauma porn" issue, either for my students or for myself. But I have found myself turning to Ramzi Fawaz's notion of "affective curation," a pedagogical model "that centralizes the value of intentionally eliciting, or 'triggering,' uncomfortable affective responses from students in the classroom in order to develop new strategies for returning, rerouting, or altogether altering students' sense perceptions of the world."[27] In this model, the issue is not whether or not the painful material is triggering; instead, it is about how that triggering gets framed and how we train students to develop critical thinking skills that help them make sense of their affective responses—whether outrage, disgust, ambivalence. Many students were embarrassed about their ignorance of this history, but the pedagogical mode of affective curation is less invested in "correcting" or "exposing" ignorance than it is in working carefully through the messiness of that encounter where much is intuited and felt but not necessarily theorized. Affective curation, as I understand it, inhabits the myriad of responses to painful topics to generate interpretations and analytical frameworks grounded in those deeply personal affective responses without disavowing them.

The goal, as I have come to understand, is not to have a painless class (if that is even possible); rather, it is the cultivation of an interdependent learning community that is accountable to pain's polymorphousness and the different ways it is lived out among both teachers and students. To be accountable to pain is not the same as dwelling in it—it is to learn from it and from the longer histories of those who have suffered to begin creating what Eve Tuck has called "desire-based" frameworks that are "intent on depathologizing the experiences of dispossessed and disenfranchised communities so that people are seen as more than broken and conquered."[28] Thinking through, and with experiences of, pain in its multiple registers is thus the work of *cripistemology*: a compassionate knowledge-making process that takes pain seriously, as more than suffering, more than hurt, but instead as a robust set of embodyminded experiences that enable us to access historical structures of feeling whose politics we are just now beginning to understand.

NOTES

1. David Sweeney Coombs and Danielle Coriale, "V21 Forum on Strategic Presentism: Introduction," *Victorian Studies* 59, no. 1 (2016): 88. See also "Manifesto of the V21 Collective," V21, March 24, 2015, http://v21collective.org/manifesto-of-the-v21-collective-ten-theses/.
2. The term "bodymind" has been used in disability studies and disability communities to emphasize how disability often takes both physical and cognitive forms. I draw on Margaret Price's use of the term because it acknowledges how "mental and physical processes not only affect each other but also give rise to each other—that is, because they tend to act as one, even though they are conventionally understood as two." See Margaret Price, "The Bodymind Problem and the Possibilities of Pain," *Hypatia* 30, no. 1 (Winter 2015): 269. See also Sami Schalk, *Bodyminds Reimagined* (Durham, NC: Duke University Press, 2018) for Schalk's application of this term in relation to disability in Black women's speculative fiction.
3. Marisela Martinez-Cola, Rocco English, Jennifer Min, Jonathan Peraza, Jamesetta Tambah, and Christina Yebuah, "When Pedagogy Is Painful: Teaching in Tumultuous Times," *Teaching Sociology* 46, no. 2 (2018): 108.
4. For an account of my remote teaching and strategies for more accessible pedagogy, see Travis Chi Wing Lau, "Access from Afar: Cultivating Inclusive, Flexible Classrooms after COVID-19," *Nineteenth-Century Gender Studies* 17, no. 1 (2021), http://ncgsjournal.com/issue171/lau.html.
5. Sara Ahmed, "An Affinity of Hammers," *TSQ: Transgender Studies Quarterly* 13, no. 1/2 (2016): 22.
6. Alison Kafer, "Un/Safe Disclosures: Scenes of Disability and Trauma," *Journal of Literary and Cultural Disability Studies* 10, no. 1 (2016): 13.
7. For more on access intimacy and disability justice, see Mia Mingus, "Access Intimacy: The Missing Link," Leaving Evidence, August 15, 2017, https://leavingevidence.wordpress.com/2011/05/05/access-intimacy-the-missing-link/.
8. Elaine Scarry, *The Body in Pain: The Making and Unmaking of the World* (Oxford: Oxford University Press, 1987), 4.
9. Keith Wailoo, *Pain: A Political History* (Baltimore: Johns Hopkins University Press, 2014), 11–12.
10. William Hay, *Deformity: An Essay* (London: R. and J. Dodsley, 1859), 6. See also Kathleen James-Cavan's annotated edition of *William Hay: Deformity, an Essay* (Victoria, BC: English Literary Studies Editions, 2004).
11. Hay, *Deformity*, 26–27.
12. Alyson Patsavas, "Recovering a Cripistemology of Pain: Leaky Bodies, Connective Tissue, and Feeling Discourse," *Journal of Literary & Cultural Disability Studies* 8, no. 2 (2014): 216.
13. Mary Wortley Montagu, *Six Town Eclogues: With some other Poems* (London, 1747), 32–37; Mary Jones, *Miscellanies in Prose and Verse* (London, 1750), 79–80.
14. To provide context for this literary figure of the scarred or pockmarked woman, I paired excerpts of Felicity Nussbaum's *The Limits of the Human: Fictions of Anomaly, Race, and Gender* (Cambridge: Cambridge University Press, 2003), with David E. Shuttleton's *Smallpox and the Literary Imagination, 1660–1820* (Cambridge: Cambridge University Press, 2007).
15. Jones, "After the Small Pox," lines 10–12.
16. For an account of my own experience of reading Hay's *Essay* for the first time, see my essay "William Hay, or an Obsession," in *Valentine*, special issue 2019, *The Rambling*, February 14, 2019, https://the-rambling.com/2019/02/14/valentines-lau/.
17. Eli Clare, *Brilliant Imperfection: Grappling with Cure* (Durham, NC: Duke University Press, 2017), 112.

18. Christina Sharpe, *In the Wake: On Blackness and Being* (Durham, NC: Duke University Press, 2016), 7.
19. Ramesh Mallipeddi, *Spectacular Suffering: Witnessing Slavery in the Eighteenth-Century British Atlantic* (Charlottesville: University of Virginia Press, 2016), 3.
20. *Oroonoko*, ed. Tiffany Potter (Peterborough, ON: Broadview, 2020) 83.
21. Mallipeddi, *Spectacular Suffering*, 44.
22. Mallipeddi, *Spectacular Suffering*, 49.
23. Jennifer L. Morgan, *Reckoning with Slavery: Gender, Kinship, and Capitalism in the Early Black Atlantic* (Durham, NC: Duke University Press, 2021), 20.
24. Gretchen Gerzina's *Black London: Life before Emancipation* (New Brunswick, NJ: Rutgers University Press, 1995) remains an invaluable resource for contextualizing Black lived experience in the period.
25. Bakary Diaby, "Feeling Black, Feeling Back: Fragility and Romanticism," *Symbiosis: Transatlantic Literary and Cultural Relations* 23, no. 1 (2019): 5.
26. Diaby, "Feeling Black, Feeling Back," 10. For more on racial science and Black insensibility, see also Joanna Bourke's *The Story of Pain: From Prayer to Painkillers* (Oxford: Oxford University Press, 2014), and Andrew Curran's *The Anatomy of Blackness: Science and Slavery in an Age of Enlightenment* (Baltimore: Johns Hopkins University Press, 2011).
27. Fawaz, "How to Make a Queer Scene, or Notes toward a Practice of Affective Curation," *Feminist Studies* 42, no. 3 (2016): 760.
28. Eve Tuck, "Suspending Damage: A Letter to Communities," *Harvard Educational Review* 79, no. 3 (2009): 416.

9

ANTICOLONIAL APPROACHES TO TEACHING COLONIAL ART HISTORIES

Emily C. Casey

I HAVE BEEN EXPLORING HOW TO take an explicitly anticolonial approach to teaching the colonial art histories of the Americas in order to make transparent to students and others how these studies relate to the colonialist forms of governance and knowledge production that order the conditions of contemporary scholarship and pedagogy. The interdisciplinary approaches of eighteenth-century studies increasingly aim to "globalize" the field's historic Eurocentrism, and to speak to the polities and politics that shape the global now. However, how can we globalize eighteenth-century studies without attending to the histories of imperial violence, settler-colonization, capitalism, and white supremacy that not only shaped the period but continue to affect our contemporary world? In this chapter I discuss how I have worked to introduce decolonial thinking and anticolonial strategies into my undergraduate art history course "Colonial Art Across the Americas," which I first developed and taught while working as a tenure-track professor in art history at St. Mary's College of Maryland. I show how I relate the themes of the course to the historical and present-day built environment of the institution, and also touch on how the strategies and materials of art history, particularly the practice of prolonged visual analysis, support anticolonial thinking in the classroom and can be applied in other pedagogical contexts. Art history and material culture studies take up physical objects as aesthetic, practical, and interpretive windows onto the past. Working with them is an opportunity, as the editors of this volume put it, to make the past "matter." This not only serves to make the eighteenth century materially present in the now, but also invites consideration of the relationship between an object's presence and the contemporary moment in which we are teaching and learning. Teaching eighteenth-century colonial American art history has challenged me to remain accountable for the colonialist histories that link what happens in the classroom to the larger contexts of my students' lives and work and my own.

In this chapter, in which I share some of my efforts at decolonizing how I teach eighteenth-century colonial art histories, I start by reflecting on my particular position in relation to anticolonial practice, both as a settler-colonizer and as a participant in the colonialist structure of higher education. I am white, an early-career scholar. Since completing my PhD in 2017, I have been engaged in the dual projects of expanding my knowledge of the cultural and material histories of empire and colonialism in the Americas, and of challenging my methods of teaching this material. I began this work while teaching at St. Mary's. Designated as the public honors college for the state of Maryland, it is a small, residential liberal arts college that is also a state institution with in-state tuition. Because I was working as a pre-tenure assistant professor at a small public institution with an emphasis on undergraduate teaching, my intellectual and social commitment to decolonizing my curriculum and pedagogy was often in conflict with limited resources of time, and the weight of service and scholarship expectations. As of May 2021, when my institution eliminated its art history program and my tenure-track position, I also became contingent.

In the aftermath of my former institution's elimination of the art history program, I have been working through the question of how and whether the eighteenth-century syllabus can be decolonized alongside my own experience of academic precarity. Faced with the challenges shared by many faculty—overloaded teaching and service responsibilities, administrative hostility to the humanities, the unique hardships of working through a pandemic in academia, and professional contingency—the sense of responsibility I have each semester to challenge the colonialist biases that inform my pedagogy can seem overwhelming. In this context, the labor conditions of instructors at the front line of teaching are an increasingly important factor in how we consider the opportunities and limits of anticolonial practice in the classroom and beyond. Settling into a new institution, and getting to know its peoples and histories—especially those who have been displaced or erased—takes many years, and is an ongoing process. Being a student in relation to institutional histories and local pasts, remaining self-critical about how pedagogy and practice is tied to settler-colonial paradigms, and constantly assessing and shifting approaches to the material and students is essential but demanding work. In my own practice, it has required me to identify and incorporate materials and histories unfamiliar to me, and to trouble not only my teaching practice but my own sense of self vis-à-vis my students and course subjects. For those whose labor is contingent, these are especially challenging practices, even as they become more urgent. What is more, for those who are pre-tenure, are on short-term contracts, or are otherwise working without a permanent commitment from the institution, offering anticolonial pedagogy that might implicate the institution and its systems in the historic and ongoing project of Western colonization is a risky move. Higher education's investment in a capitalist profit model that exploits underpaid intellectual and physical labor, promotes diversity and inclusion while undercutting its resources, and fosters asymmetrical relationships with the land and local communities, stems from the institution's settler-colonial legacy. Making transparent the relationship between the colonial past that we teach and the spaces and conditions of our classrooms requires reckoning with the colonialist dimensions of contemporary higher education.

The purpose of this chapter is to provide a reflection and road map for how decolonization theory can be incorporated into teaching the eighteenth century. Decolonization theory emphasizes the relationship between the intellectual labor of academia and the positionality of its subjects in relation to colonial systems. It offers those who engage with it guidance and examples of how to position oneself in relation to the places, communities, and resources that make academic work possible.[1] Here, I show how I work to enact this praxis in the classroom with students, specifically through the prism of material history and the built environment. Each class, each term, is part of an iterative process. Unlearning the standards of mastery and expertise that order Western academia involves adopting a more humble relationship to my teaching: one in which I don't expect to do it all at once, but also am motivated by a sense of responsibility to histories and communities beyond the institution. As Diana Epelbaum describes in chapter 6, such engagement not only enhances how I teach the eighteenth century but also transforms my scholarship on the period, as it challenges me to consider my own position in relation to the materials and communities for which and to whom I speak. This process requires that I as the teacher-scholar dwell in the discomfort of my own involvement in settler-colonialism's ongoing irresolution, through my position—however contingent—of institutional power in the classroom.

Throughout this chapter, I use both the terms "decolonial" and "anticolonial" to describe thoughts and actions that seek to unsettle colonialist histories. I use "decolonial" to describe the social praxis of dismantling colonialism, and its associated body of thought; and I characterize my pedagogical interventions as "anticolonial." Like recent discussions about the term "antiracist," "anticolonial" refers to actions or strategies that resist or unsettle settler-colonization, rather than to a consistent state of being.[2] Especially in relation to my own identity as a white person who has at times—whether intentionally or not—benefited from and upheld the colonialist enterprise, my use of the term "anticolonial" as opposed to "decolonial" in relation to my pedagogy is an effort to identify the ongoing, and always partial, nature of these efforts. Decolonial thinkers, particularly Eve Tuck and K. Wayne Yang, have rightfully argued that decolonization is not a metaphor for diversity and inclusion efforts. Rather, decolonization refers to the returning of colonized lands to their Indigenous communities, who have been violently displaced, disenfranchised, and slaughtered by settler-colonizers.[3] Another important distinction between anticolonial interventions and decolonial theory is the direction that they face. Anticolonial approaches still to a greater or lesser degree center colonialism, and the colonizing power. By contrast, decolonization theory decenters the colonial power by refusing its self-declared primacy in Indigenous people's histories, and instead directs itself toward a present and future of Indigenous sovereignty. A risk in anticolonial work is recursively uplifting colonialism simply by continuing to give it sustained attention, even if it is with the goal of critiquing it. At this time, while my courses on colonial American art histories create room to discuss contemporary Indigenous calls for the return of land and resources, advocating for these aims is not the class's primary objective. As I continue to learn how to orient my own thinking and pedagogy toward solidarity with Indigenous peoples, I am working to incorporate more ways to emphasize decolonial futurities. For now, in a class devoted to the study of the past, introducing anticolonial means of studying colonial histories—which are largely unknown in their specifics to undergraduate students—is still an important intervention; in this context, anticolonial, rather than decolonial, better describes the nature of my teaching. Having taught this course over the first five years of my teaching career, I have experienced firsthand that it takes time and patience to do this work.

As an art historian, my approach to introducing decolonial and anticolonial ways of thinking to students is rooted in the methods of the discipline. One aim of my course "Colonial Art Across the Americas" is to introduce students to art historical practices that can pose an intervention in the dynamics of power and control enacted on and in colonial spaces. Unlike literature or history, art history is rarely offered in public high schools, and therefore often entirely new to students in my classroom. Art history's hallmark practice, that of close looking, provides students with an accessible means of analyzing and critiquing the forms and structures of colonialism. As complex cultural objects, the visual and material cultures of colonialism often communicate more than they intend, especially in the context of the archive's violent erasures and silences. The practice of visual analysis, which I'll unpack later in this chapter, involves identifying and interpreting the significance of a work's formal aspects, including its composition, representation, and material. The process equips students with the skills to engage and question a diverse range of cultural forms. Sustained, collaborative visual analysis unfolds over time, fostering organic classroom discussion in which students learn from each other and build their knowledge together. This practice can be a tool for anticolonial thinking in the classroom. Another goal of this chapter, then, is to illuminate how art historical strategies like visual analysis and the practice of close looking have their own distinct place in anticolonial approaches to eighteenth-century scholarship and pedagogy.

In my pedagogy, I see the practice of collective visual analysis of colonial objects in the classroom as a model for other anticolonial strategies that likewise benefit from gestation over the course of the semester. One of these is the practice of land acknowledgment—identifying the history of the land that we occupy, and honoring the Indigenous people, past and present, of that particular place. In her essay on land acknowledgments, Eugenia Zuroski notes that while common practice places the acknowledgment in the preface, disconnected from the body of scholarship, acknowledging the place and peoples in which one works isn't something that should just be dispensed with up front, but instead ought to "frame and weave its way into your work."[4] For students, land acknowledgments can become a method of deeply looking at the landscape and its history. As another means of close looking—at the environment around us, at our own involvement in the histories that we are studying—conversations about our local context can unfold over weeks, evolving and deepening as students' knowledge and understanding grows. Both land acknowledgments and visual analysis ask students to look differently, or to search for more than meets the eye.

As an ongoing component of the course, acknowledging the history of the land upon which we study challenges assumptions that the classroom is a "neutral," context-less bubble in which learning happens. As Travis Chi Wing Lau notes in chapter 8 in this volume, many students may approach the eighteenth century as a time and place far removed from the concerns of their present. The process of learning and acknowledging the history of the land we stand on, and its peoples, urges students and instructors to connect the past and present and understand their position, and responsibility, within a wider network of relationships. I am not from Maryland—and did not live there most of the time I taught the course; however, the St. Mary's students are primarily drawn from across the state. St. Mary's in-state tuition has traditionally made a liberal arts education accessible to a student population that would find private colleges financially out of reach. For this reason, emphasizing the geographic and historic specificity of our colonial study charged students not only to consider the institutional context of their classroom learning, but also to reflect on their lifelong relationship to the colonial legacies of the state. By prompting students and teachers to look differently at the local landscape, land acknowledgments call in considerations of the colonial pasts and presents that shape the conditions of our learning.

Zuroski describes the work inherent in placing academic practice in connection with the land and its peoples as "illuminating relationships of responsibility and calling people into them."[5] Relationships of any kind are never one-and-done transactions. Rather, they unfold over time, through an accumulation of exchanges and experiences. They are expanded by gestures of generosity, and tested by mistakes and failures. Classrooms are like this as well. They are communities founded on relationships between faculty and students that take time to establish and grow. Good teaching involves not only expertise, but also curiosity and a willingness to learn. Research shows that successful pedagogy balances preparation with improvisation.[6] Colonialist strategies of mastery—be it of material or students—leads to worse, not better, learning outcomes. Instead, cultivating intentional communities founded on respect and reciprocity leads to more engaged students who better retain what they learn. The inherent power dynamic between students and teachers in the classroom only makes more urgent this responsibility to foster reciprocity rather than control. For teachers of the eighteenth century, engaging with decolonization theory and practice is imperative, not only because, as Zuroski notes in the same essay, "there is nothing from the eighteenth century to which the history of colonization is not relevant, and that history generates a web of present relations that demand our attention," but also because the classroom is the space in which we already should be weaving webs of association and relationship.[7]

ART HISTORICAL VISUAL ANALYSIS AS AN ANTICOLONIAL STRATEGY

Close study of objects and landscapes affords an opportunity to think both through and outside the bounds of empire when considering the diverse and overlapping colonial cultures of the Americas. While the movements of specific materials—an Indian textile or a Japanese folding screen—were instigated by global imperial networks designed to produce capital and power for the Europeans who oversaw them, the resulting creation and use of objects can be an expression of survival and resistance for colonized peoples. To unpack this tension, I devote significant amounts of class time to extended visual analysis of art works and objects. Here again, the chief factor is time, as deep looking requires students to sit with an image for an extended period. Art historian Jennifer Roberts has written about the effect of this patient looking. In her classes at Harvard, she takes advantage of the local art museums to assign students the task of sitting for three hours in person in front of a work of art that they plan to write about.[8] While Roberts's method is on the extreme end, I frequently will spend forty-five minutes or more of class time with a single image up on the screen, which students will describe, question, and interpret, as a means of exploring the main issues of a course. For literary scholars, this practice is akin to that of close reading, where the same sort of process takes place with a text. However, for undergraduate students the visual image can provide an immediate entry-point that the parsing of period language often precludes. This accessibility in itself has the potential to make visual analysis an anticolonial practice, as it belies the knowledge hierarchies that often make classrooms exclusionary places. When I simply ask students to tell me what they see, everyone can participate.

In "Colonial Art Across the Americas," I begin the semester with Stradanus's *Allegory of America* (1587–1588), which depicts Amerigo Vespucci "awakening" the continent of America, personified as a nude Indigenous woman arising from a hammock (figure 9.1).

Images like these are masterworks in colonial ideology, casting European arrival in the Americas in terms that are masculine, Christian, and martial.

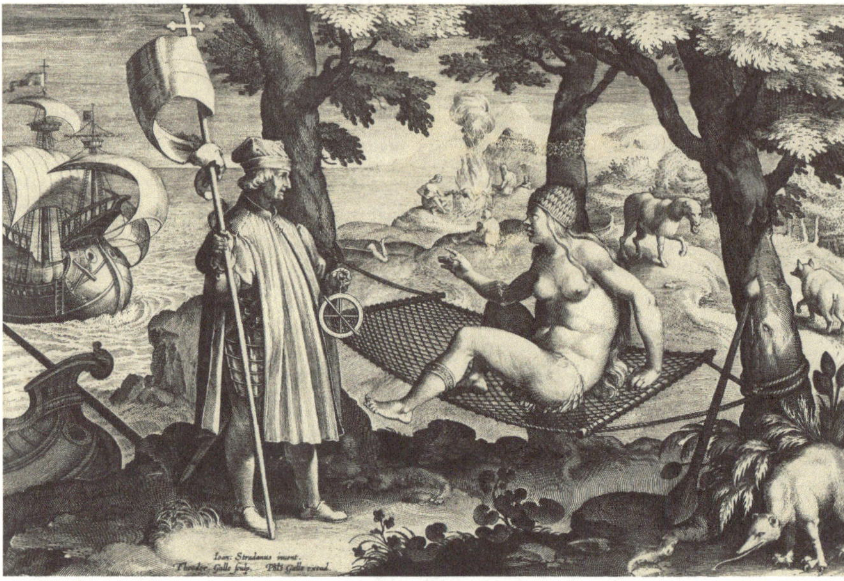

Figure 9.1 Theodoor Galle (engraver) after a drawing by Jan van der Straet, called Stradanus; published by Philips Galle, *Allegory of America*, from *New Inventions of Modern Times (Nova Reperta)*, plate 1 of 19, ca. 1690, Netherlandish. Engraving, 10⅝ × 7⅞ in. Courtesy of The Metropolitan Museum of Art, Elisha Whittelsey Collection, Elisha Whittelsey Fund, 1949.

By contrast, Indigenous peoples are depicted as effeminate, uncivilized, and a mixture of innocent and savage. Behind America, another group of Native figures is shown roasting human body parts over a bonfire. Part of what makes the work a successful starting point for students is how blatant its colonialist meaning is. The objects and symbols in the work are quickly identifiable, and contrasts like that between America's nude woman's body and Vespucci's clothed man, can be easily interpreted.

Learning the visual language of colonialism creates a foundation for dismantling its logic as the course proceeds. Stradanus's print is an opportunity to overlay the historic formation of colonialist ideology with its present-day effects in higher education. Western approaches to learning, rooted in Enlightenment philosophy, assume that all forms of knowledge can and should be acquired and "mastered" by the scholar, who, like Vespucci, is historically coded as white, European, and male. This way of thinking mirrors the logic of colonialism, which sees desirable territories as "empty land" open and welcome to the claims of the colonizer. What is missing from these Western constructions of knowledge-formation is an awareness of culturally situated forms of knowledge, and a conception of reciprocity between the scholar and their material. In Western higher education today, this colonial approach to subject mastery is evident when white scholars claim expertise over histories and ideas related to Indigenous and other colonized peoples without considering their subjective position in relation to that body of knowledge, or the peoples who are its caretakers. In this way, white academics often perpetuate the harms of colonialism by re-instantiating colonialist forms of mastery and control in their scholarly work. Examining the colonial eighteenth century alongside my students through the close study of objects and images prompts me to remain aware of and resistant to those pedagogical modes of expertise and mastery that are tied to colonialist forms of surveillance and control.

Works like *Allegory of America* allow students to question Western European intellectual and political modes of mastery and control by teaching them to not take images at face value. Learning about the practice of early modern image production teaches students that Stradanus, and many other European artists and publishers like him, never traveled to the Americas or saw the flora and fauna that they depict. This mediation between colonized spaces and their images encourages students to question the perspective of the settler-colonial eye, which sees selectively and from a distance. Learning to be skeptical of what colonial art shows us also allows my students and me to be mindful of the biases we bring with us to our looking. When do we see or not see the contributions and perspectives of colonized peoples? How do we use a visual and material culture of colonialism to see past master narratives of colonial control? In their article "Hybridity and Its Discontents," scholars of colonial Latin America Carolyn Dean and Dana Leibsohn argue that postcolonial studies' formulation of "hybrid" to describe objects and things of mixed European and non-European descent risks flattening out the complexity of exchanges within the uneven power relations of colonization.[9] Further, they critique the art historical assumption that hybridity can always be visually identified, offering examples of how material practices and knowledge ways might introduce Indigenous influences into objects that have a normative European form: "The deception of visibility . . . permits the denial of indigenous activity in building the colonial world."[10] With this prompt to question the ways in which the very practices of art history can also have a colonizing effect, my students can begin to consider how Indigenous and Black ways of knowledge, experiences, and creative expressions are present in the colonial landscape in ways visible and invisible, documented and undocumented.

Our practice of close looking, and our critical approach to the practice of looking, come to fruition when we encounter works made by colonized peoples. Among these works is a portrait of Scottish textile merchant William Duguid painted in Boston in 1773 by Prince Demah—an enslaved man of African descent (figure 9.2).

Demah's enslaver, Henry Barnes, took Demah to England where he received some artistic training; back in North American, Barnes hired Demah out to other

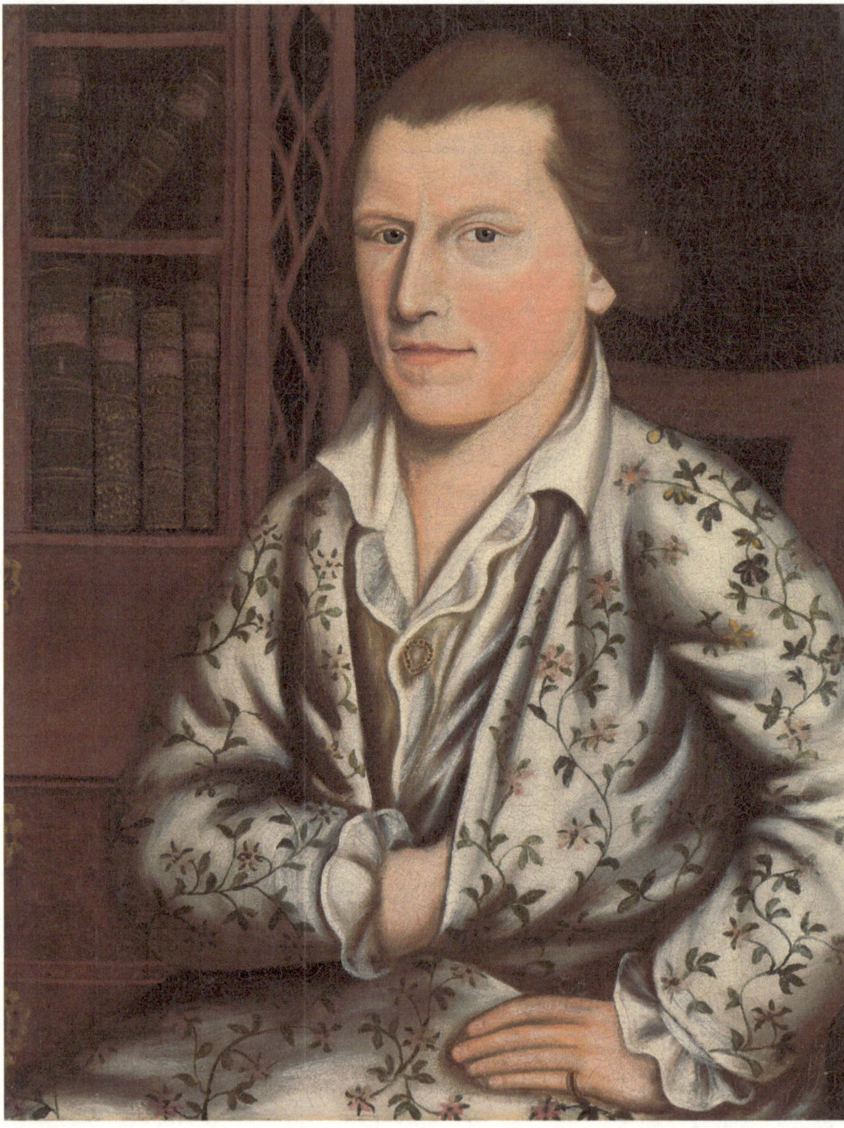

Figure 9.2 Prince Demah Barnes, *Portrait of William Duguid*, 1773, American. Oil on canvas, 20¾ × 15¾. Courtesy of The Metropolitan Museum of Art, Friends of the American Wing Fund, 2010.

white colonial Bostonians to paint their portraits.[11] When I introduce this painting to my students, their knowledge of colonial self-fashioning helps them to quickly identify the ways in which the sitter asserts his status and wealth. They note that he displays his cosmopolitan identity through imported clothes and books. They point to the authority of his posture and gaze. Using the art historical strategy of comparison, they can liken the portrait's composition and presentation of its subject to other colonial portraits made by artists of European descent across the colonized Americas, from Mexico City to New York. As they learn more about the context of the painting's creation and continue to look, they also use visual analysis to introduce anticolonial interpretations to the work. They question the uneasy relation between sitter and painter that permeates the picture. What is the effect of Demah's gaze? What might it mean for him to behold and render the image of a white oppressor? What was it like for Duguid to be seen by Demah—to place his image in the power of an enslaved person? Even as my students understand the exceptionalism in Prince Demah's access to artistic training, and the role of the man who claimed ownership of him in shaping his artistic career, they also register the anticolonial possibilities of his agency within the singular event of this portrait. Analysis of the portrait, and of the imagined dynamics between its painter and sitter, allows students to critique the totalizing effects of imperial power. Having recognized that objects and images themselves embody strategies of imperial control, they begin to identify the visible fault lines of colonial power. In the case of Prince Demah's portrait of Duguid, the uneasy relations across lines of race and freedom that bind the portrait's actors together become emblematic of the disjunctures that persist in the colonial project. Deconstructing these imperial fictions gives students a new view on their present.

THE SYLLABUS

"Colonial Art Across the Americas" takes a trans-imperial approach to the study of art and material culture in North and South America as well as the Caribbean. The globality of the eighteenth century is made visible through the frame of the colonial Americas, in which the movement of peoples, objects, and ideas from the Pacific, Asia, Africa, and the Middle East influenced the productions of diverse colonial identities. The success of the course lies as much in the multiplicity of its materials and makers—paintings, prints, architecture, and decorative arts, made by Anglo-American, Spanish, African American, and Indigenous artists—as in its geographic and cultural breadth. In counterpoint to the breadth of the vast early Americas, the course has moments of much more local focus. Through engagement with the colonial environment of the campus—in the case of St. Mary's College, the historic site of the first capital of the Maryland colony in the seventeenth century—we apply critical inquiries to our own context of learning. Asking questions about the place that organizes our studies emphasizes learning's site-specificity. In the United States, a settler-colonial state, this is especially important. These more local examinations help to keep the stakes and costs of settler-colonialism, as we encounter it in the larger course, specific and urgent.

The course was inspired by a 2011 special issue of *Winterthur Portfolio*, "Objects in Motion: Visual and Material Culture Across Colonial North America," co-edited by Wendy Bellion and Monica Domínguez Torres.[12] Their work provided an example for how to think materially about cross-cultural currents of early America. Since this landmark publication, the charge to expand the borders of colonial American histories has been taken up by interdisciplinary scholars. More importantly, scholars have increasingly taken seriously their prompt to consider how art and material objects "help produce early North American cultures."[13] As J. M. Mancini has argued, examining the movement of things across colonial borders offers insight into the multiplicity of exchanges and sites for the creation of colonial culture. Not merely trade and civil forms of exchange, but also theft, looting, and violent conflict, were ways in which objects changed hands, expanding and further entangling colonial peoples and regions.[14]

One of the greatest insights I have gained from teaching this class is realizing how wholly unknown these histories and material artefacts are to many of my students. Many have never been introduced to the global dimensions of colonization in the Americas, or asked to consider the depth of its lasting effects on the hemisphere. Students are often unaware of instances of resistance and rebellion by Indigenous and Black actors in the colonial Americas. They are emboldened to look differently and ask new questions when they discover how material objects can hold histories that might not be recorded elsewhere. Simply exposing students to this material, and teaching it from a perspective that does not privilege European governance and culture, is an anticolonial action. However, while this expanded curriculum has profound effects, within the classroom this more "diverse" coverage of colonial makers and objects can quickly amount to a settler move to innocence. It has the potential to instill in students, and me, the reassurance that mastering more material is sufficient to expand our frame of reference on the past. Tuck and Wang refer to this as "conscientization," writing that "the front-loading of critical consciousness building can waylay decolonization, even though the experience of teaching and learning to be critical of settler colonialism can be so powerful it can feel like it is indeed making change. Until stolen land is relinquished, critical consciousness does not translate into action that disrupts settler colonialism."[15] Simply presenting a plurality of eighteenth-century colonial voices doesn't fundamentally shift the balance of power that defines this period, and certainly doesn't change the settler-colonial dynamics that shape the institutions under whose auspices we study. It leaves unresolved our class's relation to the colonialist forms of governance and knowledge production that order our learning.

To respond to this difficulty, in "Colonial Art Across the Americas" and other courses, I have drawn a history of the institution itself—examined through college archives—into class discussions, and invited students to reflect on how the residues of historic colonialism and racial oppression remain present on the campus they know today.

For a course that treats the colonial Americas broadly, a primary challenge is scale. In addition to a geographic sweep that covers North, Central, and South America as well as the Caribbean, the colonial Americas also extend across centuries of time. The class's temporal scope spans the early modern period of European conquest and colonization, beginning with Columbus's voyage in 1492, and ending with the Haitian Revolution in 1804, with much of the semester focused in the long eighteenth century. In my course, ending with the Haitian Revolution reframes student perspectives on the historic colonial period by emphasizing the actions and agency of oppressed colonial communities, in this case the members of the African diaspora living enslaved and free in the French colony of Saint-Domingue who enacted the largest-scale successful uprising of enslaved Black people in the Americas. It also complicates students' understanding of the "Age of Revolutions," which typically they have been taught only in relation to France and the United States, by showing how Black activists instigated and inspired anticolonial calls for independence in the Atlantic world. Of course, the Haitian Revolution does not mark the end of colonization. Spanish American colonies continued to struggle for independence through the nineteenth century. Likewise, Indigenous sovereignty and resistance to settler-colonization in both North and South America stretches from the earliest moments of contact through to the present, making it clear that we are still living in a colonial period. In a similar fashion, nineteenth- and twentieth-century U.S. imperial actions in the Caribbean and Pacific also trouble the notion that colonialism is only a phenomenon of the past.

Over the course of the semester, we remain critical of the temporal and geographic borders that organize the course, as each reveals presumptions and biases that my students and I have about colonial pasts and presents. As Katherine Binhammer argues in her essay "Is the Eighteenth Century a Colonizing Temporality?," periodization centers Western colonial forms of knowledge production and organization, further marginalizing other ways of knowing, particularly Indigenous practices of memory and record keeping.[16] Discussing with students the various potential time frames of a course on the colonial Americas problematizes the colonialist dimensions of periodization and the assumptions of fields like eighteenth-century studies that rely on them. Not only does study of the colonial Americas require the context of earlier modern histories; it also reveals that colonial conditions are not only past, but also present.

While empires connect far-distant places, and adapt themselves to local contexts, they privilege the overarching perspective of the imperial center, which sees from a distance. A primary colonialist strategy of empire is to suppress local and Indigenous cultural forms and relationships in favor of the totalizing dynamic of imperial power.[17] In teaching colonial American histories, I aim to focus on local forms of colonial or colonized cultures that counteract the hegemonic lens of imperial colonialism. Doing so highlights the relationship between the "global turn" of early modern European empires, and the cultural and economic networks they engendered, and the grounded, specific forms of culture developed by colonized peoples that grew up in local contexts in response or resistance to them. The overlap between these dimensions of time and space is itself a testimony to how the "colonial period" is not past. As I will discuss later in this chapter, incorporating examples of contemporary colonial legacies or commemorations into course material can support class discussions about the continued endurance of colonial structures on local and global levels.

INCORPORATING LOCAL HISTORIES IN CLASS ASSIGNMENTS

In "Colonial Art Across the Americas," I invite students to connect their study of the colonial Americas broadly to our local and contemporary context through class assignments and field trips. While the assigned reading on the syllabus relates to the place and topic of our focus any given week, the main writing and research assignments ask students to observe their local landscape and consider ways in which the region's colonial histories are made visible or suppressed. Other assignments prompt students to unpack these questions through comparative study of other institutions commemorating colonial histories on their campuses. Teaching the course at St. Mary's, I was inspired to highlight contemporary memorials of colonial legacies because just such a project was being undertaken on campus over the four years that I was teaching there. Observing the ongoing process of designing and installing a monument to the enslaved peoples who lived and worked in the region also prompted me to think in a new way about another Maryland-specific artistic intervention marking colonialist histories—Fred Wilson's landmark exhibition *Mining the Museum* from 1992, which took place in Baltimore. Over the course of the semester at St. Mary's, I guided students in connecting local colonial histories with their contemporary markers by introducing them to the practice of land acknowledgments, assigning them local archaeological reports from the immediate region, taking them on field trips to the neighboring living history museum, and inviting the design team for what became the campus memorial to speak to the class.

Historic St. Mary's

At St. Mary's, acknowledging local colonial legacies begins by unsettling the familiar landscape of the campus. St. Mary's has a rich connection to its landscape on the shores of the St. Mary's River, which acts as an important signifier of identity for the students, and which the institution celebrates in its promotional materials. The college is situated on the traditional lands of the Piscataway and Yaocamico peoples, Algonquin-speaking members of the Confederacy of Tribes, who occupied territories spread across the area between the western Chesapeake Bay and the Potomac River. In the seventeenth century their lives were disrupted and dislocated by the colonial encroachments of English colonists who established the first capital of Maryland there, in a town they called St. Mary's City. While governmental treaties were established between Lord Baltimore and the Piscataway peoples, the ongoing threats of colonization, including broken treaties and land encroachment, forced many Piscataway and Yaocamico peoples to leave the area or retreat to the fringes of their traditional territories. Through the nineteenth century, land that is now in the college's holdings formed plantations that were worked by enslaved African laborers. The Piscataway Conoy Tribe was only formally recognized by the state of Maryland in 2012.[18] Similarly, the college only came to terms with its own legacy of slavery in the last few years, marked today by a commemorative monument to the enslaved peoples of southern Maryland.

The settler-colonial sites in and around the college campus are today commemorated by the living history museum Historic St. Mary's City. The museum includes indoor and outdoor interpretive spaces related to Maryland's early colonization in the seventeenth century. Areas of the outdoor museum highlight the *Dove*, a sailing ship that transported colonists and trade goods to Maryland shores in the seventeenth century, the colonial administration at the state house, and the production of cash crops such as tobacco. Significant to Historic St. Mary City's interpretation of settler-colonialism and its legacies is the museum's choice to focus primarily on the city's mid-seventeenth-century colonial history. Enslaved Africans were transported to the colony as early as 1642; in1663 the Maryland Assembly voted that all people of African descent who were transported to the colonies should be enslaved for life. This law prompted a shift in the colony, and in St. Mary's in particular, away from the indentured labor of English and Irish settlers to reliance on involuntary labor from people of African descent. By locating the focus of its interpretation to a moment at the midcentury, Historic St. Mary's City for a long time avoided discussing how the colony's wealth was tied to its investment in the institution of slavery.[19] Similarly, the museum's "Woodland Indian Hamlet" highlights the Indigenous group of the Yaocamico, who lived in the region in the period of colonization. However, the interpretation at the site focuses on a precontact moment, and does not explore the impacts of colonization on the community. The most recent addition to the interpretive sites at Historic St. Mary's is the "Struggle for Freedom" exhibit in a building that was the home of enslaved and free peoples of African descent who worked on a plantation in the area during the nineteenth and twentieth centuries. This exhibit is the first significant inclusion of African American history and histories of enslavement on the site. While recent changes to the museum's sites, programming, interpretive strategies, and staffing have introduced a more complicated treatment of Maryland's history of slavery, and the experiences of enslaved and free Black people in the region, this shift is slow and ongoing.

Many students in my classes were already familiar with Historic St. Mary's City because it is the site of an annual field trip for elementary school classes in the state's public school system. Students have recounted to me their memories of these field trips, including the experience of churning butter, visiting with the heritage breed cattle and pigs on the plantation, and speaking with white costumed interpreters. Returning to Historic St. Mary's as college students, and in the context of a class on the colonial Americas, caused them to reflect on how their knowledge of colonialism has been shaped by long-standing American myths about quaint European colonial cultures. Contrasting their childhood experiences of the museum with what they were learning as college students enabled them to think critically about how and for whom colonial histories are visible in the present.

Visiting the museum's plantation complex introduced students to the physical labor involved in tobacco cultivation, and offered insight into the global networks of trade that brought livestock, plants, housing goods, and more from all corners of the world to rural Maryland in the seventeenth and eighteenth centuries. However, it also prompted them to question the relative absence of histories of enslavement in museum interpretation, and the museum's choice to focus on a time period before large-scale plantation production prompted white colonists to turn to unfree African labor. Similarly, students learned how colonial visual media, such as John White's watercolor depictions of Algonquin-speaking Indians published in Theodor de Bry's *A briefe and true report of the new found land of Virginia* (1590), informed the design of interpretive sites at the museum. This inclusion of colonial archives also led students to wonder about the lack of discussion of the complex negotiations between Indigenous peoples and English colonizers in these same sites. My students' preparation to make these critiques stemmed both from our practice of close visual analysis in the classroom—which had taught them to look carefully and consider the meaning of every detail they saw—and from the openness of Historic St. Mary's educators to share the process and challenges of interpreting in the museum context. While I encouraged students to bring a critical lens to our visits, my ability to guide them through unpacking what was present and absent in the museum's installations came from my own collaboration with the staff on site.

Exhibit: Mining the Museum

Visiting Historic St. Mary's in person enabled us to question how colonial histories are being shaped in the twenty-first century for learning audiences that included children, college students, and adults. We contextualized our reckoning with very local colonial legacies through a study of a landmark reinterpretation of Maryland history that took place in Baltimore in 1992. Fred Wilson's *Mining the Museum* is a classic case study in the practice of institutional critique. Wilson, an African American artist from New York, staged an installation about race and material culture at the Maryland Historical Society, through collaboration with The Contemporary—a noncollecting Baltimore museum without its own dedicated space. In preparation for the show, Wilson explored the on-view collection of the Historical Society, as well as its vast storage, looking for objects that spoke to histories of race and identity. He then recontextualized these objects in the Society's galleries using curatorial strategies such as layout, lighting, and labels. Examples of the resulting installation included a display case labeled "Metalwork" that included elaborate sterling silver tea services alongside iron manacles used to shackle enslaved people. Another room exhibited colonial and early national portraits of white families and children, with gallery spotlights redirected to illuminate the Black children relegated to the paintings' margins. Wilson wrote new labels and recorded audio to reinterpret these works, giving a voice to these long-ignored subjects, and probing their status as attendants, servants, and pets in the pictures.[20] I introduced students to the exhibition through photographs of the gallery installation and written and recorded interviews with Wilson, who has spoken widely on the project.

While the exhibition is frequently cited in academic and museum settings, for students at St. Mary's who have been raised learning Maryland history as local history, it was additionally illuminating. In his work at the Historical Society, Wilson used the institution's own collection to highlight slavery's ubiquitous presence in the fabric of Maryland history, effectively undercutting narratives that painted Maryland as an antislavery state because it joined the Union cause during the Civil War. Similarly, Wilson revealed and questioned the erasure of Indigenous lives from the state's history. When Wilson began working on *Mining the Museum*, people at the museum told him that there were no longer Indigenous people in Maryland. This claim, from the predominantly white museum leadership, was indicative of the state's larger erasure of Indigenous people from its polity and history. During his time at the Historical Society, Wilson conducted community outreach that connected him with Indigenous communities in the Baltimore area. Community members shared with Wilson photographs that documented their peoples' presence and survivance in the region.[21] Wilson incorporated these materials into a gallery of the exhibition that contrasted stereotyped sculptures of "cigar store Indians" with the living history of Maryland's Indigenous communities.[22] In the installation, the sculptures are turned with their back to the viewer, facing the photographs of Indigenous Marylanders that are hung on the wall. This gesture appropriates the caricatured figures for an expression of community identity and solidarity. With their backs turned, their forms are not available for consumption in the way that they were designed to be as advertisements at the front of Euro-American stores; rather, they are in intimate communication with a living Native history represented by the materials that community members shared with Wilson. Just as a class visit to Historic St. Mary's made students rethink their experiences of the living history museum on elementary school field trips, studying Wilson's exhibition of Maryland history gave them new insight into their own understanding of the place where they had grown up.

My own approach to Wilson's work—which I have been familiar with since I was a college student myself—changed while I taught it in a Maryland college. Prior to this I had too often considered *Mining the Museum*'s Maryland context as incidental to its broader themes and national importance. Focusing on its rootedness in specific regional histories illuminated its relationship to the city in which it was exhibited. Students shared with me their perceptions of how legacies of slavery and racial oppression had shaped the landscape of the Baltimore in which they lived today, and how the state's inconsistent acknowledgment of its Black and Indigenous histories informed their own cultural formations. In this respect, Wilson—a New Yorker, and therefore also an outsider to Maryland culture and politics when he curated the exhibit—became a model to me of how to engage with local peoples and histories in critical as well as community-focused ways. Speaking with my students about their own associations with Maryland history made me more mindful of how these local narratives inform individual perspectives on the material encountered in the classroom. In the classroom the students, who came from diverse regional and cultural backgrounds across the state, shared with each other their own Maryland experiences, gaining new perspectives on the uneven legacies and visibility of settler-colonialism.

Exhibit: Commemorative to the Enslaved Peoples of Southern Maryland

My commitment to dedicating significant classroom time to exploring local colonial legacies was in part generated by an ongoing process of recovering these histories that was unfolding on campus during my time at St. Mary's. In 2016, archaeological evidence indicating the site of living quarters for enslaved families was uncovered on campus during routine excavation in preparation for building a new athletic stadium. These artifacts, including ceramics, bottle glass, and tobacco pipes, dated from the eighteenth and nineteenth centuries when the land was part of plantation properties worked by enslaved African American laborers.[23] While these remains predated the foundation of the college, their presence on what is today college-owned land sparked a discussion about Maryland's legacy of slavery and the college's historic complicity in practices of enslavement. At about the same time, the college archivist identified documentary evidence that in the nineteenth century, enslaved persons resided at the women's seminary that later became St. Mary's College, as servants to student boarders.[24]

Like other higher educational institutions who have histories of enslavement, St. Mary's took the decision to establish a memorial to those African Americans who had lived and worked the land in bondage. After a design competition, the artistic team Re:Site was selected to make the monument that is known as the Commemorative to the Enslaved Peoples of Southern Maryland. Their design, titled *From Absence to Presence*, consists of a simple, reflective metal house structure meant to evoke the dwellings of the enslaved inhabitants, and intentionally echoes the "ghost frames" marking other colonial buildings that dot the landscape at Historic St. Mary's. The exterior of the house is punctured by an erasure poem created by the African American writer Quenton Baker that draws from eighteenth- and nineteenth-century runaway slave advertisements that were local to the region. The intention of the poem is to repurpose these documents of oppression into a lyric expression of the Black people who lived and resisted in the area. Like Wilson's installation of the cigar store Indians, the enclosed, reflective structure of the house is meant to make visible the presence of historically erased community members—in this case enslaved people of Africa descent—while also emphasizing their autonomy. The house-like structure remains a private space that cannot be entered, thus preserving the internal life of its inhabitants from the eyes of visitors. By day, the mirrored surface of the monument reflects the faces of its visitors, asking them to consider their place in the history it commemorates. By night, interior lights in the structure shine through the apertures made by the text, casting the form of the poem onto the surrounding land. Re:Site characterized this effect as recalling the illumination of the North Star, which led Black freedom seekers to safety. The unfolding of the design process allowed students in my classes to engage critically with it from beginning to end. Working with the visual documentation offered by the design team, we analyzed the form and meaning of the monument, considering how it meshed with existing interpretations of the colonial past, as well as how it made visible the legacies of oppression and resistance that had long been obscured. Crafting written assignments that analyzed the form and effect of the design allowed me to link this contemporary monument with the course's broader historical study. Students delivered presentations about other monuments commemorating those who were enslaved on college campuses, including Martin Puryear's monument at Brown University and Do Ho Suh's monument at the University of North Carolina. Considering the designs, interpretation, and siting of these monuments brought up important considerations of how this history would be remembered at St. Mary's.

Consistently over the course of our study, students expressed concern over the location of St. Mary's memorial next to the new athletic stadium. While this situation reflected where the archaeological remains were found, the juxtaposition of sporting events—and all that they represent within college culture—with the somber tone of the monument troubled students. It was a reminder that the stadium was in fact physically built upon land that had once housed enslaved people, and held some of the only material evidence of their presence in the region. Students' discussion of how the activities of the stadium might dilute the reflective nature of the monument led into a broader consideration of how monuments alone do not ensure remembrance. Similarly, we sought to work through the tension between the college's promotional, celebratory goals of the stadium and the monument's call to self-reflection and responsibility. Athletic stadiums are linked to fundraising, recruitment, and prestige, because of the outsized importance of college athletics in American culture. While these impulses are at odds with the purpose of a commemoration of enslaved people, they also echo the historic intertwining of profit, culture, and human oppression in the production of settler-colonial states.

The methods I used to incorporate discussions of local and contemporary colonial histories included partnering with neighboring cultural institutions; inviting students to research the Indigenous history of the area, reflect on the practice of land acknowledgments, and analyze how these colonial histories were visible or invisible on campus; and examining contemporary memorial and artistic productions illuminating local colonial contexts. Incorporating contemporary artistic and memorial works that touch on colonial history into the study of historic materials provides a tangible way to connect the study of the past with ongoing colonialities.[25] If some of these strategies seem unavailable to you in your context, first give yourself time to discover resources or connections that might not be immediately apparent. If some of the resources I have mentioned don't exist for your campus, create class assignments where your students produce them. Have students research colonial histories, and propose ways of marking them on campus, either materially or virtually. Seeing the colonial eighteenth century in the present is necessary for connecting the work that happens in the classroom to the visceral here and now of where students and teachers live and work. Grounding undergraduate courses that are designed to cover a breadth of historic material in the contemporary and local can seem counterintuitive, and it is largely not how academics are trained. However, with these connections to the present, students can create a conceptual map for locating the legacies of eighteenth-century colonialism in their own environments.

DECOLONIAL FAILURES

When I was first invited to write this chapter, I was excited to reflect on the work I had been doing with my students at St. Mary's, and to imagine how I could deepen the relationship between the course content of my class on the art and culture of the colonial Americas, and the colonial legacies of the place and institution where we gathered. Writing this chapter in the aftermath of the college's elimination of art history and my teaching position prompted me to think in new ways about the failure of institutions to recognize and sustain efforts to unsettle colonial histories. Importantly, my critique here is wider than the personal harm I experienced when my tenure-track appointment was eliminated. Rather, it is about the contradiction of contemporary institutions that adopt the language and optics of reckoning with systemic inequality even as they downsize or eliminate the programs, disciplines, and staff that do this very work. On this point, eighteenth-century studies scholar Robbie Richardson writes that the project of building anticolonial, radically inclusive structures or curriculums will necessarily fail while the humanities are under attack and in collapse. Meanwhile, institutions of higher learning are appropriating decolonizing language to justify austerity measures that do not actually support BIPOC faculty and students or foster critical, anticolonial considerations of the past.[26] As I continue to explore how to responsibly bring anticolonial approaches to my scholarship and teaching in the next stage of my career, I return often to those moments of failure in the project of opposing colonization's history and present. In addition to the work of academics, my thoughts here are informed by the insights of contemporary curators whose work within and beyond museum institutions brings fresh insight to the praxis of decolonization.

In a widely distributed online article and short documentary film, both titled *The Museum Will Not Be Decolonised,* independent curator Sumaya Kassim shared her challenges co-developing an exhibition at the Birmingham Museum and Gallery in the United Kingdom as a woman of color. Kassim speaks about her experience working within a historically white institution on a show related to the history of race and empire in Britain. In the article Kassim described the labor and contributions of the guest curatorial team, who were all women of color, and the systemic limitations of the museum in critiquing its own racist histories, and noted: "Decoloniality is challenging because it is necessarily unreachable and necessarily indefinable. The legacies of European colonialism are immeasurably deep, far-reaching, and ever mutating, so decolonial resistance must take on different forms, methods, and evolve accordingly."[27] In considering the settler-colonial legacies that pervade higher education, settler-colonialism's infinite ability to mutate is visible in budget cuts, program cuts, and corporate-style diversity initiatives. At a place like St. Mary's College of Maryland, it seems all too fitting that the choice to decimate humanities programs took place in the academic year when the college unveiled in the same location both a new athletic stadium and a memorial to the enslaved people who struggled and resisted on the college's colonized land.[28] Deprioritizing the disciplines and fields of study that encourage us to place ourselves in responsibility to the land and its peoples is everywhere present in higher education at this moment. As colleges and universities enact austerity measures that diminish faculty members and pedagogical resources, while also aggressively pursuing profits on the backs of students, they are simply re-instantiating the exploitative and capitalistic strategies of settler-colonialism. In fields like eighteenth-century studies, it is important to continue to initiate conversation about how anticolonial or decolonial turns in the field necessarily relate to the still-existing settler-colonial conditions that structure the manner and contexts in which scholars do their work.

Of course, in weaving these threads together, I am not equating my job loss to the harms of colonization on Indigenous peoples and land, or to the nation's historic oppression of it BIPOC citizens. Returning to Tuck and Yang's formulation: decolonization is not a metaphor for other worthy justice movements, and neither is colonization a metaphor for other kinds of harm. Indeed, my newfound precarity made me see more clearly how I have benefited from allying myself with settler-colonial institutions that have rewarded my whiteness and my complicity. Given the systemic exclusion and under-representation of BIPOC faculty in higher education, I ask myself what it even means for me as a white person to tie my desire for a secure job and my future contributions to the field to the project of anticolonialism. While I don't have an answer to this yet, I have found that making visible to students in the classroom my own questions about my relationship to settler-colonialism made me accountable in new ways for my role in contemporary colonialist structures. It made the conditions of the classroom, and the inherent biases of a syllabus that I wrote, based on what I did and didn't know, more transparent, while also inviting students to consider their own agency in relation to the course and its material. Some of the best, most challenging moments in the classroom came when students were able to critique my own methods, including what I had included and excluded in our course of study.

Following the positive reception to her article and film, Kassim acknowledged that the popularity of her critique was co-opted by museums as part of an effort to seem progressive without doing the deep work of decolonization.[29] Tracing the relationship between the institution of the museum and white colonial narratives, she argues that the project of decolonizing the museum is ultimately unattainable: "We must accept that the museum is not the place for these conversations, because the museum will never be decolonized."[30] More succinctly, in a Museum Studies roundtable that I moderated as my final public event at St. Mary's, in April 2021, independent curator La Tanya Autry observed that "we *could* decolonize the museum . . . but then it would be something else."[31] In the case of both the museum and the university, the prospect that this something else will be established in our lifetimes seems distant. The experiences of these curator-scholars are a reminder that in the face of the resistance of institutions—be they museums, colleges and universities, or academic fields like eighteenth-century studies and their attendant professional organizations—decolonization risks being a deferred or unachievable project. And indeed, as scholars of institutional diversity efforts in higher education have shown, any absorption of decolonial thinking into university systems that does not result in their dismantling is merely a strategy for controlling and minimizing decolonization's demands.[32] What, then, are the anticolonialist strategies faculty can enact in the classroom in the unjust meantime? And how do they relate to the direction of the institutions under whose auspices this learning happens? The future of academic and activist efforts at decolonizing the curriculum are in relationship to the modern-day business of higher education. While the tensions between the opposing goals of the anticolonial classroom and the colonialist institution cannot and should not be resolved, the future of our fields demands that we think through them together.

CODA

I first drafted this chapter in the summer of 2021, in the immediate aftermath of St. Mary's elimination of the art history program and termination of my tenure-track position. That fall, like so many academics across the country, I went on the job market seeking a position that would financially and professionally support me in continuing this work. As the outcome of that search, I was offered a tenure-track position at the University of Kansas as the Hall Assistant Professor of American Art and Culture in the Kress Department of Art History, which I began in the fall of 2022.

This new role has prompted another phase of reflection on the future of my course "Colonial Art Across the Americas," as I adapt it to be taught in a different part of the country, at a different type of institution. Relocating to Lawrence, Kansas—my first time not living on the East Coast—has once more challenged my biases over where and when we locate colonial histories past and present. This land was occupied before and during colonization by both settled and seminomadic Indigenous communities. From the sixteenth century, Spanish, French, and British settler-colonizers have claimed and occupied parts of the region. The land that is now eastern Kansas was acquired by the United States through the Louisiana Purchase, while western portions of the state were annexed by the United States during the Mexican-American war. Kansas's entry into the Union was defined by debates over whether slavery would be legal or abolished in the territory, and was a catalyst for the Civil War. Over the long period of Euro-American settlement of this territory, then state, Native peoples have both been violently displaced from this, their traditional land, and forcibly relocated here from other regions of the settler nation. These histories trouble linear narratives of colonization that are clearly demarcated by chronology or culture. As I explore the area, nineteenth-century histories are readily visible—the Kansas-Nebraska Act establishing the territory; the Indian Removal Act, which established reservations across the region; and Bleeding Kansas, defined by John Brown's radical abolitionism. However, seventeenth- and eighteenth-century histories that predate the incorporation of the region into the U.S. nation-state are comparatively less visible. As I plan to evolve the course at KU, I am considering how student research can make these colonial legacies more visible on campus and in the community. As I approach the university, town, and state as a newcomer and outsider, I am also actively looking for those spaces and communities in which I can be a student of colonial history, rather than an expert.

This new position has not changed my thoughts on the urgent crisis in higher education. While I recognize the skill and preparation that earned me this position, I also know that while I occupy a professional field with many qualified candidates, I am one of very who have been offered the privilege of a tenure-track position. My previous experience has also taught me that in the twenty-first century the promised security of the tenure system is an illusion—and dangerous for any of us to believe in. I am still contingent. Indeed, we are all contingent. Without question, those who have a contract within the tenure-track system certainly have more stability, support, and opportunity than those working outside of it. However, whether each of us from our varied backgrounds and positions within the Academy feel it or not, all of our work is contingent on institutional structures that today are defined by dwindling support for the humanities, increasing reliance on adjunct labor, and the contradiction between institutional desires to incorporate diversity, equity, and inclusion efforts into the curriculum and the profit model that organizes university and college systems. Teaching the eighteenth century—a period of intense intellectual advancement achieved only through dependence on violent colonial systems and investment in an extractive, exploitative model of capitalism—must occur in dialogue with these present-day conditions that create and inform our classrooms.

NOTES

I would like to acknowledge with utmost gratitude the many people who have informed my thinking, and guided my writing. First and foremost, I thank the students at Saint Mary's College of Maryland (SMCM) who took the course "Colonial Art across the Americas" during the three semesters I taught it in—Fall 2017, Fall 2019, and Spring 2020. They were my teachers and inspiration. Their inquiries and insights continue to challenge me to develop the class and my approach to the material. Thank you also to SMCM faculty members Beth Charlebois and Joe Lucchesi, who observed my teaching in these classes and have been generous mentors and friends as I have developed my pedagogy. Janine Yoritomo Boldt and Dana Leibsohn both provided invaluable feedback at different stages that shaped my thinking about this chapter. Finally, my sincere thanks to editors Kate Parker and Miriam Wallace for including this chapter in their volume, and offering incisive comments and questions during the revision stages. Much of this chapter explores how the pedagogy I discuss is in relation to the historic lands of the Piscataway and Yaocamico peoples. Here, I would also like to acknowledge my own position on the lands of the Lenni-Lenape people, now called Philadelphia, during the period of time that I remotely taught "Colonial Art across the Americas," and while I drafted this chapter.

1. Key contributions in this scholarship include Eve Tuck and K. Wayne Yang, "Decolonization is not a metaphor," *Decolonization: Indigeneity, Education and Society* 1, no. 1 (2012): 1–40; and Leanne Betasamosake Simpson, "Anticolonial Strategies for the Recovery and Maintenance of Indigenous Knowledge, in *The Recovery of Indigenous Knowledge*, special issue, *American Indian Quarterly* 28, no. 3/4 (Summer–Autumn, 2004): 373–384. For a focused exploration of how decolonization theory can shape eighteenth-century studies, see *The Indigenous Eighteenth Century*, ed. Eugenia Zuroski, special issue, *Eighteenth-Century Fiction* 33, no. 2 (Winter 2021).
2. In his book *How to Be an Antiracist*, Ibram X. Kendi describes how antiracism is a "radical reorientation of our consciousness" that is about pursuing antiracist policies, rather than a static condition. For more, see "Definitions" in *How to Be an Antiracist* (New York: One World), 2019: 13–23.
3. Tuck and Yang, "Decolonization."
4. Eugenia Zuroski, "Academic Land Acknowledgements for Settler Scholars: A Guest Post by Dr. Eugenia Zuroski," American Society for Eighteenth-Century Studies Graduate and Early Career Caucus (blog), February 25, 2020, https://asecsgradcaucus.wordpress.com/2020/02/25/academic-land-acknowledgment-for-settler-scholars-a-guest-post-by-dr-eugenia-zuroski/.
5. Zuroski, "Academic Land Acknowledgements."
6. In his work on faculty effectiveness, Robert Boice describes this as "finding imagination" or "reinforcing acts of discovery." See Robert Boice, "Developing Writing, Then Teaching, amongst New Faculty," *Research in Higher Education* 36, no. 4 (August 1995): 447, 421. Broadly, Boice argues that moderate approaches to teaching that include communication with the professor's audience—students—are most effective. His guidance on relations between students and teachers emphasizes the collective sense of purpose that comes when students feel involved in their learning and heard by their professors.
7. Zuroski, "Academic Land Acknowledgements."
8. Jennifer Roberts, "The Power of Patience," *Harvard Magazine*, November–December 2013, https://www.harvardmagazine.com/2013/11/the-power-of-patience.
9. Carolyn Dean and Dana Leibsohn, "Hybridity and Its Discontents: Considering Visual Culture in Colonial Spanish America," *Colonial Latin American Review* 12, no. 1 (2003): 5–35.
10. Dean and Leibsohn, "Hybridity and Its Discontents," 15. The example that Dean and Leibsohn use here is the construction of Cuzco Cathedral in Peru. The cathedral itself is a clear adaptation of European Catholic architecture forms, but the authors show how it was constructed using the traditional building practices of Indigenous laborers. Although the markers of these knowledge-ways were removed as the structure was completed, Dean and Leibsohn argue that their influence on the building and its meaning persists.
11. For more on Prince Demah Barnes and this portrait, see *Portrait of William Duguid*, The Collection: Met American Wing, Metropolitan Museum of Art, https://www.metmuseum.org/art/collection/search/20517; and Amelia Peck, ed., *Interwoven Globe: The Worldwide Textile Trade, 1500–1800* (New York: Metropolitan Museum of Art, 2013), 291–292.
12. Wendy Bellion and Mónica Domínguez Torres, "Editor's Introduction," *Winterthur Portfolio* 45, no. 2/3 (Summer/Autumn 2011): 101–106.
13. Bellion and Domínquez Torres, "Editor's Introduction," 103.
14. J. M. Mancini, "Introduction," in *Art and War in the Pacific: Making, Breaking, and Taking from Anson's Voyage to the Philippine-American War* (Berkeley: University of California Press, 2018).
15. Tuck and Yang, "Decolonization," 19.
16. Katherine Binhammer, "Is the Eighteenth Century a Colonizing Temporality?," *Eighteenth-Century Fiction* 33, no. 2 (Winter 2020–2021): 199–204.
17. Emmanuel Wallerstein introduced the center/periphery model for understanding imperial colonialism in his book *The Modern World System* (New York: Academic Press, 1975).

While subsequent scholarship has complicated the reductive notion that culture and governance only flow from the metropolitan capital outward, world-systems theory to a certain extent reflects the ways in which early modern European empires sought to order and manage their global control. For more on empire's strategies of disconnecting colonial sites and seeing at a distance, see Michael Hardt and Antonio Negri, *Empire* (Cambridge MA: Harvard University Press, 2000); Lisa Lowe, *The Intimacies of Four Continents* (Durham, NC: Duke University Press, 2015).

18. "Piscataway Conoy Tribe—History," http://www.piscatawayconoytribe.com/history.html, accessed October 23, 2021.
19. Suzanne Ellery Chapelle, *A History of Maryland and Its People* (Baltimore: Johns Hopkins University Press, 2018), 24. Julie King notes that although there were few African people in southern Maryland prior to the turn of the eighteenth century, "beginning in the first half of the seventeenth century, racial separation and racial exclusion characterized colonial decision making in the Chesapeake" (King, *Archaeology, Narrative, and the Politics of the Past* [Knoxville: University of Tennessee Press, 2017], 10).
20. Fred Wilson and Howard Halle, "Mining the Museum," *Grant Street*, no. 44 (1993): 151–172.
21. Gerald Vizenor coined this portmanteau term, signifying "an active sense of presence, the continuance of native stories, not a mere reaction, or a survivable name. Native survivance stories are renunciations of dominance, tragedy and victimry" in *Manifest Manners: Narratives on Postindian Survivance* (Lincoln: University of Nebraska Press, 1999), vii.
22. Wilson and Halle, "Mining the Museum."
23. Catherine C. Dye, Julia King, Lauren McMillan, Scott Strickland, and Rebecca Webster, "Landscape of Slavery: Exploring a Portion of the Hicks-Mackall-Brome Plantation," *Exploring a Portion of the Hicks-Mackall-Brome Plantation: Phase I and II Archaeological Investigations for the Jamie L. Roberts Athletic Stadium Project*, October 17, 2022, https://www.academia.edu/44555410/Landscape_of_Slavery_Exploring_a_Portion_of_the_Hicks_Mackall_Brome_Plantation.
24. About St. Mary's "History Archive," "Slavery Found in Seminary History," St. Mary's College of Maryland website, April 7, 2017, https://www.smcm.edu/about/tag/history/.
25. In the course, I cover the work of other contemporary artists, such as Coco Fusco and Titus Kaphar, who intentionally engage with the histories and materials of the colonial pan-American past.
26. Robbie Richardson, "Some Observations on 'Decolonizing' the University," in "Antiracism in the Contemporary University," ed. Tita Chico, *Los Angeles Review of Books*, July 6, 2021, https://lareviewofbooks.org/article/antiracism-in-the-contemporary-university/#_ftn9. See also Richardson, "Decolonizing ASECS: An Indigenous Perspective," in *Decolonization and Eighteenth-Century Studies*, eds. Emily C. Casey and Tita Chico, special issue, *Studies in Eighteenth-Century Culture* 52 (April 2023): 35–39.
27. Sumaya Kassim, "The Museum Will Not Be Decolonised," *Media Diversified*, May 7, 2022, https://mediadiversified.org/2017/11/15/the-museum-will-not-be-decolonised/.
28. In the same academic year as the unveiling of the Commemorative to Enslaved People of Southern Maryland and the program cuts, the college also announced that it had been awarded a National Endowment for the Humanities grant to support programming and community engagement around the artwork. The funding will support long-term planning of "humanities activities and public outreach" and a one-year public humanities position that will spearhead the outreach. Funding mechanisms like the NEH are unquestionably vital for supporting the humanities in American culture. However, the college's depletion of humanities representation in the curriculum through its elimination of humanities programs, faculty, and faculty lines in the same year that it creates a term-contract public humanities position is an example of how powerful institutions manage the threat of structural change. Term-limit positions displace the labor of reckoning with the past and incorporating diversity, equity, and inclusion values into the curriculum onto contingent scholars

as the institution diminishes the number of full-time, long-term faculty who can have a stake in the process. In 2021 the board of trustees unanimously voted to eliminate majors and minors in art history, German, Latin American studies, fundamental physics, religious studies, and film and media. They also eliminated minors in democracy studies, applied mathematics, astrophysics, and dance. See "St. Mary's College of Maryland Receives National Endowment for the Humanities Grant," Office of Research and Sponsored Programs (ORSP), October 11, 2021, https://www.smcm.edu/research/2021/10/st-marys-college-of-maryland-receives-national-endowment-for-the-humanities-grant/; and "St. Mary's College Board of Trustees Approves Academic Program Changes for Fall 2021," St. Mary's College of Maryland, https://inside.smcm.edu/news/2021/02/st-marys-college-board-trustees-approves-academic-program-changes-fall-2021, accessed June 28, 2021.

29. Research Center for Material Culture, "(De)coloniality as Unfinished Story: What Artists and Writers Can Teach Museums about 'Decolonial' Praxes," https://www.materialculture.nl/en/events/decoloniality-unfinished-story-what-artists-and-writers-can-teach-museums-about-decolonial, accessed June 28, 2021.
30. Kassim, "The Museum Will Not Be Decolonised."
31. "Communities of Care: How Museum Workers Build Structures of Care and Advocacy," Museum Studies Roundtable, moderated by Emily C. Casey and featuring La Tanya Autry, Nicole Cook, and Paula Santos, St. Mary's College of Maryland, April 1, 2021.
32. Sara Ahmed, *On Being Included: Racism and Diversity in Institutional Life* (Durham, NC: Duke University Press, 2012).

CODA

Teaching (in) the Eighteenth(-)Century Now

Eugenia Zuroski

Like so many scholars trained as a specialist in eighteenth-century studies, I was encouraged early on to recognize myself as a researcher first and foremost, and a teacher as a matter of professional necessity, though this did not necessarily mean not taking pedagogy seriously. Also like so many scholars who have made our way along one path or another into an academic career, I have found that the professional respect—including material support and institutional recognition—given to my labor as teacher has never felt commensurate with what is asked of us as teachers, or what we bring to our courses, our students, our classrooms. As the chapters in this volume show, practicing teacher-scholars are keenly aware that research and pedagogy are deeply intertwined aspects of an active knowledge practice. These reflections aim not simply to vindicate teaching as intellectual endeavor, but to call us as scholars back to the specific space of classroom relations—to its constraints and possibilities; to the myriad knowledges and expectations that encounter one another there; to the frustrations it inevitably hosts, as well as its excitements and joys—as a site where we can most fruitfully ask: What are my capabilities and responsibilities as a scholar? What do I know, where do I know from, and with whom do I practice that knowledge? For what, and for whom, is my work done, and how do I move it toward those purposes?

Each of these questions carries the implicit temporal modifier of *now*. Such reflections belong to a moment of crisis—not (only) in the sense of perilous uncertainty, but in the broader etymological sense of a turning point requiring decisive action to assess how we have arrived where we are, and how to move deliberately forward from here, toward newly perceived ends. The title of this collection has had me meditating for days on the instructive slippage of object that I hear as I repeat the phrase in my head: "Teaching the eighteenth century now" can refer to teaching, right now, this thing called the "eighteenth century," but it can also refer to teaching a different thing called "the eighteenth-century now"—that is, teaching our *now* as an eighteenth-century phenomenon. Every contribution to the collection illuminates the author's way of approaching both of these pedagogical tasks: introducing students to texts, figures, people, and problems from the long eighteenth century through frameworks attuned to the context of our unevenly shared present; and, simultaneously, urging students to take their own world and their situation in it as a primary object of study, through which they may come to distinguish how the world as we know and experience it is, in many ways, an eighteenth-century project.

Wedding *now* to the field of *the eighteenth century* opens up numerous possibilities for teachers to frame texts, cultures, and encounters of the past not as universal icons of academic and cultural capital but as invitations to engage in explicitly site-specific inquiry. As a point of temporal orientation, in other words, *now* entails a spatial orientation to *here*. Site-specificity is a principle of numerous anticolonial pedagogies. To name only a few examples from my own syllabuses: Leanne Betasamosake Simpson details "land as pedagogy" in Anishinaabe teachings toward "rebellious transformation" of settler-colonial state education systems; Vanessa Watts explains the centrality of "Place-Thought" to Haudenosaunee and Anishinaabe cosmologies in which all human and nonhuman intellectual activity is an expression of a *place, thinking*—of land that "tries to speak through us"; and Sylvia Wynter insists that one of the foundational moves of Euro-Western colonial ideology was to "induce the subjects of [colonial] order to experience their own placement in the structuring hierarchies of the order as having been extrahumanly . . . designed and/or determined, rather than as veridically or systemically produced by our collective human agency."[1] To take our own material and ideological placements as the first object, the first consideration of all intellectual exercise, is a technique for understanding that thought is a material endeavor, that it *takes place* within particular conditions and material circumstances, among specific interlocutors, and that every one of us who participates in acts of thinking as they take place has agency and bears responsibility for how knowledge is generated and circulated around and among us.

To teach the "eighteenth century now" necessarily means, especially for those of us teaching in North American and other settler-colonial states, teaching how the eighteenth century is *here* with us, how it came to be so, and what is at stake in reproducing or disrupting its presence. Possibilities for teaching eighteenth-century art and material culture in North America through an explicitly anticolonial framework are spelled out with extraordinary care by Emily Casey (chapter 9). I am particularly struck by how her course "Colonial Art Across the Americas," which covers a vast range of materials and geographies, makes time for students to dwell on "the colonial environment of the campus" of St. Mary's College in Maryland, "the historic site of the first capital of the Maryland colony in the seventeenth century." A similar attention to place appears in Christine Myers's chapter

(chapter 5), in which she describes teaching Monmouth College's own mission statement as a primary text to illuminate the ways in which the college as it defines itself now—including the students who belong to it now—is very much part of the ongoing project of the Scottish Enlightenment.

Site-specific teaching and attention to place and placement are not limited, however, to studying particular geographic and institutional sites. Diana Epelbaum's discussion (chapter 6) of how she strives toward universal design in the structure of her course shows that equitable accessibility requires minute attention to the particular ways in which individual students access and move through pedagogical spaces, both material and conceptual. Epelbaum's account of how she designs her course "Race and Place in Natural Histories of the Americas" to provide "many entry points for exploration and connection" as well as "key lines of inquiry that build upon one another, and that also function iteratively" so that primary texts can be revisited and newly illuminated by a growing "understanding of the period's colonialist framework" reminds me of what Cynthia Wall, in her study of eighteenth-century landscaping, calls "grammars of approach."[2] The picturesque spatial design of English estates that Wall examines produced an epistemology of discovery, surprise, and gradual revelation; it also linked the intellectual experience of aesthetic perception to the embodied experience of moving through and about a specific landed site. While the politics of the British picturesque undeniably collude with the colonization of Indigenous lands by positing all land as potential British property, both material and intellectual, its grammars of approach can also be placed within a genealogy of "thinking on the ground" that has gathered conceptual and political challenges to top-down arrangements of power and authority. Epelbaum's emphasis on the shared and reciprocal activities of student-scholars and teacher-scholars in the classroom is consistent with this more radical tradition that seeks to level traditional arrangements of power rather than reinvent and reinvigorate them. I found her example of assigning "social annotation" instead of the more familiar exercise of "peer review" especially instructive. Where "peer review" encourages students to mimic positions of authority that currently structure academic power relations by "assessing" the quality of another's work, social annotation asks students to think with and alongside someone else's writing, finding their way into it, noting points of tension and resonance, and weaving their own thoughts into another's text.

All of the examples of teaching and learning gathered in this collection evince pedagogical practice as a kind of *weaving together*. The classroom is a space where strands of knowledge become identifiable, where students and teachers test the strength and pliability of these strands, and where, together, they cultivate techniques for bringing multiple strands together into new formations. For students conditioned to approach their education in the neoliberal terms of "gain," "reward," competitive "excellence," and individual "success," the methods detailed in this collection offer a fundamental reframing: learning as *making* rather than acquiring something of value. From this perspective, education is less about "getting ahead" (of what? of whom?) than it is a process of knitting oneself into relation to other people, to institutions, to shared histories, to collective movements.

Tiffany Potter (chapter 1) approaches this pedagogical practice through the exercise of editing critical editions of primary texts. This exercise emphasizes collaboration not only among students but also between students and the eighteenth-century texts they study; students are invited not merely to consume the literary text but to cultivate a relationship to it through the process of weaving their own knowledge into it, as it weaves its knowledge into them. Potter's efforts to move away from "disposable" assignments, whose primary function is to generate a grade, reveal the importance of recognizing every class as a practicum, a space where students are not absorbing information but cultivating a knowledge *practice.* Honoring the lateral relations that define these classroom experiences requires that the practical details of working together *here, now*—what we often refer to as the "housekeeping" details—come to be recognized as crucial components of the knowledge relations that are formed in the classroom, rather than as a backdrop to scholarly work. Understanding the housekeeping—how a space is envisioned and maintained, to what purpose, who does that work, and under what conditions—is, after all, a basic element of gaining critical purchase on how the institution operates as lived space.

Kate Parker (chapter 3) offers an especially resonant example of how and why the "technical" aspects of a course must be woven into its intellectual content. A specialist in feminism and sexuality who had been tasked with "teaching sex online" during the COVID-19 closures, Parker attends carefully to the particular pressures a virtual classroom imposes on course content that directly addresses sex, gender, their various embodiments, and sex- and gender-based forms of violence. Her keen awareness of "the nonconsensual aspects of the COVID-19 moment" and her commitment to clarifying, for her students, "how I will repair the harm done if I make a mistake" are vital examples of how making a place for teaching and learning to play out requires instructors to take direct responsibility for the contours of the space and the dynamics of the relations that are enacted there.

These pedagogical responsibilities, this collection shows, also call upon teachers to recognize knowledge practice as a profoundly embodied activity. This is another form of site-specificity in the classroom: recognizing not only the built and cultivated environment of learning as part of how, and what, one comes to know, but recognizing each scholar inhabiting that space as a whole human being, and recognizing all intellects as "bodyminds." Travis Chi Wing Lau (chapter 8) reminds us that, in current institutional hegemonies of "proper bodily form and function," "we remain remarkably indebted to the eighteenth-century's grammars of the flesh." These grammars yield the cultural matrices of gender, sex, and race that each of us lives at the same time that we study them; they also yield the logics of ability and disability, illness and wellness, and normality and abnormality that intersect all other aspects of lived experience *now*. Noting his students' expectation that reading literatures of the past would be an "escape" from the "pandemic present," Lau trains their focus on bodies and embodiment as a way of showing how eighteenth-century thought reproduces itself in our visceral arrangements, not merely in our mental furniture. This attention to the bodymind resonates throughout this collection. When, for example, Ziona Kocher (chapter 2) asks their students to consider "how we are supposed to feel about" various plot and character details in Behn's *The Widdow Ranter*, they foreground literature's appeal to our feelings as a technique for producing historical and other forms of knowledge. And Teri Doerksen's delightful "Chocolate Project" (chapter 4) fashions a new sensorium of eighteenth-century studies that overtly invites students to think with their whole bodymind about the kinds of cultural formations that took shape through the eighteenth century's imperial flows of commercial goods—assemblages that included the noses, the palates, the guts of consumers. The detail of her students' "audible gasp" when the historical confluence of the taste in their mouths and the institution of transatlantic slavery lands on them also calls us to consider the pedagogical sensorium—what learning and knowing feels like, and how we register and communicate this experience with the entire instrument of the bodymind.

Lau's particular focus on *pain* as both object and condition of pedagogical engagement raises an important ethical question for how we teach the eighteenth century now: How do we insist that the eighteenth-century studies classroom is no "escape" from the pressures of the present without overwhelming students with the dreadful feeling that there can be no respite from systemic violence? How might we make the classroom a space where one can reckon with the forms of violence that link *then* and *now* in ways that feel viable—that are revitalizing, fortifying, and ultimately hopeful as we orient ourselves toward the future? Questions of this scale require ongoing consideration, but one of Lau's techniques brings us back to the crucial work of classroom housekeeping. By inviting students and others in the classroom to "inhabit our bodyminds in whatever ways we might need"—standing and stretching; taking a break for the bathroom, for food, or for emotional regrouping; stimming; turning one's camera off; and so on—underscores the classroom as a site of care, even when it asks students to grapple with problems of harm. Pedagogy informed by disability studies insists that illness, disability, rest, and care (of the self and others) are not anathema to teaching, learning, and knowledge practice—and that to presume that they are reproduces the punishing and exclusionary knowledge schemes that eighteenth-century colonial epistemology has bequeathed us.

There is perhaps no better course content than eighteenth-century writing to nurture classroom considerations of how ableist definitions of intellectual activity and knowledge-work collude with racial capitalism and settler-colonialism to generate and reinforce the very forms of cultural capital the Euro-Western university is designed to reproduce. Matthew Reznicek (chapter 7) illustrates this point beautifully in his discussion of teaching the link between sickness and poverty in Austen's *Emma*. Income inequity and the costs of health care are issues that the vast majority of current students know a lot about. Yet in the mythical stream of "upward mobility" that has compelled generations of students through university educations, this knowledge is likely to seem anathema to academic learning, something to be suppressed in the effort to become a successful, employable graduate who doesn't have to worry about such things anymore.

As Edward Said influentially noted, for as long as Austen has been recognized as part of the English literary canon, her novels have played a particular role in upholding imperial ideals amid various political challenges to the empire.[3] Teaching Austen *now* thus presents a particular challenge, given that it may be material that students already turn to for an escape from politics, or material that students recognize as part of an imperial, white supremacist project. Reznicek meets this challenge by approaching *Emma* not as a token and artifact of cultural power and privilege but as a way to address—in the interest of transforming—systemic inequities passed down and reproduced since the eighteenth century. The association of *health* with *wealth* that structures so much of the novel is a cultural formation brought to what is currently known as North America by eighteenth-century capitalist colonial expansion. To make this association legible, to attend to how it shapes and conditions lives, and to place it in historical context—a context in which *then* and *now* overlap in potentially startling ways—is to draw Austen's writing fully into a present moment when the intertwined phenomena of poverty and illness are more pressing issues than ever for a growing number of people in North America and beyond.

When I consider this collection as a whole, I am perhaps most struck by the astounding generosity of it—by the care with which each example of instruction approaches its students and course material alike; by the assignments and course designs that are shared in such detail that readers can take them up in their own teaching practice; and by the extraordinary glimpses into the vulnerable processes of teaching in action. Kocher remarks on the pedagogical value of "misfires and slip-ups" in performance exercises, and, as every teacher knows, this fact of the work applies to teaching as well—nowhere do we learn most immediately how to teach *now* than in those awkward and often excruciating moments of failure. There is generosity as well as deep honesty in how this collection addresses itself to eighteenth-century specialists *as teachers*, and in how this mode of address reveals that our specialized knowledge is put to the test and revitalized nowhere so much as in our exchanges with students.

From Doerksen's discussion of institutional curricular restructuring, to Lau's disclosure of the physical pain of sitting through a remote workday on

Zoom, to Casey's account of her tenure-track position suddenly becoming contingent, the collection acknowledges the immense difficulty of teaching (in) the eighteenth(-)century now. Yet it also takes this moment to ask: What do we as eighteenth-century specialists know, where do we know from, and what can that knowledge be for, beyond reproducing the field known as eighteenth-century studies and the forms of cultural and institutional capital that once assembled in and around fields like it? Our students who have little to no interest in becoming experts in this field prompt us to imagine our knowledge for broader and better purposes. As Doerksen shows, the urgent strategic thinking compelled by moments of institutional crisis can also be a laboratory for swift pedagogical action usually foreclosed by the slow pace of institutional transformation. Disability justice advocates have remarked repeatedly on how changes that they have requested for years, such as remote learning, were routinely deemed "unfeasible" as a form of accommodation but suddenly materialized (through the compelled efforts of instructors following emergency mandates) as components of emergency pandemic teaching. Institutional and cultural transformation, we now know, is not only possible, it is inevitable. Pedagogical thinking "on the ground" through the COVID-19 pandemic has meant accepting drastic re-spatialization of the classroom and the modes of relation we foster there. It has meant becoming attuned to new limitations to shared knowledge practices as well as new possibilities as remote learning reconfigures the contours of pedagogical encounter. It has also been an opportunity to reflect that the colonial movements of the eighteenth century were a global emergency that we are still very much in, and that *emergency pedagogy* is the rule, not the exception of teaching (in) the eighteenth(-)century now. There is struggle in this collection, and immense clarity of purpose. Teaching the eighteenth century now means, fundamentally, gathering critical perspective on how to take responsibility for how we move together into a livable future. I am grateful for these starting points.

NOTES

1. Leanne Betasamosake Simpson, "Land as Pedagogy: Nishnaabeg Intelligence and Rebellious Transformation," *Decolonization: Indigeneity, Education & Society* 3, no. 3 (2014): 1–25; Vanessa Watts, "Indigenous Place-Thought and Agency amongst Humans and Non Humans (First Woman and Sky Woman Go on a European World Tour!)," *Decolonization: Indigeneity, Education & Society* 2, no. 1 (2013): 20–34; Sylvia Wynter, "Unsettling the Coloniality of Being/Power/Truth/Freedom: Towards the Human, after Man, Its Overrepresentation—An Argument," *CR: The New Centennial Review* 3, no. 3 (2003): 257–337.
2. Cynthia Wall, *Grammars of Approach: Landscape, Narrative, and the Linguistic Picturesque* (Chicago: University of Chicago Press, 2019).
3. Edward Said, *Culture and Imperialism* (New York: Knopf, 1993).

ACKNOWLEDGMENTS

As editors, we are grateful for the wonderful work that our colleagues across the teaching world shared with us to bring this collection into the world. This process has both revitalized our own thinking about teaching and given us the space to take seriously the labor and scholarship of teaching itself.

We want to thank our respective academic institutions and programs—the Division of Humanities at the New College of Florida and the Department of English at the University of Wisconsin La Crosse—for their support. We also want to thank the reviewers for this project; their generous thinking and insightful feedback made this a stronger and more ambitious collection, one that is more than the sum of its parts. As always, the director of Bucknell University Press, Suzanne Guiod, and the managing editor, Pamelia Dailey, were delightful to work with—patient and professional and encouraging as we needed. And finally, we must thank our students—who are after all the reason we show up every day, and who continue to challenge us to think hard about the collaborative work of the classroom and what it means to aim for generous and ethical teaching.

BIBLIOGRAPHY

About St. Mary's "History Archive." "Slavery Found in Seminary History." St. Mary's College of Maryland website, April 7, 2017.

Ahmed, Sara. "An Affinity of Hammers." *TSQ: Transgender Studies Quarterly* 13, no. 1/2 (2016): 22–34.

———. *On Being Included: Racism and Diversity in Institutional Life*. Durham, NC: Duke University Press, 2012.

Alston, David. *Slaves and Highlanders: Silenced Histories of Scotland and the Caribbean*. Edinburgh: Edinburgh University Press, 2021.

Aphra Behn Online (ABO): Interactive Journal for Women in the Arts, 1640–1830. University of South Florida Digital Commons. https://scholarcommons.usf.edu/abo/.

Arrupe, Pedro, S.J. "Men for Others." Speech, Valencia Spain, July 31, 1973. https://jesuitportal.bc.edu/research/documents/1973_arrupemenforothers/.

Ashford-Rowe, K., J. Herrington, and C. Brown. "Establishing the Critical Elements That Determine Authentic Assessment." *Assessment & Evaluation in Higher Education* 39, no. 2 (2013): 205–222.

Austen, Jane. *Emma*. 1815. Edited by Fiona Stafford. New York: Penguin, 2015.

———. *Mansfield Park*. 1813. Edited by James Kinsley. New York: Oxford University Press, 2008.

———. *Sense and Sensibility*. 1811. Edited by John Mullan. New York: Oxford University Press, 2017.

Bailey, Cathryn. "Online Feminist Pedagogy: A New Doorway into Our Brick-and-Mortar Classrooms?" *Feminist Teacher: A Journal of the Practices, Theories, and Scholarship of Feminist Teaching* 27, no. 2–3 (2017): 253–266.

Barker, Kim, and Olga Jurasz. "Online Misogyny: A Challenge for Digital Feminism?" *Journal of International Affairs* 72, no. 2 (Spring/Summer 2019): 95–114.

Bartoszyńska, Katarzyna. "Texts in Context: Manu Samriti Chander on *Brown Romantics*." *Asymptote* (December 8, 2022). https://www.asymptotejournal.com/blog/2022/12/08/texts-in-context-manu-samriti-chander-on-brown-romantics/.

Bartram, William. "Alegator." In *Botanical and Zoological Drawings of William Bartram, 1756–1788*. London: Trustees of the Natural History Museum, ____.

———. "Alligators on the St. John's River." In *Travels through North and South Carolina, Georgia, East and West Florida and Other Writings*. Plate no. 9. 1791.

———. "American Lotus or Water Chinquapin Seed Vessel with Snail and Black Root." In *Travels through North and South Carolina, Georgia, East and West Florida and Other Writings*, edited by Thomas P. Slaughter. Plate no. 25. Washington, DC: Library of America, 1996.

Behn, Aphra. *Oroonoko*. Edited by Tiffany Potter. Peterborough, ON: Broadview, 2020.

———. *Oroonoko, The Rover, and Other Works*. Edited by Janet Todd. London: Penguin Books, 2003.

———. *The Widdow Ranter or, The History of Bacon in Virginia*. 1690. In *The Routledge Anthology of Restoration and Eighteenth-Century Drama*, edited by Kristina Straub, Misty G. Anderson, and Daniel O'Quinn, 234–274. New York: Routledge, 2017.

———. *The Widdow Ranter, or, The History of Bacon in Virginia*. 1690. In *Electronic Texts in American Studies*, edited by Paul Royster. UNL Digital Commons, 2008. https://digitalcommons.unl.edu/etas/45/.

Bellion, Wendy, and Mónica Domínguez Torres. "Editor's Introduction." *Winterthur Portfolio* 45, no. 2/3 (Summer/Autumn 2011): 101–106.

Bennie, Lynn. "New Scottish Government: Key Takeaways from the SNP Deal with the Greens." *The Conversation*. August 31, 2021. https://theconversation.com/new-scottish-government-key-takeaways-from-the-snp-deal-with-the-greens-166841.

Binhammer, Katherine. "Is the Eighteenth Century a Colonizing Temporality?" *Eighteenth-Century Fiction* 33, no. 2 (Winter 2020–2021): 199–204.

Boice, Robert. "Developing Writing, Then Teaching, amongst New Faculty." *Research in Higher Education* 36, no. 4 (August 1995): 415–456.

Bourke, Joanna. *The Story of Pain: From Prayer to Painkillers*. Oxford: Oxford University Press, 2014.

Bowden, Martha. "Avoiding *Oroonoko* Syndrome—Teaching Haywood and *Fantomina* in Context." In *Approaches to Teaching the Works of Eliza Haywood*, edited by Tiffany Potter, 44–49. New York: MLA Press, 2020.

Bowers, Terence N. "*Travels through France and Italy* by Tobias Smollett" (Review). *Eighteenth-Century Fiction* 25, no. 4 (2013): 798–800.

Boyer, Ernest L. "The Scholarship of Engagement." *Bulletin of the American Academy of Arts and Sciences* 49, no. 7 (1996): 18–33. https://www.jstor.org/stable/3824459.

———. *Scholarship Reconsidered: Priorities of the Professoriate*. New York: Carnegie Foundation for the Advancement of Teaching, 1990.

Brooks, Lisa. *The Common Pot: The Recovery of Native Space in the Northeast*. Minneapolis: University of Minnesota Press, 2008.

Buis, Joris J. W., Ger Post, and Vincent R. Visser. "Chapter 13: Reflection." In *Academic Skills for Interdisciplinary Studies*, 116–123. Amsterdam: Amsterdam University Press, 2015.

Burgess, Miranda. "On Being Moved: Sympathy, Mobility, and Narrative Form." *Poetics Today* 32, no. 2 (2011): 289–321.

Castelli, Frank R., and Mark A. Sarvary, "Why Students Do Not Turn On Their Video Cameras during Online Classes and an Equitable and Inclusive Plan to Encourage Them to Do So." *Ecology and Evolution* 11, no. 8 (January 2021): 3565–3576.

Center for Engaged Learning. "What Is SoTL?" October 7, 2021. https://www.centerforengagedlearning.org/studying-engaged-learning/what-is-sotl/.

Chander, Manu Samriti, and Patricia A. Matthew. "Abolitionist Interruptions: Romanticism, Slavery, and Genre." *European Romantic Review* 29, no. 4 (2018): 431–434.

Chapelle, Suzanne Ellery. *A History of Maryland and Its People*. 2nd edition. Baltimore: Johns Hopkins University Press. 2018.

Christie's (christiesinc). "Finch and Co's Cabinet of Curiosities." *Instagram*. October 14, 2020. https://www.instagram.com/p/CGUng3yHb8F/?utm_source=ig_web_button_share_sheet.

Clare, Eli. *Brilliant Imperfection: Grappling with Cure*. Durham, NC: Duke University Press, 2017.

"Communities of Care: How Museum Workers Build Structures of Care and Advocacy." Museum Studies Roundtable, moderated by Emily Casey and featuring La Tanya Autry, Nicole Cook, and Paula Santos. St. Mary's College of Maryland, April 1, 2021.

Cook-Sather, Alison, Catherine Bovill, and Peter Felten. *Engaging Students as Partners in Learning and Teaching*. San Francisco: Jossey-Bass, 2014.

Coombs, David Sweeney, and Danielle Coriale. "V21 Forum on Strategic Presentism: Introduction." *Victorian Studies* 59, no. 1 (2016): 87–89.

Cooper, Richard (Buz). *Poverty and the Myths of Health Care Reform*. Baltimore: Johns Hopkins University Press, 2016.

Coronado, Jorge. "On Entrenched Inequalities in the Research University: Activism and Teaching for Tenured Faculty Members." *PMLA* 136, no. 3 (May 2021): 441–446.

Cottom, Tressie McMillan. "Dying to Be Competent." In *Thick and Other Essays*, 73–97. New York: New Press, 2019.

Curran, Andrew. *The Anatomy of Blackness: Science and Slavery in an Age of Enlightenment.* Baltimore: Johns Hopkins University Press, 2011.

Dean, Carolyn, and Dana Leibsohn. "Hybridity and Its Discontents: Considering Visual Culture in Colonial Spanish America." *Colonial Latin American Review* 12, no. 1 (2003): 5–35.

Deb, Basuli. "Transnational Complications: Reimagining *Oroonoko* and Women's Collective Politics in the Empire." *Frontiers: A Journal of Women Studies* 36, no. 1 (2015): 33–56.

Devine, T. M. *Recovering Scotland's Slavery Past: The Caribbean Connection*. Edinburgh: Edinburgh University Press, 2015.

Diaby, Bakary. "Feeling Black, Feeling Back: Fragility and Romanticism." *Symbiosis: Transatlantic Literary and Cultural Relations* 23, no. 1 (2019): 1–22.

Dorn, Lori. "Lin-Manuel Miranda Premiering His Song 'Alexander Hamilton' at a 2009 Poetry Jam at The White House." Laughing Squid, July 8, 2020. https://laughingsquid.com/lin-manuel-miranda-alexander/.

Dwyer, John. "Henry Mackenzie, *The Man of Feeling*. Edited by Maureen Harkin" (Review). *Eighteenth-Century Scotland: Newsletter of the Eighteenth-Century Scottish Studies Society* 20 (2006): 28.

Dye, Catherine C., Julia King, Lauren McMillan, Scott Strickland, and Rebecca Webster. "Landscape of Slavery: Exploring a Portion of the Hicks-Mackall-Brome Plantation." *Exploring a Portion of the Hicks-Mackall-Brome Plantation: Phase I and II Archaeological Investigations for the Jamie L. Roberts Athletic Stadium Project*, 2020 https://www.academia.edu/44555410/Landscape_of_Slavery_Exploring_a_Portion_of_the_Hicks_Mackall_Brome_Plantation.

Facing History and Ourselves. "Teaching Strategy: Fishbowl." October 19, 2009. https://www.facinghistory.org/resource-library/teaching-strategies/fishbowl.

Falconer, I., and A. Littlejohn. "Designing for Blended Learning, Sharing, and Reuse." *Journal of Further and Higher Education* 31, no. 1 (2007): 41–52.

Fawaz, Ramzi. "How to Make a Queer Scene, or Notes toward a Practice of Affective Curation." *Feminist Studies* 42, no. 3 (2016): 757–768.

Fitzpatrick, Kathleen. *Generous Thinking: A Radical Approach to Saving the University*. Baltimore: Johns Hopkins University Press, 2019.

Flippo, Rona F., Victoria Appatova, and David M. Wark. "Test Preparation and Test Taking." In *Handbook of College Reading and Study Strategy Research*, edited by Rona F. Flippo and Thomas W. Bean, 241–278. New York: Taylor and Francis, 2018.

Foucault, Michel. *Security, Territory, Population: Lectures at the Collège de France, 1977–78.* Translated by Graham Burchell. Basingstoke: Palgrave, 2007.

Frankel, Valerie Estelle, ed. *Outlander's Sassenachs: Essays on Gender, Race, Orientation and the Other in the Novels and Television Series*. Jefferson, NC: McFarland, 2016.

Freire, Paolo. *Pedagogy of the Oppressed*. 1968. Translation, 1970, by Myra Bergman Ramos. New York: Continuum, 1986.

Gerzina, Gretchen. *Black London: Life before Emancipation*. Reprint. New Brunswick, NJ: Rutgers University Press, 1995.

Gliserman Kopans, Dana. "*Sense and Sensibility: An Annotated Edition* by Jane Austen" (Review). *Eighteenth-Century Fiction* 28, no. 1 (2015): 207–209.

Grisham, Leah. "'Yield It Up Cheerfully': Teaching Consent, Violence, and Coercion in Samuel Richardson's Pamela." *ABO: Interactive Journal for Women in the Arts, 1640–1830* 10, no. 2, Article 5 (2020). http://doi.org/10.5038/2157-7129.10.2.1237.

Hardt, Michael, and Antonio Negri. *Empire*. Cambridge, MA: Harvard University Press, 2000.

Hartman, Saidiya. *Lose Your Mother: A Journey along the Atlantic Slave Route*. New York: Farrar, Straus and Giroux, 2008.

Hay, William. *Deformity: An Essay*. London: R. and J. Dodsley, 1859.

Hendricks, Christina. "Renewable Assignments: Student Works: Adding Value to the World." *Flexible Learning*. University of British Columbia. October 29, 2015. https://flexible.learning.ubc.ca/news-events/renewable-assignments-student-work-adding-value-to-the-world/.

Hendricks, Margo. "Civility, Barbarism, and Aphra Behn's *The Widow Ranter*." In *Women, "Race," and Writing in the Early Modern Period*, edited by Margo Hendricks and Patricia Parker, 225–239. London: Routledge, 1994.

Herman, Arthur. *Scottish Enlightenment: The Scots' Invention of the Modern World*. New York: HarperCollins, 2003.

Hirji, Faiza. "Claiming Our Space: Muslim Women, Activism, and Social Media." *Islamophobia Studies Journal* 6, no. 1 (Spring 2021): 78–92.

hooks, bell. "Feminism: A Movement to End Sexist Oppression." In *The Feminist Theory Reader: Local and Global Perspectives*, edited by Carole R. McCann and Seung-Kyung Kim, 50–56. New York: Routledge, 2003.

———. *Teaching Critical Thinking*. New York: Routledge, 2007.

Hoover, Eric. "The Demographic Cliff: 5 Findings from New Projections of High-School Graduates." *The Chronicle of Higher Education*, December 15, 2020. https://www.chronicle.com/article/the-demographic-cliff-5-findings-from-new-projections-of-high-school-graduates.

Hunt, Lynn. "Against Presentism." *Perspectives on History: The Newsmagazine of the American Historical Association*, May 2002. https://www.historians.org/publications-and-directories/perspectives-on history/may-2002/against-presentism.

Hutchings, Pat, et al. "The Scholarship of Teaching and Learning in an Age of Accountability: Building Bridges." *Teaching & Learning Inquiry: The ISSOTL Journal* 1, no. 2 (2013): 35–47. https://www.jstor.org/stable/10.2979/teachlearninqu.1.2.35.

Hutner, Heidi. "Aphra Behn's *The Widow Ranter*." In *Colonial Women: Race and Culture in Stuart Drama*, 89–106. Oxford: Oxford University Press, 2001.

Instructure. "Teaching and Learning: To the Power of Canvas LMS." https://instructure.com/canvas.

James-Cavan, Kathleen Viola, ed. *William Hay: Deformity: An Essay*. Victoria, BC: English Literary Studies, 2004.

Jenkins, George. "Dedication to *The Widdow Ranter*." In *The Routledge Anthology of Restoration and Eighteenth-Century Drama*, edited by Kristina Straub, Misty G. Anderson, and Daniel O'Quinn, 234–235. New York: Routledge, 2017.

Johnson, Barbara. "Headnotes." *College English* 66, no. 2 (November 2003): 177–185.

Jones, Mary. *Miscellanies in Prose and Verse*. London, 1750.

Kafer, Alison. "Un/Safe Disclosures: Scenes of Disability and Trauma." *Journal of Literary & Cultural Disability Studies* 10, no.1 (2016): 1–20.

Kahan, Lee. "*Moll Flanders* by Daniel Defoe" (Review). *Eighteenth-Century Fiction* 25, no. 3 (2013): 639–641.

Kassim, Sumaya. "The Museum Will Not Be Decolonised." Media Diversified. May 7, 2022. https://mediadiversified.org/2017/11/15/the-museum-will-not-be-decolonised/.

Kay, Matthew R. *Not Light, but Fire: How to Lead Meaningful Race Conversations in the Classroom*. Portland, ME: Stenhouse, 2018.

Keenleyside, Heather. "*The History of Pompey the Little*, by Francis Coventry, edited by Nicholas Hudson" (Review). *Eighteenth-Century Fiction* 23, no. 3 (2011). https://ecf.humanities.mcmaster.ca/book-reviews-2011/.

Kelly, Helena. *Jane Austen: The Secret Radical*. New York: Alfred A. Knopf, 2017.

Kelly, T. Mills. *Teaching History in the Digital Age*. Ann Arbor: University of Michigan Press, 2013.

Kendi, Ibram X. *How to Be an Antiracist*. New York: One World, 2019.

King, Julia. *Archaeology, Narrative, and the Politics of the Past: The View from Southern Maryland*. Knoxville: University of Tennessee Press, 2017.

Knipe, Charles. *A City Ramble: or The Humours of the Compter*. London, 1715.

Lau, Travis Chi Wing. "Access from Afar: Cultivating Inclusive, Flexible Classrooms after COVID-19." *Nineteenth-Century Gender Studies* 17, no.1 (2021). http://ncgsjournal.com/issue171/lau.html.

———. "William Hay, or an Obsession." In *Valentine*. Special issue, *The Rambling*. February 14, 2019. https://the-rambling.com/2019/02/14/valentines-lau/.

Leitch, Victor B. "Editing a *Norton Anthology*." *College English* 66, no. 2 (November 2003): 172–177.

LePage, Brooke. "These Are the States That Passed Laws Restricting the Teaching of Racial History." *The 74* (September 3, 2021). https://www.the74million.org/article/these-are-the-states-that-passed-laws-restricting-the-teaching-of-racial-history/.

Levin, Kate. "'The Only Beguiled Person': Accessing Fantomina in the Feminist Classroom." *ABO: Interactive Journal for Women in the Arts, 1640–1830* 2, no. 1 (2012). http://dx.doi.org/10.5038/2157-7129.2.1.5.

London Stage Database. "London Stage Event: 20 November 1689 at Drury Lane Theatre." n. d. https://londonstagedatabase.uoregon.edu/event.php?id=1732.

Long, Heather. "The World's Top Economists Just Made the Case for Why We Still Need English Majors: English Majors Are Down 25.5 Percent since the Great Recession, Just as World's Top Economists Say We Need More 'Storytellers.'" *Washington Post*, October 19, 2019. https://www.washingtonpost.com/business/2019/10/19/worlds-top-economists-just-made-case-why-we-still-need-english-majors/.

Louden, Robert. *The World We Want: How and Why the Ideals of the Enlightenment Still Elude Us*. Oxford: Oxford University Press, 2010.

Lowe, Lisa. *The Intimacies of Four Continents*. Durham, NC: Duke University Press, 2015.

Lubey, Kathleen. "*Memoirs of a Woman of Pleasure* by John Cleland" (Review). *Eighteenth-Century Fiction* 32, no. 3 (2020): 521–523.

Major, Melissa. "7 Ways 'Hamilton' Has Impacted America." PBS/Great Performances, November 16, 2017. https://www.pbs.org/wnet/gperf/hamilton-american-musical-changed-musical-theater/5224/.

Mallipeddi, Ramesh. *Spectacular Suffering: Witnessing Slavery in the Eighteenth-Century British Atlantic*. Charlottesville: University of Virginia Press, 2016.

Mancini, J. M. "Introduction." In *Art and War in the Pacific: Making, Breaking, and Taking from Anson's Voyage to the Philippine-American War*, edited by J. M. Mancini, 1–26. Berkeley: University of California Press, 2018.

Manne, Kate. *Entitled: How Male Privilege Hurts Women*. New York: Random House, 2020.

Marsh, Sarah. "Changes of Air: The Somerset Case and *Mansfield Park*'s Imperial Plots." *Eighteenth-Century Studies* 53, no 2 (2020): 211–233.

Martinez-Cola, Marisela, Rocco English, Jennifer Min, Jonathan Peraza, Jamesetta Tambah, and Christina Yebuah. "When Pedagogy Is Painful: Teaching in Tumultuous Times." *Teaching Sociology* 46, no. 2 (2018): 97–111.

Matar, Nabil. *"The Turkish Embassy Letters: Lady Mary Wortley Montagu,"* (Review) *The Scriblerian and the Kit-Cats* 47, no. 2 (2015): 100–101.

McEwen, Nicola. "The Union: New (and Old) Challenges for the New Prime Minister." *UK in a Changing Europe*. August 16, 2022. https://ukandeu.ac.uk/challenges-for-the-union/.

McInnis, David. "Virginian Culture and Experimental Genre in Aphra Behn's *The Widow Ranter*." In *Early Modern Englishwomen Testing Ideas*, edited by Jo Wallwork and Paul Salzman, 84–104. Farnham: Ashgate, 2011.

McKinney, Kathleen. "Searching for Prior Literature for SoTL Projects: Beyond Electronic Data Bases." *The SOTL Advocate*, ISUSOTL. April 29, 2015, https://illinoisstateuniversitysotl.wordpress.com/2015/04/29/searching-for-prior-literature-for-sotl-projects-beyond-electronic-data-bases.

Merian, Maria Sibylla. "Surinam Common or Spectacled Caiman with South American False-Coral Snake," ca. 1705–1710. RCIN 921218, Royal Collection Trust, London. https://www

.rct.uk/collection/921218/common-or-spectacled-caiman-with-south american-false-coral-snake.

Mingus, Mia. "Access Intimacy: The Missing Link." May 5, 2011. https://leavingevidence.wordpress.com/2011/05/05/access-intimacy-the-missing-link.

Mitsein, Rebekah. "Teaching Eighteenth-Century British Literature beyond the Pale." *Studies in Eighteenth-Century Culture* 49 (2020): 131–136.

MLA (Modern Language Association). "The MLA Job List, 2018–19." Natalia Lusin, MLA Office of Programs. November 2020. https://www.mla.org/content/download/134145/file/Job%20List_2018-19_Linked.pdf.

———. "Report on the MLA Job Information List, 2012–13." MLA Office of Research. October 2013. https://www.mla.org/Resources/Career/Job-List/Reports-on-the-MLA-Job-List.

———. "Tables and Figures on the MLA *Job List*, 2019–20." Reports on the MLA Job List. https://www.mla.org/Resources/Career/Job-List/Reports-on-the-MLA-Job-List.

Monmouth College. "Our Mission & Values." n.d. https://www.monmouthcollege.edu/welcome-home/our-mission-values/, accessed June 22, 2021.

Morgan, Jennifer L. *Reckoning with Slavery: Gender, Kinship, and Capitalism in the Early Black Atlantic*. Durham, NC: Duke University Press, 2021.

Mowry, Melissa. "'Past Remembrance or History': Aphra Behn's *The Widdow Ranter*, or, How the Collective Lost Its Honor." *ELH* 79, no. 3 (Fall 2012): 597–621.

Myers, Christine D. *University Coeducation in the Victorian Era: Inclusion in the United States and the United Kingdom*. New York: Palgrave Macmillan, 2010.

Nagle, Christopher. "Beyond Victims & Villains: Teaching Cleland with Haywood & Behn." *ABO: Interactive Journal for Women in the Arts, 1640–1830* 10, no. 2 (2020). http://doi.org/10.5038/2157-7129.10.2.1239.

National Center for Education Statistics. "Table 22:10: Bachelor's Degrees Conferred by Postsecondary Institutions, by Field of Study: Selected Years, 1970–71 through 2016–17." Digest of Education Statistics. https://nces.ed.gov/programs/digest/d18/tables/dt18_322.10.asp?current=yes.

New, Melvyn. "Thoughts on Reviewing Textbook Editions and Student Companions." *The Scriblerian and the Kit-Cats* 52, no. 1 (2019): 77–82.

Newbould, M.-C. "*Tristram Shandy* ed. by Judith Hawley" (Review). *Eighteenth-Century Studies* 54, no. 2 (2021): 512–515.

Norton Critical Editions. https://wwnorton.com/catalog/college/norton-critical-editions.

Nosowitz, Dan. "How the English Failed to Stamp Out the Scots Language." *Atlas Obscura*, September 28, 2018. https://www.atlasobscura.com/articles/scots-language?utm_source=facebook.com&utm_medium=atlas-page.

Nussbaum, Felicity. *The Limits of the Human: Fictions of Anomaly, Race, and Gender*. Cambridge: Cambridge University Press, 2003.

Office of Research and Sponsored Programs (ORSP). "St. Mary's College of Maryland Receives National Endowment for the Humanities Grant." October 11, 2021. https://www.smcm.edu/research/2021/10/st-marys-college-of-maryland-receives-national-endowment-for-the-humanities-grant/.

Ogilvie, Brian. *The Science of Describing: Natural History in Renaissance Europe*. Chicago: University of Chicago Press, 2006.

Patsavas, Alyson. "Recovering a Cripistemology of Pain: Leaky Bodies, Connective Tissue, and Feeling Discourse." *Journal of Literary & Cultural Disability Studies* 8, no 2 (2014): 203–218.

Pauley, Benjamin F. "Daniel Defoe, *Robinson Crusoe*. (Review). Ed. Evan R. Davis." *Digital Defoe: Studies in Defoe & His Contemporaries* 5, no.1 (2013): 152–156.

Peck, Amelia, ed. *Interwoven Globe: The Worldwide Textile Trade, 1500–1800*. New York: Metropolitan Museum of Art, 2013.

Phillips, Lynn. *Flirting with Danger: Young Women's Reflections on Sexuality and Violence*. New York: NYU Press, 2000.

Phillipson, Nicholas. *Adam Smith: An Enlightened Life*. New Haven, CT: Yale University Press, 2010.

Piketty, Thomas. *Capital in the Twenty-First Century*. Translated by Arthur Goldhammer. Cambridge, MA: Belknap Press of Harvard University Press, 2017.

Pinch, Adela. "Recent Studies in the Nineteenth Century." *Studies in English Literature, 1500–1900* 54, no. 4 (2014): 943–1002.

"Piscataway Conoy Tribe—History." n.d. http://www.piscatawayconoytribe.com/history.html.

"Portrait of William Duguid." The Collection: Met American Wing, Metropolitan Museum of Art. https://www.metmuseum.org/art/collection/search/20517.

Price, Margaret. "The Bodymind Problem and the Possibilities of Pain." *Hypatia* 30, no. 1 (Winter 2015): 268–284.

Pulsipher, Jenny Hale. "*The Widow Ranter* and Royalist Culture in Colonial Virginia." *Early American Literature* 39, no. 1 (2004): 41–66.

Ratcliff, Kathryn Strother. *The Social Determinants of Health: Looking Upstream*. Medford, MA: Polity Press, 2020.

Research Center for Material Culture. "(De)coloniality as Unfinished Story: What Artists and Writers Can Teach Museums about 'Decolonial' Praxes." https://www.materialculture.nl/en/events/decoloniality-unfinished-story-what-artists-and-writers-can-teach-museums-about-decolonial.

Richardson, Robbie. "Decolonizing ASECS: An Indigenous Perspective." In *Decolonization and Eighteenth-Century Studies*, edited by Emily C. Casey and Tita Chico. Special issue, *Studies in Eighteenth-Century Culture* 52 (April 2023): 35–39.

———. "Some Observations on 'Decolonizing' the University." In "Antiracism in the Contemporary University," edited by Tita Chico. *Los Angeles Review of Books*, July 6, 2021, https://lareviewofbooks.org/article/antiracism-in-the-contemporary-university/#_ftn9.

Roberts, Jennifer. "The Power of Patience." *Harvard Magazine*, November–December 2013. https://www.harvardmagazine.com/2013/11/the-power-of-patience.

Ross, Sara E. E., and Paul Salzman, eds. *Editing Early Modern Women*. Cambridge: Cambridge University Press, 2016.

Rothman, Barbara Katz. *The Book of Life: A Personal and Ethical Guide to Race, Normality, and the Implications of the Human Genome Project*. Boston: Beacon Press, 2001.

Saez, Emmanuel, and Gabriel Zucman. *The Triumph of Injustice: How the Rich Dodge Taxes and How to Make Them Pay*. New York: Norton, 2019.

Said, Edward. *Culture and Imperialism*. New York: Alfred A. Knopf, 1993.

Scarry, Elaine. *The Body in Pain: The Making and Unmaking of the World*. Oxford: Oxford University Press, 1987.

Schalk, Sami. *Bodyminds Reimagined: (Dis)ability, Race, and Gender in Black Women's Speculative Fiction*. Durham, NC: Duke University Press, 2018.

Schwartz, Sarah. "Lawmakers Push to Ban '1619 Project' from Schools." *EducationWeek*, February 3, 2021. https://www.edweek.org/teaching-learning/lawmakers-push-to-ban-1619-project-from-schools/2021/02.

Seraphin, S. B., J. A. Grizzell, A. Kerr-German, M. A. Perkins, P. R. Grzanka, and E. E. Hardin. "A Conceptual Framework for Non-Disposable Assignments: Inspiring Implementation, Innovation, and Research." *Psychology Learning and Teaching* 18, no. 1 (2019): 84–97.

Shapiro, Johanna, Jack Coulehan, Delese Wear, and Martha Montello. "Medical Humanities and Their Discontents: Definitions, Critiques, and Implications." *Academic Medicine* 84, no. 2 (2009): 192–198.

Sharpe, Christina. *In the Wake: On Blackness and Being*. Durham, NC: Duke University Press, 2016.

Shuttleton, David E. *Smallpox and the Literary Imagination, 1660–1820*. Cambridge: Cambridge University Press, 2007.

Simpson, Leanne Betasamosake. "Anticolonial Strategies for the Recovery and Maintenance of Indigenous Knowledge." In *The Recovery of Indigenous Knowledge*, edited by Waziyatawin

Angela Wilson. Special issue, *American Indian Quarterly* 28, no. 3/4 (Summer–Autumn, 2004): 373–384.

———. "Land as Pedagogy: Nishnaabeg Intelligence and Rebellious Transformation." *Decolonization: Indigeneity, Education & Society* 3, no. 3 (2014): 1–25.

Smith, Adam. *Lectures on Justice, Police, Revenue and Arms: Delivered in the University of Glasgow*. 1763. Oxford, 1869.

———. *The Theory of Moral Sentiments*. 1759. Edited by Ryan Patrick Hanley. New York: Penguin, 2009.

Smith, Cassander L. "*The Interesting Narrative by Olaudah Equiano*" (Review). *Eighteenth-Century Fiction* 31, no. 4 (2019): 767–768.

Spratt, Danielle. "Denaturalizing Lady Bountiful: Speaking the Silence of Poverty in Mary Brunton's *Discipline* and Jane Austen's *Emma*." *The Eighteenth Century* 56, no. 2 (2015): 193–208.

St. Mary's College of Maryland. "St. Mary's College Board of Trustees Approves Academic Program Changes for Fall 2021." https://inside.smcm.edu/news/2021/02/st-marys-college-board-trustees-approves-academic-program-changes-fall-2021.

Stott, Anne. "Hannah More and the Blagdon Controversy, 1799–1802." In *Evangelicalism in the Church of England, c.1790–c.1890*, edited by Mark Smith and Stephen Taylor. Church of England Record Society vol. 12. Woodbridge, UK: Boydell Press, 2004: 1–50.

Strother Ratcliff, Kathryn. *The Social Determinants of Health: Looking Upstream*. Medford, MA: Polity Press, 2020.

Student 1 (Ashleyj Pavia). "Race and Science as Tools of Empire: Connecting Climate Perspectives: An Interactive Museum Exhibit," https://www.artsteps.com/embed/5fd9679ad0a711628df1389d/560/315.

Student 3 (William Bryan). "The Colonialist Oppression of the 'Other': TikTok Cosplay #rpnh," https://www.youtube.com/watch?v=FbygTDd7o0g.+6.

Swaminathan, Srividhya. "*Captain Singleton* by Daniel Defoe" (Review). *Eighteenth-Century Fiction* 33, no. 2 (2021): 325–327.

———. *Debating the Slave Trade: Rhetoric of British National Identity, 1759–1815*. New York: Routledge, 2009.

Sweeney Coombs, David, and Danielle Coriale, "V21 Forum on Strategic Presentism: Introduction." *Victorian Studies* 59, no. 1 (2016): 87–89.

Tikkanen, Roosa, and Melinda K. Abrams. "U.S. Health Care from a Global Perspective, 2019: Higher Spending, Worse Outcomes?" January 30, 2020. https://www.commonwealthfund.org/publications/issue-briefs/2020/jan/us-health-care-global-perspective-2019.

Tuck, Eve. "Suspending Damage: A Letter to Communities." *Harvard Educational Review* 79, no. 3 (2009): 409–427.

Tuck, Eve, and K. Wayne Yang. "Decolonization Is Not a Metaphor." *Decolonization: Indigeneity, Education and Society* 1, no. 1 (2012): 1–40.

Tyler, Imogen. *Revolting Subjects: Social Abjection and Resistance in Neoliberal Britain*. New York: Zed Books, 2013.

University of Edinburgh. "Edinburgh Lectures: Nicholas Phillipson." YouTube. March 17, 2011. https://www.youtube.com/watch?v=INiybcmN-YY.

University of Wisconsin La Crosse. CATL Teaching Improvement Guide. "Teaching in a Crisis." Updated December 2022, https://www.uwlax.edu/catl/guides/teaching-improvement-guide/how-can-i-improve/crisis/.

———. Institutional Research, Assessment, and Planning (IRAP). "UWL Factbook." Updated December 2022. https://www.uwlax.edu/institutional-research/data-resources/fact-book/.

V21. "Manifesto of the Collective." March 24, 2015. http://v21collective.org/manifesto-of-the-v21-collective-ten-theses/.

Vizenor, Gerald. *Manifest Manners: Narratives on Postindian Survivance*. Lincoln, NE: University of Nebraska Press, 1999.

Wailoo, Keith. *Pain: A Political History*. Baltimore: Johns Hopkins University Press, 2014.

Wald, Priscilla. *Contagious: Cultures, Carriers, and the Outbreak Narrative*. Durham, NC: Duke University Press, 2008.

Wall, Cynthia. *Grammars of Approach: Landscape, Narrative, and the Linguistic Picturesque*. Chicago: University of Chicago Press, 2019.

Wallerstein, Emmanuel. *The Modern World System*. New York: Academic Press, 1975.

Watts, Vanessa. "Indigenous Place-Thought and Agency amongst Humans and Non Humans (First Woman and Sky Woman Go on a European World Tour!)." *Decolonization: Indigeneity, Education & Society* 2, no. 1 (2013): 20–34.

Wiley, David. "What Is Open Pedagogy? Killing the Disposable Assignment." Improving Learning. October 21, 2013. https://opencontent.org/blog/archives/2975.

Wilson, Fred, and Howard Halle. "Mining the Museum." *Grant Street*, no. 44 (1993): 151–172.

Wiltshire, John. *Jane Austen and the Body: The Picture of Health*. Cambridge: Cambridge University Press, 1992.

Wortley Montagu, Mary. *Six Town Eclogues. With Some Other Poems*. London, 1747.

Wright, Nicole Mansfield. "Resisting 'Resistance': Presentism and Its Discontents." Paper presented at the conference "Resistance in the Spirit of Romanticism," University of Colorado, Boulder, September 6, 2018, and at the conference of the American Society for Eighteenth-Century Studies, "Mind Yore Business" panel, Orlando, Florida, March 23, 2018.

Wright, Nicole Mansfield, and Suvir Kaul. "ASECS at 50: Interview with Suvir Kaul." *Eighteenth-Century Studies* 53, no. 1 (2019): 31–42.

Wynter, Sylvia. "Unsettling the Coloniality of Being/Power/Truth/Freedom: Towards the Human, after Man, Its Overrepresentation—An Argument." *CR: The New Centennial Review* 3, no. 3 (2003): 257–337.

Zuroski, Eugenia. "Academic Land Acknowledgements for Settler Scholars: A Guest Post by Dr. Eugenia Zuroski." *American Society for Eighteenth-Century Studies Graduate and Early Career Caucus* (blog), February 25, 2020. https://asecsgradcaucus.wordpress.com/2020/02/25/academic-land-acknowledgment-for-settler-scholars-a-guest-post-by-dr-eugenia-zuroski/.

———, ed. *The Indigenous Eighteenth Century*. Special issue, *Eighteenth-Century Fiction* 33, no. 2 (Winter 2021).

———. "Where Do You Know From?: An Exercise in Placing Ourselves Together in the Classroom." MAI: Feminism & Visual Cultures. January 27, 2020. https://maifeminism.com/where-do-you-know-from-an-exercise-in-placing-ourselves-together-in-the-classroom/.

NOTES ON CONTRIBUTORS

EMILY C. CASEY, Hall Assistant Professor of American Art and Culture, teaches the art history of the Americas and early modern Atlantic world in the Kress Foundation Department of Art History at the University of Kansas in Lawrence. She recently edited a colloquium, *When and Where Does Colonial America End?*, and coedited a collection of essays, *Decolonization and Eighteenth-Century Studies*. Her most recent article, "A More Perfect Atlantic World: Abolition, Liberty, and Empire in Art after the American Revolution," critically reevaluates Samuel Jennings's *Liberty Displaying the Arts and Sciences*, considered to be the earliest abolitionist painting in the United States.

TERI DOERKSEN, professor of English, teaches long-eighteenth-century British literature and cultural studies at the Mansfield University campus of Commonwealth University of Pennsylvania, a small, regional, public university in the Pennsylvania State System of Higher Education (PASSHE). She is part of a small curricular team working to implement a new general education program and oversee the creation of all new courses, programs, majors, and minors for three universities that have been integrated into a single institution.

DIANA EPELBAUM is an associate professor and director of the Academic Writing Program at Marymount Manhattan College, a small creative arts college in New York City. Her teaching and scholarship are interdisciplinary, bridging eighteenth-century cultures of transatlantic science, writing and rhetoric, and early American literature. She has published on Maria Sibylla Merian, a pioneering naturalist, and on best practices in writing, reading, and thinking pedagogies. As part of her current role, Diana trains faculty in writing pedagogy and classroom metacognition.

ZIONA KOCHER is a postdoctoral lecturer in the English department at the University of Tennessee in Knoxville, where they teach composition and introduction to women, gender, and sexuality studies. While a graduate student, they co-taught "Restoration and Eighteenth-Century British Drama: Staging Political Change" at New College of Florida. Their research explores queerness throughout the long eighteenth century, with recent and forthcoming publications on Centlivre's *The Wonder*, Sheridan's *The Memoirs of Miss Sidney Bidulph*, and Wycherley's

The Country Wife. They are the recipient of the 2022 Catharine Macaulay Prize, 2021 SEASECS Graduate Student Essay Prize, and a Lewis Walpole Library Fellowship.

TRAVIS CHI WING LAU, assistant professor of English, teaches eighteenth- and nineteenth-century British literature and culture, health humanities, and disability studies at Kenyon College, a small liberal arts college in central Ohio. Dr. Lau won Kenyon College's LGBTQ+ Faculty Advocate Award in Spring 2022. He is also a prize-winning poet.

CHRISTINE D. MYERS is an American historian who completed her master's and doctorate degrees in comparative gender history at the University of Strathclyde in Glasgow, Scotland. After two decades of teaching all manner of British, European, U.S., and transatlantic topics, she stepped away from academia and is now an independent scholar and freelance writer. She presents regularly at conferences, and her most recent publication is a coauthored chapter, "From Chemistry to History to Psychology: Creating a Multidisciplinary Minor in Investigative Forensics," in the volume *The Synergistic Classroom: Interdisciplinary Teaching in the Small College Setting.*

KATE PARKER, professor and chair of English at the University of Wisconsin-La Crosse, a regional comprehensive university in the University of Wisconsin System, teaches pre-1800 English and European cultural studies and feminism and sexuality studies.

TIFFANY POTTER, professor of teaching in the Department of English Language and Literatures at the University of British Columbia in Vancouver, teaches courses on the theater, popular culture, and fiction of the British eighteenth century, and representations of gender and indigeneity in what is now called North America. She has edited several critical and classroom editions, including fiction (Eliza Haywood's *The Masqueraders;* Aphra Behn's *Oroonoko*), plays (Elizabeth Cooper's *The Rival Widows, or Fair Libertine;* Robert Rogers' *Ponteach, or the Savages of America*), and a Seneca biography (James Seaver's *A Life of Mrs. Mary Jemison*). She was awarded Canada's 3M National Teaching Prize in 2020.

MATTHEW L. REZNICEK is an associate professor of medical humanities at the University of Minnesota School of Medicine, Twin Cities, in the history of science, technology, and medicine program. He has recently published articles on disability and the Irish gothic as well as death and citizenship in the National Tale. He currently serves as president of the American Conference for Irish Studies.

MIRIAM L. WALLACE, incoming dean of the College of Liberal Arts and Social Sciences at the University of Illinois-Springfield, taught English literature and culture from 1660 forward at New College of Florida, a public liberal arts honors college, from 1995 to 2023. In 2022, she completed a yearlong NEH Planning

Grant working with colleagues across the college and local professionals to develop a new Health-Culture-Societies minor for students in sciences, social sciences, and humanities/arts.

EUGENIA ZUROSKI is an associate professor of English and cultural studies at McMaster University, which is located on the colonized territories of the Mississauga and Haudenosaunee peoples, a site currently known as Hamilton, Ontario. She teaches literature in English from the long eighteenth century to the present, as well as courses in cultural studies, critical theory, and creative writing practice.

INDEX

Note: Page numbers in italics indicate figures.